LOST IN TRANSLATION

ACKNOWLEDGMENTS

The author wishes to thank Matthew Hazell, Richard Chonak, Peter Kwasniewski, and sundry online commentators on *New Liturgical Movement* and the Facebook page of the Society for Catholic Liturgy for their assistance with this volume, and especially Gregory DiPippo, the editor of *New Liturgical Movement*, for his outstanding feedback and corrections. Any mistakes that remain are entirely mine.

spiritual exercises, that is, in a prayerful frame of mind with sufficient time to meditate on the passage before encountering the prayer during Mass. It is our hope that these reflections will also be of use to the clergy in crafting their homilies.

INTRODUCTION

The Beguiling Roman Orations (and the Purpose of This Book)

 R. KIERAN J. O'MAHONY, O.S.A., WAS not happy. The 2011 English edition of the Roman Missal had recently come out, and it was, in his opinion, so bad that it was beyond repair. The Augustinian friar used three criteria to reach this conclusion: exclusion, catechesis, and poor theology. In case you were wondering how it might be that *accurate* translations of the Orations of the Roman Rite, many of which date back to the earliest centuries of the Church, could be examples of poor theology, Fr. O'Mahony charges that they "border on the heretical" because their talk of merit contradicts "our fully signed up [1999] agreement with the World Lutheran Federation on justification by faith and grace"![1]

As for exclusion and catechesis, the author writes:

> Only people of a certain background and a relatively high level of education can make any sense of [the new translation]. In your ordinary congregation, many are excluded: the young, people whose first language is not English,

---

1 "Note on the English Roman Missal (2011)," https://www.tarsus.ie/resources/000-PDFs/Roman-Missal-Letter.pdf. Ironically, Fr. Mahony's understanding of what borders on the heretical borders on the heretical. There are degrees of authority with respect to magisterial documents, and an agreement such as the Joint Declaration on the Doctrine of Justification, which was ratified by the Lutheran World Federation and the Pontifical Council for Promoting Christian Unity (rather than an ecumenical council or a pope acting *ex cathedra*) does not outweigh the Council of Trent's Decree Concerning Justification.

Second, Fr. Mahony is part of a larger group of liturgists who mistakenly equate all talk of merit with Pelagianism, failing to grasp the (paradoxical) concept of merit formulated by St. Augustine in his battles against Pelagianism and kept by orthodox Catholicism ever since—namely, that merit is both individual achievement and divine gift, and that when God crowns our merits, He crowns His own gifts. See chapter 52, "The Theological Virtues and the Thirteenth Sunday After Pentecost," and Thomas Kocik's review of Gerald O'Collins' *Lost in Translation: The English Language and the Catholic Mass* (Collegeville, MN: Liturgical Press, 2017) in *Antiphon* 22.1 (2018): 107–13, esp. 111.

people whose education stopped after primary school or early in secondary school. Also excluded, as far as the responses go, are people who attend church only for Baptisms, weddings and funerals. It has pushed some people finally to stop attending Mass at all.[2]

I would love to see the good father's evidence for his claim that attendance dropped as a result of the 2011 translation, and I hardly think that the entire worship of the Catholic Church should be specifically tailored to those who "attend church only for Baptisms, weddings and funerals." But what struck me most of all in the argument is the implicit assumption that elevated language is exclusive language. Is that really so?

In her 1938 study *Rhetoric in the Sunday Collects of the Roman Missal*, Sr. Mary Gonzaga Haessly writes that the three purposes of classical rhetoric—teaching, delighting, and persuading—are on full display in the Church's liturgical prayer:

> All these devices of the art of language are necessary for us, for they enable us: (1) to grasp clearly the lessons embodied in the Prayers (*docere*); (2) to make these lessons more acceptable to us through the charm of diction and structure, in a word, through their appeal to our aesthetic sense (*delectare*); (3) to persuade us (*movere*) to mold our conduct in accordance with the principles of faith set forth in the Prayers. This explains why rhetoric is, and must be, found in the liturgy: it is to dispose us to pray "ut oportet," as we ought to pray.[3]

And it is often through making diction and structure somewhat complex that that "charm" is produced. The complexity may, of course, engender some initial frustration, but that can be intentional, for a little frustration goads the reader or listener to push on and figure it out. And when it is figured out, there is an "Aha!" moment that brings a delight greater than that which comes from understanding something easy. If adults only used baby talk, it might be effective, but it would hardly be delightful. "What is sought with some difficulty," St. Augustine observes, "is attained with more pleasure."[4] And what is attained with more

---

2 Mahony, "Note."
3 Sr. Mary Gonzaga Haessly, *Rhetoric in the Sunday Collects of the Roman Missal* (Cleveland, OH: Ursuline College for Women, 1938), 5.
4 *On Christian Doctrine* 2.6.8, translation mine.

pleasure, we might add, has a deeper impact on our souls. The rhetorical goal of delighting is intimately bound up with the goal of persuading, of "molding our conduct." And since one of the purposes of sacred liturgy is the formation of souls, liturgical composers are wise not to neglect this connection.

Used properly, then, elevated language does not exclude but extends to all an invitation to understanding, just as the dense imagery of poetry is not meant to rebuff but to awaken in the reader a deeper meaning. And just as poetry is not for the few (even if few today, alas, pay it any attention), neither is liturgical prayer, which by its very nature is solemn, public, and rhetorical. There is something condescending about thinking of either poetry or sonorous public discourse as the sole possession of the elite, and it is—historically, at least—inaccurate. The Lincoln-Douglas debates, each of which was replete with lofty rhetoric and lasted three hours, took place before the "common man" who, though often illiterate, had a longer attention span and a greater comprehension than most of our college graduates today. Even the least cultivated or educated among us has a greater capacity for the sublime than his well-intentioned but patronizing patrons give him credit for. The same error, incidentally, occurs in discussions about other forms of beauty as well. Some people seem to think that because the wealthy build beautiful churches, beautiful churches are only for the wealthy. They forget the service that the wealthy provide the poor in creating the conditions for them to worship in a world of beauty, and they forget that in the days when the poor saved their nickels and dimes to build churches in their ghettoes, they too chose to build ones that were beautiful. To follow, then, a lowest-common-denominator approach and to flatten all signs and symbols during the most important and solemn act that man can do is both mystagogical suicide and a sin against the great artistic gifts with which God has endowed us. It is also to deny the so-called uneducated an experience of beauty on the grounds that they are too dumb to appreciate it. To me, that is the ultimate exclusion.

Of course, if the entire liturgy were nothing but fancy rhetoric, it could indeed become overwhelming. But the beauty of the traditional Roman Rite (and the other apostolic liturgies as well) is the diversity of strategies by which it endeavors to catch and form souls. Saint Augustine writes that good rhetoric consists of an artful blend of styles: the subdued, the temperate, and the grandiose.[5] The traditional Roman Rite reflects this blend of high and low, contemplative and active, verbal and silent. With some exceptions—like the Epistles of the rhetorically-gift Saint Paul—the biblical readings tend to be simple in diction and syntax. The Offertory Prayers, composed in the Middle Ages, betray a medieval love of florid yet precise eloquence, and the Canon is a magnificent example of late Roman courtly rhetoric.

And then there are the Orations, the subject of this volume. The Collects, Secrets, and Postcommunion Prayers of the 1570/1962 Roman Missal—and, to a lesser extent, of the 1970 Missal—are a unique species of rhetoric that ingeniously combines tight structure, poetic rhythm, literary order, succinct imagery, and a panoply of human experience.

Tight structure. The Orations have three basic parts:

1. A *protasis* or first part that usually invokes God and includes a description of His actions or attributes in a subordinate clause: "O God, You who do A, B, and C."
2. An *apodosis* or second part that usually includes a petition followed by a purpose clause: "Please give us U, V, and W so we may attain X, Y, and Z."
3. And an *adjuration* to the Holy Trinity.

Poetic rhythm. The Orations have a pattern that is called a *cursus* which, though derived in some respects from Cicero, branches out in new directions. Grammarians and liturgists further identify a *cursus planus, cursus tardus*, and *curus velos*.[6] We do not in this book go into the rhythmic nuances of the original Latin, but they are there and should be respected as part of the genius of the Roman Rite.

Literary order. The Orations employ a number of subtle literary devices like chiasm (an ABCCBA sequence), antithesis, and juxtaposition.

---

5 *On Christian Doctrine* 4.20.39–4.27.60.
6 See Adrian Fortescue, *The Mass: A Study of the Roman Liturgy* (London: Longmans, Green, and Co., 1912), 251, and Sr. Mary Pierre Ellebracht, *Remarks on the Vocabulary of the Ancient Orations in the* Missale Romanum (Nijmegen: Dekker & Van de Vegt, 1963), 9.

Succinct imagery. In part because of the nature of Latin, the Orations can convey two different images with one word.

Finally, *human experience.* To trigger a more vivid insight into the supernatural mysteries, the Orations draw from concrete realms of daily life: agriculture, warfare, sickness, navigation, commerce, politics, childbirth, feasting, stargazing, etc. (Although these experiences draw from a pre-industrial age, they can still resonate with modern audiences yearning for a connection with nature.)

Indeed, because of their structure, order, imagery, and universality, we are tempted to call the Orations examples of poetry rather than oratory. Think of them, if you will, as pious Roman haikus. And it is the poetic quality of these prayers that makes them particularly difficult to translate. What award-winning translator Edith Grossman observes of all language is especially true of poetry:

> A translation is not made with tracing paper. It is an act of critical interpretation. Let me insist on the obvious: Languages trail immense, individual histories behind them, and no two languages, with all their accretions of tradition and culture, ever dovetail perfectly. They can be linked by translation, as a photograph can link movement and stasis, but it is disingenuous to assume that either translation or photography, or acting for that matter, are representational in any narrow sense of the term.... Words or syntax...are peculiar to specific languages and are not transferable.[7]

Hence the need for a book such as this. *Lost in Translation* examines one or more of a liturgical occasion's prayers in the original Latin with an eye towards revealing images or meanings that typically elude even the best of translations. The book is greatly indebted to pioneering commentators such as Sr. Mary Gonzaga Haessly and Sr. Marie Pierre Ellebracht,[8] but it differs from earlier treatments in four respects.

First, greater attention is paid to the impact of the context on the meaning. In the 1962 Missal, the same Collect can be used one year for the Fifth Sunday after Epiphany and next year for the Twenty-Fourth Sunday after Pentecost. In such a case, the

---

7   Edith Grossman, "Narrative Transmutations," PEN American Centre, www.scribd.com/document/230692721/Edith-Grossman.
8   See Haessly, *Rhetoric in the Sunday Collects* and Ellebracht, *Vocabulary of the Ancient Orations.*

meaning of the Collect both is and is not the same.[9] Similarly, we view Collects differently when we see a theme emerge among them Sunday after Sunday. When they are part of a pattern (as we will see with both the last and the first Sundays of the calendar), they accrue an extra meaning.

Second, we betray an interest in what we call "spiritual eructation" (see Ps. 44:2). Whereas modern liturgists often try to insert as many direct biblical passages into prayers or ceremonies as possible (with the laudable goal of making the people of God more biblically literate), ancient liturgies "ingested" the Word of God, ruminated on it, and then "belched" out a scripturally-informed prayer. Ancient worship, in other words, was the result of a kind of *lectio divina* rather than an intentional quilt of quotes.

Third, apropos of Sr. Haessly's comment about delighting and shaping, we follow the ways in which the Orations contribute to what Pope Benedict XVI calls the "school of love."[10] The Orations do not simply petition God for the things that we love; they teach us what to love and how to love. The Collects do not simply collect our desires; they rearrange them and school them. Meditating on this aspect of the Orations thus becomes a kind of spiritual therapy.

Finally, *Lost in Translation* is less technical than earlier treatments of the subject in order to make it more spiritually and pastorally useful. Although we occasionally use grammatical terms like hyperbaton or asyndeton, we generally try to avoid words that preachers themselves will want to avoid in their homiletic efforts to bring the hay down to the sheep. Our hope is that this book will help lovers of the traditional Latin Mass gain a deeper appreciation of the treasures of the classical Roman Missal, and that it will help in the areas of homiletics and catechesis as well. Or, to paraphrase Sr. Haessly, by recovering the original charm of these prayers, we aspire to increase delight and mold conduct.

---

9 See chapter 63, "New Meanings and the 'Leftover' Sundays."
10 Pope Benedict XVI, "Message of the Holy Father Benedict XVI to the Youth of the World on the Occasion of the 22nd World Youth Day, 2007," www.vatican.va/content/benedict-xvi/en/messages/youth/documents/hf_ben-xvi_mes_20070127_youth.html.

I

ADVENT

The Tempestuous Collect of the First Sunday of Advent

HE FIRST SUNDAY OF ADVENT IS THE first day of a new liturgical year, and as such it is roughly the sacred equivalent of New Year's Day. The Romans named the month that greets the new year January after their two-faced god Janus, one of whose faces looks forward and the other backward. The traditional Roman Rite makes an even stronger claim to this double awareness, and on two levels. First, the end of the liturgical year (the final Sundays after Pentecost) looks ahead to the end of the world while the season of Advent continues this theme and hence looks back at it. Second, Advent itself looks back to the historic birth of Jesus Christ (ironically, with anticipation) and looks ahead to the Second Coming of Jesus Christ.

One way to think about the transition from the old year to the new is that the Sundays during this period function as an interlocking clasp that ties the two ends together into a beautiful necklace. The last Sundays, as we mention later, have an apocalyptic theme, and that theme grows in intensity until it crescendos with the Last Sunday after Pentecost and its Gospel reading about the fall of Jerusalem and Doomsday.[1] The first Sunday of Advent has a nearly identical Gospel and thus continues the apocalyptic theme, and it adds a penitential spirit: during the "green Sundays" we were made aware of the End Times; now in this time of violet we are asked to do penance in preparation for them.

Another way in which the two ends of the year interlock is with their Collects. The Collects of the first, second, and fourth Sundays of Advent are "Stir up" prayers, Orations beginning with *Excita* or "stir up" that petition the Lord to arouse either the people or His own power. Sometimes the prayers are addressed

---

1 The relationship between the last Sundays after Pentecost and the season of Advent are explained in greater detail in chapter 5, "The Key to the Season: The Collect for the Vigil Mass of Christmas Eve."

And so, in those moments when we are prone to fear and apt to doubt the "sleeping Lord," let us recall the end of St. Mark's story:

> And rising up, He rebuked the wind, and said to the sea: "Peace, be still." And the wind ceased: and there was made a great calm. And He said to them: "Why are you fearful? Have you not faith yet?" (4:39–40)

2

The Heartfelt Collect of the Second Sunday of Advent

OR THE THIRD WEEK IN A ROW, THE 1962 Roman Missal uses an *Excita* or "Stir Up" Collect during the Sunday Mass:

> *Excita, Dómine, corda nostra ad præparándas Unigéniti tui vias: ut per ejus advéntum, purificátis tibi méntibus servíre mereámur. Qui tecum vivit et regnat.*

Which I translate as:

> Stir up our hearts, O Lord, to prepare the ways of Thine only begotten Son; that through His coming we may deserve to be in Thy service with purified minds. Who with Thee liveth and reigneth.

On the Last Sunday after Pentecost, the Church prayed to the Father to stir up our wills. On the First Sunday of Advent, she prayed to the Son to stir up His power and come. Now, during the Second Sunday of Advent, she prays to the Father to stir up our hearts in preparation for "the ways of" His Son. The phrasing has a nice seasonal ring to it: preparing the ways of the Only-Begotten is evocative of the Forerunner of Christ, who figures prominently during Advent. Like St. John the Baptist, we are called to prepare the ways of the Lord (Luke 1:76).

The order of Collects also makes sense. Last week we inaugurated Advent by asking the Son to come; this week we get ready for His arrival. But instead of asking God to stir up our wills as we did two weeks ago (during the Last Sunday after Pentecost), we now ask Him to stir up our hearts. Because the Last Sunday after Pentecost betokens the end of time, it is appropriate that we prayed then for more willpower to help us rise to the challenge of the final struggle. Now, however, we want our hearts to be ready, which I take to include not only our will but our desires.

This Sunday's Postcommunion Prayer provides an excellent example of a heart that is ready: it is one that has learned to look down on earthly things and love the heavenly (*terrena despicere et amare cælestia*). The often-misunderstood concept of *contemptus mundi* or disdain for the world simply means a realignment of one's subjective desires with the objective hierarchy of goods.[1] The heart that has its act together is the heart that loves the higher goods more and the lower goods less. As St. Augustine writes:

> Now he is a man of just and holy life who forms an unprejudiced estimate of things and keeps his affections also under strict control, so that he neither loves what he ought not to love, nor fails to love what he ought to love, nor loves that more which ought to be loved less, nor loves that equally which ought to be loved either less or more, nor loves that less or more which ought to be loved equally.[2]

Such a heart, for example, is ready to renounce physical safety at the drop of a hat to profess its faith in Jesus Christ, because it loves Christ far more and is not encumbered by an excessive attachment to other things.

Finally, the Collect's main petition, which requests that we may deserve to be in the service of God the Father with purified minds, is distinctive in two ways. First, whereas some Roman Orations ask for pure minds (*mentes puræ*), others such as this Collect ask for purified minds (*mentes purificatæ*), thereby drawing attention to a process of purgation. During Advent we are in a special kind of training that, we pray, has purgative results. Second, instead of asking to serve God, the Collect asks to deserve or merit (*mereamur*) serving God. Serving God is an honor and a privilege, of which we must ask to be deserving since our own merits fall short. In the succinct wording of this Sunday's Secret: "no influence from our merits is sufficient (*nulla suppetunt suffragia meritorum*)."

---

1   On this theme, see Peter Kwasniewski, "Should We 'Despise Earthly Goods and Love Heavenly Ones'? A Liturgical Lesson for Lent," *OnePeter Five*, March 2, 2022, https://onepeterfive.com/despise-earthly-goods/.
2   *On Christian Doctrine* 1.27.28, trans J. F. Shaw (Mineola, NY: Dover Publications, 2009).

3

The Accommodating Collect of the Third Sunday of Advent

SIMPLE BUT BEAUTIFUL COLLECT GATH-ers our prayers for the Third Sunday of Advent:

Aurem tuam, quǽsumus, Dómine, précibus nostris accóm-moda: et mentis nostrœ ténebras grátia tuœ visitatiónis illús-tra: Qui vivis.

Which I translate as:

Accommodate Thine ear to our prayers, we beseech Thee, O Lord; and enlighten the darkness of our minds by the grace of Thy visitation: Who livest.

The Collect joins those of the First and Fourth Sundays of Advent in addressing God the Son; common during Advent, this address is rare during other seasons.[1] In another way, the Collect breaks rank. For three Sundays in a row, the Collect has begun with *Excita* or "Stir up," but that streak ends here. The desire for the Messiah to rouse up and come, however, is transferred rather than suppressed. "Stir up, O Lord, Thy might and come to save us" (Ps. 79:2–3), the inspiration behind the Collects of the First and Fourth Sundays of Advent, appears in this Sunday's Grad-ual and Alleluia. Instead of the imagery of rousing, the prayer employs the language of accommodation and illumination. While our hearts are stirred up by Gaudete Sunday's theme of rejoicing, the Collect strikes a more irenic note.

The Collect may not incorporate Psalm 79:2, but it does draw from another biblical convention. "Inclining one's ear," which is no doubt the inspiration behind the English expression "to bend an ear," is used several times in the Old Testament, including

---

1 For more on the Christocentric prayers of Advent, see Peter Kwas-niewski, "The Collects of Advent: Who is Being Addressed, and What Difference Does It Make?," *New Liturgical Movement*, December 19, 2016, www.newliturgicalmovement.org/2016/12/the-collects-of-advent-who-is-being_19.html.

invocations to God.[2] In the Vulgate translation, the idiom is translated with *inclino* as the verb. In this Sunday's Collect, the Church uses the less common *accommodo*, which literally means "to fit or adapt one thing to another." Hence the prayer asks God not simply to bend an ear to our prayers, but to reshape His ear in such a way that it conforms to our prayers.

Another biblical influence is evident in the choice of *visitatio*. Saint Peter writes of the "day of visitation" (1 Pet. 2:12) and the "time of visitation" (ibid. 5:6), presumably with respect to the glorious return of the Son of Man. Here the Church speaks of the illuminating grace of visitation enlightening our darkened minds. The Advent and Christmas seasons essentially celebrate three comings: the coming of Our Lord to Bethlehem, His coming into our hearts, and His coming at the end of time. This Sunday's Collect indirectly references the middle coming and indirectly alludes to the third.

Some Collects, such as this one, contain two separate petitions, one in the protasis and one in the apodosis (the first and second parts). The petition of the protasis is for accommodation; the petition of the apodosis is for illumination. Note that the author has put both of these imperatives (*accommoda* and *illustra*) at the end of each part. This figure of speech is called a homoioteleuton: in pairing the two words, it more forcefully brings them to the reader's or listener's attention.

The Collect begs for an audience with God so that He may accommodate our prayers. Prayer is an important theme of this Sunday: both the Introit and the Epistle implore us to make our petitions known to God. The Collect uses the word *preces* (plural) to denote prayer. *Prex* is different from other Latin words for prayer such as *oratio*, *votum*, and *supplicatio* insofar as it does not have a public meaning (the other words were originally tied to formal events or ceremonies).[3] And the author may have simply acted out of customary usage when he put the word in the plural, but even if he did, both the plural voice and the choice of the "private" *prex* remind us of the mystagogical function of the Collect in the Mass, which is "to collect" the myriad private prayers of the individuals who have assembled for the sacrifice and to

2 See Ps. 16:6, 70:2, 85:1, 87:3, 101:3.
3 Haessly, *Rhetoric in the Sunday Collects*, 125.

unite them into a single coordinated public petition. Whatever our hopes, fears, and wishes we bring with us to this Sunday, they will be made better by the gentle and illuminating grace of Christ when He visits our hearts.

4

The Indulgent Collect of the Fourth Sunday of Advent

HE FOURTH SUNDAY OF ADVENT resumes the pattern of *Excita* or "Stir Up" Collects begun on the Last Sunday after Pentecost and carried over into the Advent season before the "interruption" of Gaudete Sunday last week:

> *Excita, quǽsumus, Dómine, poténtiam tuam, et veni: et magna nobis virtúte succúrræ; et per auxílium grátiæ tuæ, quod nostra peccáta præpédiunt, indulgéntia tuæ propitiatiónis accéleret: Qui vivis.*

Which I translate as:

> Stir up Thy power and come, we beseech Thee, O Lord, and with great might run to our aid; that by the help of Thy grace, Thy merciful forgiveness may accelerate what our sins are impeding. Who livest.

The Collect contains three imperatives. The first and second, "stir up and come," are lifted verbatim from the Collect of the First Sunday of Advent (which in turn is inspired by Ps. 79:2). The third, "run to our aid," is mildly pleonastic, that is, it can be characterized as using more words than are absolutely necessary. I say "mildly," however, because power (*potentia*) and might (*virtus*) are close in meaning but not synonymous. In liturgical Latin, *virtus* has the more specific meaning of "the supernatural force of God which is productive of wonderful effects."[1] The repetition also adds urgency, as does the use of *succurre*, which literally means to run under and denotes rushing to the aid of another. Further, the repeated request for God's power echoes the yearning of the generations waiting for Christ. "Just as of old, when the pagan world was sunk in degradation," writes Sr. Mary Gonzaga Haessly, "the Patriarchs prayed for an all-powerful Savior, so in this Collect the Church calls upon the Omnipotence

---

1 Ellebracht, *Vocabulary of the Ancient Orations*, 128.

of God to save her children by the might of His grace."[2] Finally, the repetition of *et* before and after *magna nobis virtute succurre* likewise conveys a certain rushed breathlessness.

All told, it is a unique Collect. As Sr. Haessly observes:

> In no other of the Sunday Collects do we find three imperatives. On this last Sunday before the feast of Our Lord's coming, the Church, fearing lest we should miss the fulness of His grace, multiplies her petitions, uttering her desires in varied expressions. First she repeats the prayer made on the first Sunday: "Rouse Thy might, and come." As if this were not urgent enough, she adds in more persistent tone: "with great might hasten to our assistance" before it is too late.[3]

The second half of the prayer consists of a purpose clause (even though there is no *ut*). Emphasis is placed on the help of God's grace by the prominent position of *per auxilium gratiæ tuæ*. Again Sr. Haessly: "It is through grace that the first Advent of the Savior is perpetuated"[4]—that is, carried through into His second Advent (His visitation to our heart[5])—and it is through grace that we are prepared for His third Advent (aka, His Second Coming) at the end of time. In the syntax of the prayer, grace is contrasted with what comes next: that which our sins impede (*quod nostra peccata præpediunt*). What our sins impede is left undefined, but we can hazard a guess in light of the current season: it is, among other things, progress in being ready for Christ's coming. There is also a subtle contrast between God's running to our aid (*succurre*) and our sins tripping us up: *præpedio*, which is from the Latin for "in front of the foot," means to fetter or shackle. The choice of *accelero* for hasten or accelerate also adds to the pedal motif of the prayer.

Finally, we come to the phrase *indulgentia tuæ propitiationis*, which occurs two other times in the 1962 Roman Missal. *Indulgentia* means forgiveness, and in at least one case it refers specifically to the forgiveness of sins committed after Baptism.[6]

---

2 Haessly, *Rhetoric in the Sunday Collects*, 29.
3 Haessly, 29.
4 Haessly, 30.
5 See, for instance, the Collect of the Third Sunday of Advent.
6 *Missa ad postulandam continentiam.* See Ellebracht, *Vocabulary of the Ancient Orations*, 156.

Providentially, this Sunday's Gospel describes St. John the Baptist "preaching the Baptism of penance for the remissions of sins." (Luke 3:3). John's baptisms were not efficacious in removing sins, but thanks be to God, our sacraments of Baptism and Confession are. The faithful can therefore fruitfully use this Collect as a reminder to be shriven before they celebrate the great feast of the Nativity. May the remission of our sins and the accelerant of grace quickly return us to a life that makes straight the way of the Lord.

5

The Key to the Season: The Collect of the Vigil Mass of Christmas Eve

N ORDER TO UNDERSTAND THE MEANing of Christmas, let us turn to the Collect for December 24:

> *Deus, qui nos redemptiónis nostræ ánnua exspectatióne lætíficas: præsta; ut Unigénitum tuum, quem Redemptórem læti suscípimus, veniéntem quoque júdicem secúri videámus, Dóminum nostrum, Jesum Christum, Filium tuum: Qui tecum.*

Which I translate as:

> O God, who makest us glad with the yearly expectation of our redemption, grant that we who now joyfully receive Thine only-begotten Son as our Redeemer, may also confidently behold Him coming as our Judge, Our Lord Jesus Christ Thy Son: Who with Thee.

Even though December 24 in the 1962 Calendar is a vigil Mass and is thus penitential in character (prior to Vatican II, December 24 was a day of complete fast and abstinence), the Church cannot hide her joy about the impending arrival of the Messiah. The Secret tells of "the soon-to-be-adored birthday" (*adoranda natalitia*) of the Son of God, while the Postcommunion prays that we may "catch our breath again" (*respirare*) by celebrating the Nativity.

The Collect is also joyful albeit with a twist. God "makes us glad" each year with an annual expectation of our redemption. *Redemptionis nostræ annua exspectatio* can be taken in two ways. The predominant meaning is an expectation of the *feast* of our redemption, namely, Christmas Day (the Roman Orations often speak in shorthand). On the other hand, it can also mean an expectation of Doomsday, which St. Paul calls the "day of redemption" (Ephesians 4:30). Both meanings are the subject of the Collect's apodosis (second half): just as we are currently glad about celebrating Christ as our Redeemer who has come, we pray that we may be glad to meet Him as the Judge who is to come.

The ambivalence of *redemptionis nostræ annua exspectatio* is, I suspect, deliberate. The Church wants us to blur the lines between the two events in order to indicate a relation between Christ's three comings. The purpose of annually celebrating Christ's earthly Nativity is to renew our faith and receive Christ more fully into our hearts; and the more fully Christ has come into our hearts, the more we will be ready for His Second Coming. The goal, as the Collect implies, is to be so well prepared that seeing Jesus Christ as our Judge on the Last Day will be no more fearful than seeing Him as a Babe in the manger.

That is quite a goal! Although as Christians we should be looking forward to the end of the world and Christ's glorious return, it is understandable if most of us are not exactly giddy with excitement at the prospect of Armageddon. Moreover, anyone with an ounce of self-knowledge has cause for concern about meeting Christ in all His terrifying splendor on Judgment Day. As St. Augustine writes:

> And when men look for Him to come from heaven as the judge of the quick and the dead, it strikes great terror into the neglectful, so that they wheel themselves around to a diligent [preparation] and [learn how] to long for His approach by acting well rather than fearing it by acting badly.[1]

As we explain elsewhere,[2] the last Sundays after Pentecost and the entire Christmas season are designed to offer "diligent preparation" that can convert a terrified and "negligent" person into a holy soul "who longs for His approach." Beginning around the Eighteenth Sunday after Pentecost, the Mass propers address the fears of a negligent person as they take on an apocalyptic note that crescendos with the Last Sunday after Pentecost and its Gospel reading, St. Matthew's detailed description of the end of the world (24:15 35). The next week, the First Sunday of Advent, continues the theme of holy terror; on the other hand, the Gospel reading for that Sunday is St. Luke's description of the end of the world, which is shorter and arguably less frightening. A

---

1   *On Christian Doctrine* 1.15.14, translation mine.
2   See chapter 1, "The Tempestuous Collect of the First Sunday of Advent" and chapter 68, "The Stirring Collect of the Last Sunday after Pentecost."

shift is therefore underway, and by the time we get to Christmas Day, fear has been replaced by joy, even to the point that we can imagine ourselves so transformed by our ongoing redemption that we are actually looking forward to Doomsday: as the Collect puts it, we aspire to be confident or *securi*, which literally means "without a care" (*sine cura*) in the world. (I punted somewhat when I translated *læti* and *securi* as "joyfully" and "confidently." They are not adverbs but adjectives, attributes of our state of being [real or aspirational], not mere qualifiers of a passing action.)

What a Christmas present it would be to be truly *securus*! And happily, it is one which Almighty God, through the conditioning of His Church's calendar, makes possible every year.

II

CHRISTMAS

6

The Three Nativities of the Three Christmas Masses

N THE *SUMMA THEOLOGIAE*, ST. THOMAS Aquinas explains the tradition in the Roman Rite of having three different Masses on Christmas Day:

> On Christmas Day... several Masses are said on account of Christ's threefold Nativity. Of these the first is His eternal birth, which is hidden in our regard, and therefore, one Mass is sung in the night, in the Introit of which we say, "The Lord said unto Me: Thou art My Son, this day have I begotten Thee." The second is His Nativity in time, and the spiritual birth, whereby Christ rises "as the day-star in our hearts" (2 Pet. 1:19), and on this account the Mass is sung at dawn, and in the Introit we say, "The light will shine on us today." The third is Christ's temporal and bodily birth, according as He went forth from the virginal womb, becoming visible to us through being clothed with flesh: and on that account the third Mass is sung in broad daylight, in the Introit of which we say, "A child is born to us." Nevertheless, on the other hand, it can be said that His eternal generation, of itself, is in the full light, and on this account in the Gospel of the third Mass mention is made of His eternal birth. But regarding His birth in the body, He was literally born during the night, as a sign that He came to the darknesses of our infirmity; hence also in the Midnight Mass we say the Gospel of Christ's Nativity in the flesh.[1]

In sum, Aquinas claims that:

1. The Midnight Mass primarily celebrates Christ's eternal birth from the Father, the Dawn Mass Christ's spiritual birth in our hearts, and the Daytime Mass Christ's historic birth in Bethlehem.
2. Each Mass, however, also alludes to one or more of the other births.

---

1 *Summa theologiae* III, Q. 83, art. 2.

Aquinas rightly looks to the Introits of each Mass in support of this interpretation, but the Collects also play a role in elucidating the three Nativities.

The Collect of the Midnight Mass is:

> *Deus, qui hanc sacratíssimam noctem veri lúminis fecísti illustratióne claréscere: da, quǽsumus: ut, cujus lucis mystéria in terra cognóvimus, ejus quoque gáudiis in cǽlo perfruámur. Qui tecum vivit.*

Which I translate as:

> O God, who hast made this most sacred night to shine with the brightness of the True Light, grant, we beseech: that we who have known the mysteries of His light on earth may also relish His joys in Heaven. Who with Thee.

On its own, the Collect is a reference to the tradition that Our Lord was born in Bethlehem in the middle of the night; but juxtaposed with the Introit ("Thou art My Son, this day have I begotten Thee"), it can also betoken the Son's eternal generation from the Father. To know the mysteries of the Light is to know that that Light proceeds from the Father for all eternity and to know that the Beatific Vision, where we "relish His joys in Heaven," consists of seeing that eternally-begotten Light face to face.

The Collect of the Dawn Mass is:

> *Da nobis, quǽsumus, omnípotens Deus: ut, qui nova incarnáti Verbi tui luce perfúndimur; hoc in nostro respléndeat ópere, quod per fidem fulget in mente. Per eúndem Dóminum.*

Which I translate as:

> Grant, we beseech Thee, almighty God: that we, upon whom is poured forth the new light of Thy Incarnate Word, may show forth in our work that which shineth by faith in our minds. Through the same Our Lord.

With the spiritual birth of Christ on our minds, the Collect can be seen as a gloss on this mystery. The Incarnation in the womb of the Blessed Virgin Mary makes possible Christ's temporal birth in Bethlehem, and Christ's temporal birth makes possible His spiritual birth in our hearts. With the Light now born internally in our hearts, we ask that it show forth externally in our work.

The Collect of the Daytime Mass is:

Concéde, quǽsumus, omnípotens Deus: ut nos Unigéniti tui nova per carnem natívitas líberet; quos sub peccáti jugo vetústa sérvitus tenet. Per eúndem Dóminum.

Which the *St. Andrew's Daily Missal* translates as:

Grant, we beseech Thee, almighty God, that the new birth in the flesh of Thine only-begotten Son may set us free, whom the old bondage doth hold under the yoke of sin. Through the same Our Lord.[2]

The Collect focuses on the historic birth of Jesus Christ in Bethlehem (rather than His eternal generation or His spiritual birth in our hearts) as the agent of our liberation from the yoke of sin. Note the pleasing contrast between the new birth of Our Lord and the old bondage of sin. The Collect also has a precise use of prepositions. Jesus Christ is literally born "through the flesh" (*per carnem*), and "through" is a preposition hinting at motion. Christ's divinity fully assumes and suffuses His humanity, which then passes through the flesh of His Mother when He is born. We, however, are held down fast under the yoke of sin (*sub peccáti jugo*). A yoke is supposed to be an instrument of motion, making it possible for a plow or cart to move, but unlike the sweet yoke of Christian discipleship (see Matt. 11:30), there is no real movement under the yoke of sin. The old slavery keeps us stuck in our ways and trodden down, until the enfleshed Word, unleashed upon this sunken world, sets us free.

---

2 *The Saint Andrew Daily Missal*, ed. Dom Gaspar Lefebvre, OSB (St. Paul, MN: E. M. Lohmann Co., 1952), 73.

7

The Orations of the
Sunday after Christmas

HE MASS FOR THE SUNDAY WITHIN THE
Octave of the Nativity (which no longer exists in the
new rite) is significant for two reasons. First, as the
only Sunday within the Christmas Octave, attention is implicitly
drawn to its dominical character. According to an ancient tradition,
Our Lord was born on a Sunday, and so on those years when
December 25 does not fall on a Sunday, it is left to the Sunday
after Christmas to honor the connection between the Lord's Day
and His Nativity.[1] Second, thanks to the Epistle reading (Gal.
4:1-7), which includes the following verses, the Mass celebrates
our divine adoption:

> But when the fulness of the time was come, God sent
> His Son, made of a woman, made under the law, that
> He might redeem them who were under the law, that
> we might receive the adoption of sons. And because you
> are sons, God hath sent the Spirit of His Son into your
> hearts, crying: "Abba," Father. Therefore now he is not a
> servant, but a son: and if a son, an heir also through God.

Although the theme of divine adoption appears several times
throughout the liturgical year, this is its first and perhaps most
important appearance, for it clearly establishes the link between
the *meaning* of Christmas (the Incarnation) and its *purpose* (our
supernatural adoption). Commenting on this passage, Dom
Guéranger offers the colorful image of the Holy Infant turning
heavenward and saying "My Father!" and then turning to us and
saying "My brethren!" Guéranger continues:

> This is the mystery of adoption, revealed to us by the
> great event we are solemnizing. All things are changed,
> both in heaven and on earth: God has not only one Son,

---

1   Dom Prosper Guéranger, OSB, *The Liturgical Year*, vol. 2, trans. Dom
Laurence Shepherd (Great Falls, MT: St. Bonaventure Publications, 2000),
340-41.

He has many sons; henceforth we stand before this our
God, not merely creatures drawn out of nothing by His
power but children that He fondly loves.[2]

Similarly, the Gospel reading for this Sunday is Luke 2:33–44,
which recounts *part* of the story of the Presentation in the Temple.
Significantly, the Presentation is never mentioned; instead, the
reading is framed by the wonder that Mary and Joseph experience at the things that are said of Jesus (2:33) and by the
grace of God that was in Jesus (2:44). The result is a focus on
the marvelous identity of the God-Man rather than the specific
mystery of the Presentation, which is celebrated instead on the
Feast of the Purification (February 2). The Gospel does, however,
mention how a "sword" shall pierce the heart of Mary (2:35).
This sorrowful note in the midst of jubilance is not meant to
make us morose but to supplement the teaching of the Epistle
by identifying the price of our adoption. For "the mystery of
man's adoption by God," Guéranger explains, "is to cost this
Child of hers His life!"[3]

The doctrine of divine adoption is important because it lies at
the center of God's plan to redeem mankind. As Blessed Columba
Marmion (who, I believe, will one day be designated the Doctor
of Divine Adoption) explains, the Father out of sheer love and
generosity has willed for all eternity to extend to us His Pater-
nity, to recognize us as His sons so that we can be filled with
holiness and share in His eternal happiness. Marmion stresses
that although it is in accordance with our nature to call God
our Creator, it is *not* natural for a creature to call his Creator
"Father." That privilege is the result of a purely supernatural
act of adoption. "By *nature* God has only one Son," Marmion
observes; "by *love* He wills to have an innumerable multitude"
(emphasis added).[4]

The Orations of what we are tempted to call Divine Adoption
Sunday do not explicitly allude to this doctrine, but they can be
fruitfully read as creating a profile of what good adopted sons
of God look like. The Collect is:

---

2   Guéranger, *Liturgical Year*, 2:342–43.
3   Guéranger, *Liturgical Year*, 2:344.
4   Bl. Columba Marmion, *Christ the Life of the Soul* (Tacoma, WA:
Angelico Press, 2012), 24.

Omnípotens sempitérne Deus, dírige actus nostros in bene-
plácito tuo: ut in nómine dilécti Fílii tui mereámur bonis
opéribus abundáre. Qui tecum vivit.

Which I translate as:

Almighty, everlasting God, direct our actions in the way
of Thy good pleasure: that in the Name of Thy beloved
Son we may deserve to abound in good works. Who liveth
and reigneth with Thee.

The Collect appears to be influenced by Ephesians 1, where St.
Paul explains our predestination as divinely adopted sons through
Jesus Christ. Ephesians 1:9 uses the relatively uncommon word
beneplacitum ("good pleasure") to describe the way in which
God has made known to us the mystery of His will; the Collect
uses the same word as the means through which God will guide
our actions. Ephesians 1:8 states that Christ's grace has "super-
abounded" (*superabundavit*) in us, and in the Collect we pray
that we may abound in good works. In both cases, the Collect
redirects the language to right action; the focus here is on doing
good like our adopted brother Jesus. But we do not wish to do
good for our own sake but in the Holy Name of Jesus, a Name
that is much on our minds during this season. There is even a
bit of suspense about the Holy Name during this Sunday after
Christmas, for we know that Jesus has been born, we know that
His Name is Jesus (thanks to Saint Gabriel), but He will not
officially receive His Holy Name until his forthcoming circumcision on January 1.

The Secret is:

Concéde, quǽsumus, omnípotens Deus: ut óculis tuæ majestá-
tis munus oblátum, et grátiam nobis piæ devotiónis obtíneat,
et efféctum beátæ perennitátis acquírat. Per Dóminum.

Which I translate as:

Grant, we beseech Thee, almighty God: that the gift which
has been offered before the eyes of Thy majesty may
obtain for us the grace of pious devotion and the effect
of a blessed perennity. Through Our Lord.

This rather unusual Secret is used four times in the 1962 Missal: here, Palm Sunday, the Ember Saturday of September, and

the Eighteenth Sunday after Pentecost. The final prepositional phrase, *beatae perennitatis*, is awkward when translated literally, as I have done; "blessed eternity" will also work. *Perennitas* was a title of the Roman Emperors; you could address an emperor as "Your Perennity." Perhaps, then, the author chose the word to form a parallel with the majesty of God mentioned earlier in the prayer.

The content of the prayer is less puzzling than the diction. Of special note for our purposes is the petition for pious devotion. *Pietas* has a rich meaning in ecclesiastical Latin,[5] but it is still anchored in its original meaning of a loving loyalty to one's gods, one's family, and one's country. To ask for pious devotion is to ask for the grace of being a good son to the Father and a good brother to the Son.

The Postcommunion is:

> *Per hujus, Dómine, operatiónem mystérii, et vítia nostra purgéntur, et justa desidéria compleántur. Per Dóminum.*

Which I translate as:

> By the virtue of this mystery, O Lord, may our vices be purged away and our just desires fulfilled. Through Our Lord.

In the Collect, we prayed to acquire good works or good acts; here in the Postcommunion we pray to be rid of vices. Vices (*vitia*) are not the same as sins, for sins are bad acts while vices are bad habits. The sacrament of penance, for example, may absolve me from the lies that I have been telling, but it does not cure me of my habit of lying. In Roman medical terminology, getting sick (*morbus*) was contrasted with having a defect (*vitium*). Most sicknesses are transitory, and most defects (like blindness or deafness) are permanent.[6] In the Epistle reading St. Paul teaches that God adopted us out of pity because we were "serving under the elements of this world," that is, we were in a permanent state of vice.

Once purged of our vices, our remaining desires are *ipso facto* just, and once those desires are fulfilled, we are by definition happy. As St. Monica succinctly puts it in an early dialogue of

---

5   See chapter 50, "God Has Piety? The Collect of the Eleventh Sunday after Pentecost."
6   See Ellebracht, *Vocabulary of the Ancient Orations*, 190.

St. Augustine: "If he wants good things and has them, he is happy; but if he wants bad things, he is unhappy, even if he has them."[7] Freed from their enslavement to vice, God's happy sons have just desires and total fulfillment.

---

7 Augustine, *On the Happy Life* 2.10, translation mine.

8

The Mostly Marian Orations
of the Christmas Octave

LTHOUGH THE OFFICIAL TITLE FOR THE feast on January 1 in the 1962 Roman Missal is the Octave of Christmas, for most of liturgical history it was called the Feast of the Circumcision. In accordance with the Law, Jesus was circumcised eight days after His birth (see the Gospel reading), and thus, if He was born on December 25, He would have been circumcised on January 1. Our Lord's circumcision is an important event to commemorate: it underscores the faithful Jewish piety of the Holy Family; it is the occasion on which the Infant was, again in accordance with the Old Law, formally given the Holy Name of Jesus; and it marks the first time that Our Lord shed His Blood for humanity. The slightly dolorous note of this last fact also ties into the Church's earliest known observance of January 1 as a day of fasting and penance in opposition to the revelries of the pagans.[1]

The day also has a Marian motif. The station church on January 1 is Santa Maria in Trastevere, one of the oldest churches in Rome dedicated to the Blessed Virgin Mary, and this location no doubt influenced the choice of the Collect and Postcommunion.

The Collect for the feast, which is at least as old as the late eighth century, is:[2]

> *Deus, qui salútis ætérnæ, beátæ Maríæ virginitáte fœcúnda, humáno géneri prǽmia præstitísti: tríbue, quǽsumus; ut ipsam pro nobis intercédere sentiámus, per quam merúimus auctórem vitæ suscípere, Dóminum nostrum Jesum Christum Fílium tuum: Qui tecum.*

Which I translate as:

---

1 See Gregory DiPippo, "The Ancient Character of the Feast of the Circumcision," *New Liturgical Movement*, January 1, 2019, www.newliturgicalmovement.org/2019/01/the-ancient-character-of-feast-of.html.
2 *Corpus Orationum 3: Orationes 1708–2389* (Turnholt, Belgium: Brepols, 1993), 2113b, Br 440, 182.

29

O God, who through the fruitful virginity of blessed Mary didst bestow upon mankind the rewards of eternal salvation: grant, we beseech, that we may feel interceding for us her through whom we have been made worthy to receive the Author of life, Our Lord Jesus Christ Thy Son: Who with Thee.

The protasis or first half of the prayer includes a delightful description of Mary's virginity as fruitful. In St. Hildegard of Bingen's *Play of the Virtues*, the Devil says to the personified virtue of Chastity:

You don't know what you are nurturing, since your womb is bereft of the beautiful form that is received from a man; therefore you transgress the precept that God commanded in the sweet act of copulation; therefore you don't know what you are!

To which Chastity replies:

How on earth could this touch me, which your foul suggestion has polluted through its uncleanness? I did bring forth *one* Man, Who through His Nativity gathers mankind to Himself, against *you*.[3]

Paradoxically, chastity is a fecund virtue.

The apodosis or second half is a bit of a brain twister, but when the initial confusion gives way to comprehension, there is greater delight. Mary, who has paradoxically authored the Author of life, makes us worthy to receive Him as well through her constant intercession. And we pray not only for this continued intercession but for an awareness of it. We want to *feel* her intercession, for the experience of Mary watching over us brings with it consolation, hope, and inspiration to do better.

The Secret, on the other hand, has no explicit Marian theme:

Munéribus nostris, quǽsumus, Dómine, precibúsque suscéptis: et cæléstibus nos munda mystériis, et cleménter exáudi. Per Dóminum.

Which I translate as:

Having received our offerings and prayers, we beseech Thee, O Lord: cleanse us with these heavenly mysteries and mercifully hear us. Through Our Lord.

---

3   Saint Hildegard of Bingen, *Ordo Virtutum* 235–41, translation mine.

Curiously, the prayer appears several times elsewhere in the 1962 Missal but only for a martyr: Boniface (May 14), Romanus (August 9), Hadrian (September 8), Menna (November 11), and in the Mass for a martyr outside of Paschaltide. Perhaps on January 1 the Secret pays indirect tribute to Mary as Queen of Martyrs, who on this day felt the pain of true compassion as she saw her Son's Precious Blood shed. Or perhaps the washing or cleansing with heavenly mysteries calls to mind the Precious Blood itself.

The Postcommunion returns us to Mary as the Mother of God:

> *Hæc nos commúnio, Dómine, purget a crímine: et, intercedénte beáta Vírgine Dei Genitríce María, cœléstis remédii fáciat esse consórtes. Per eúndem Dóminum nostrum.*

Which I translate as:

> May this communion, O Lord, purge us from all guilt, and with the Blessed Virgin Mary, Mother of God, interceding for us, make us partakers of the heavenly remedy. Through the same Our Lord.

The prayer is also used for the Feast of the Maternity of the Blessed Virgin Mary on October 11 and in the Saturday Mass for Our Lady from Christmas until Candlemas (February 2). Aside from these usages, it is, as with the Secret, only used only for martyred Saints.[4]

The prayer has both medical and legal imagery: paired with "remedy," "purge" (*purget*) connotes healing, and paired with "guilt" (*crimen*), it suggests a clearing from accusation or condemnation.[5]

It is noteworthy that we ask to be made partakers of the heavenly remedy after partaking of the heavenly remedy a few moments ago in Holy Communion. The juxtaposition of "communion" and "remedy" is similar to the distinction between the *res et virtus* (reality and power) and the *sacramentum* (sacramental symbolism) of the Eucharist that St. Thomas Aquinas makes in his Prayer before Holy Communion. It is one thing to

---

4 Eusebius (December 16), Blaise (February 3), Stanislaus (May 7), Gervasius and Protasius (June 19), Januarius and Companions (September 19), Vitalis and Agricola (November 4), several martyrs, and a martyred pontiff. Only once in the 1962 Missal is the prayer used without reference to a saint's intercession: the ferial Mass of Monday during the third week of Lent.

5 Ellebracht, *Vocabulary of the Ancient Orations*, 185.

receive Holy Communion sacramentally, that is, on the tongue and under the appearance of bread; it is another to receive the power of its healing and sanctification. Having done the first, we now ask for the second.

And on January 1, we ask for it with the help of Our Blessed Lady. Most of the old hand missals translate *intercedente beata Virgine Dei Genitrice Maria* as "through the intercession of the Blessed Virgin Mary," but I prefer to translate this ablative absolute in a more dynamic way. The first translation could suggest that Mary intervened at only one point to help us get the medicine we needed, like a helpful nurse who called our pharmacist and got the prescription filled. But I believe that this clause, which is in the present tense, asks for Mary's ongoing intercession (like the Collect) so that she can advocate for us now, tomorrow, and at the hour of our death. After all, if on this day we celebrate Mary as the mother of Jesus Christ, we implicitly celebrate her as our mother as well. And a good Mom constantly has her children's back.

9

The Postcommunion of the Feast of the Holy Name of Jesus

N A SENSE, JANUARY 1 IS THE ORIGINAL Feast of the Holy Name, for this is the day, eight days after He was born, that Jesus was formally given His name by Saint Joseph on the occasion of His Circumcision. It is for this reason that the Society of Jesus (the Jesuits) continues to keep this day as their titular feast.

A celebration devoted exclusively to the Most Holy Name of Jesus was begun by the Franciscan Order in the sixteenth century and extended to the universal calendar in 1721; its final date in the *usus antiquior* was fixed by Pope St. Pius X on the Sunday between January 1 and January 6, or otherwise on January 2. In 1969, it was dropped from the calendar but later restored by Pope St. John Paul II and assigned to January 3.

The quality of the propers composed during the Counter Reformation has been the subject of some controversy. The great English liturgist Fr. Adrian Fortescue was not impressed:

> And merely from an aesthetic point of view there can be no doubt that the old propers are more beautiful than modern compositions. It is these old propers that show the austere dignity of our liturgy, that agree in feeling with the Ordinary and Canon, happily still unaltered. It is the old collects that really are collects and not long florid prayers. A tendency to pile up explanatory allusions, classical forms that savour of Cicero and not at all of the rude simplicity that is real liturgical style, florid rhetoric that would suit the Byzantine Rite in Greek rather than our reticent Roman tradition, these things have left too many traces in the later propers. It is astonishing that the people should have so little sense of congruity, apparently never think of following the old tradition, or of harmony with the old ordinary.[1]

---

1 Fortescue, *The Mass*, 212.

Fortescue does not mention the Feast of the Holy Name, but I suspect that its propers are among those that drew his ire. The Postcommunion, for example, is one of the longest in the 1962 Missal:

> Omnípotens ætérne Deus, qui creásti et redemísti nos, réspice propítius vota nostra: et sacríficium salutáris hóstiæ, quod in honórem nóminis Fílii tui, Dómini Jesu nostri Christi, majestáti tuæ obtúlimus, plácido et benígno vultu suscípere dignéris; ut grátia tua nobis infúsa, sub glorióso nómine Jesu, ætérnæ prædestinatiónis título gaudeámus nómina nostra scripta esse in cælis. Per eúndem Dóminum.

Which I translate as:

> Almighty and everlasting God, who hast created and redeemed us, graciously look upon our prayers and deign to accept with a kind and benign countenance the Sacrifice of the Saving Victim, which we have offered to Thy majesty in honor of the Name of Thy Son, Our Lord Jesus Christ: that, being infused with Thy grace in us, we may rejoice to have our names written in heaven as an inscription of eternal predestination under the glorious Name of Jesus. Through the same Our Lord.

The Postcommunion certainly seems guilty of "florid rhetoric," but perhaps we can forgive its authors and even learn to appreciate it as part of the glorious and diverse flea-market that is our liturgical patrimony. After all, the Offertory Prayers of the traditional Roman Rite are arguably florid imports from the Gallican liturgy, and yet they are now part of the family. (Whether *new* prayers should be composed in this style is a different conversation.)

At the very least, we can appreciate the Postcommunion's theological themes. We do indeed want God the Father, who created and redeemed us, to look upon us and our participation in the Sacrifice of the Mass with a kindly countenance. There is wisdom in connecting the Father's kind face to His Son's Holy Name. We learn a person's basic identity from his name, and we associate his name with his face more than with any other part of his body: both the name and the face provide a ready means of recognition. The face, in turn, often reveals what is in a person's heart (his emotions, character, etc.). The Holy Name of Jesus draws us to His Holy Face, and His Holy, suffering Face reveals the love of His most Sacred Heart. And Jesus's Holy Face also reveals the kind Face of the Father, for whoever sees the Son sees the Father (John 14:9).

The second half of the Postcommunion prays that, "being infused with Thy grace, we may rejoice to have our names written in heaven under the glorious name of Jesus." The petition hearkens to the last verse of the Epistle reading: "For there is no other name under Heaven given to men whereby we must be saved" (Acts 4:12). But it also brings out an eschatological element with the plea to have our names "written in heaven as an inscription of eternal predestination." Jesus's name, too, was once written as an inscription and placed over His Head as He writhed on the Cross. By placing our names under His, we join Him on the Cross as part of His mystical Body, and God willing, we will join Him in glory in Heaven. The association of predestination with writing can be found in the Secret for the Votive Mass for the Living and the Dead. Commenting on that Secret, Sr. Mary Ellebracht writes: "The notion of a *liber predestinationis* is a combination of the Hebrew 'Book of Works' and 'Book of Life.' Thus being inscribed in the *beatæ predestinationis liber* is a metaphorical expression for salvation by grace and good works."[2]

Finally, we pray not only to have our names written in the Book of Life, but to rejoice at having our names written. The Feast of the Holy Name is a great feast of joy. We rejoice now at the name of our Messiah, a name that means "YHWH saves," and we hope to rejoice at our eternal salvation in Heaven. "Blessed be Jesus Christ, true God and true man," we proclaim during the Divine Praises. "Blessed be the name of Jesus!"

---

2 Ellebracht, *Vocabulary of the Ancient Orations*, 152. For more on predestination, see Peter Kwasniewski, "Who's Afraid of Predestination?" *New Liturgical Movement*, January 29, 2018, www.newliturgicalmovement.org/2018/01/whos-afraid-of-predestination.html.

10

The Highly Beautiful
Collect of the Epiphany

HE DIVINE OFFICE FOR THE FEAST OF
the Epiphany commemorates three epiphanies or manifestations: the manifestation of the God-Man to the
Gentiles as represented by the Magi who brought Him gifts;
the manifestation of Christ's divinity at the Wedding of Cana;
and the manifestation of Christ's Sonship at His Baptism by
St. John the Baptist. All three are interwoven in the beautiful
Benedictus antiphon:

> This day is the Church joined unto the Heavenly Bride-
> groom, since Christ hath washed away her sins in the
> Jordan; the Magi hasten with gifts to the marriage supper
> of the King; and they that sit at meat together make merry
> with water turned into wine, alleluia.

The focus in the Epiphany Mass, however, is predominantly on
the visit of the Three Kings. Hence the Collect:

> *Deus, qui hodiérna die Unigénitum tuum géntibus stella duce*
> *revelásti: concéde propítius; ut, qui jam te ex fide cognóvimus,*
> *usque ad contemplándam spéciem tuæ celsitúdinis perducámur.*
> *Per eúndem Dóminum.*

Which I translate as:

> O God, who on this day and by virtue of a star leading the
> way didst reveal Thine only-begotten Son to the Gentiles:
> mercifully grant that we who know Thee now by faith may
> be led all the way up to a contemplation of the beauty of
> Thy Highness. Through the same.

It is difficult for the Roman Rite to resist the temptation to
allegorize altitude. The Collect for the Feast of the Ascension of
Our Lord Jesus Christ parallels His ascent into Heaven and our
mental elevation whereby we dwell amidst heavenly things.[1] On
the Feast of the Epiphany, the Star of Bethlehem likewise puts

---

1 See chapter 33, "The Elevating Collect of Ascension Thursday."

us in mind of things high above, though the parallelism here is more complicated. In the protasis or first half of the prayer, the Magi follow what is physically above them (the Star) to the Infant Jesus, who is ontologically the Highest yet physically lower on the ground.

And in the apodosis or second half, one would expect the Star to be paired with the beauty of God's height, but instead the bright Star is compared to the light of faith; it is the Only-Begotten who is equated with the beauty of God's height. That in itself is a sentiment worthy of contemplation, namely, that rather than being a divine attribute or quality, the Beauty of God's Height may be a Divine Person, the Son Himself.

There is also a lovely parallel between the star leading the Magi (*duce*) and the Faith that leads us (*perducamur*) to what is on high but once again with a difference: the star leads, but the Faith thoroughly leads, for *per-ducamur* is a more intense action than *ducamur* or the noun *dux*. The prayer goes on to identify faith as a source of knowledge. Faith and knowledge are often contrasted: faith is what we affirm despite a clear grasp of what is going on, while knowledge is what reason can affirm based on a certain comprehension of causes. Here, however, faith gives birth to knowledge: we may see through a glass darkly (see 1 Cor. 13:12), but we still see something, something that we would not otherwise have seen.

Perhaps the most difficult word in the Collect to translate is what I originally rendered as "Highness" and then called "Height." *Celsitudo*, derived from the Latin *celsus* (raised high, lofty), is rather rare in classical Latin. The Roman historian Vellejius Paterculus (19 BC–AD 31) uses the expression *celsitudo corporis* to signify a "a lofty carriage of the body."[2] Although it makes no appearance in the Vulgate, the word is common in the Patristic age: Church Fathers like Paulinus of Nola, Origen (in translation), Peter Chrysologus, and Arnobius use it, as does Augustine — eighty-three times in his case, to be precise (assuming the accuracy of the Brepols search engine). In the Theodosian Code, which is a compilation of laws under Christian Roman Emperors, *celsitudo* becomes a title, the way to say "Your Highness." If the latter is

---

2 *Lewis and Short Latin Dictionary* (Oxford: Clarendon Press, 1879), 310.

what the author of the Collect intended, then *tua celsitudo* refers to God the Father's kingship.

Celsitudo is used two other times in the 1962 Missal,[3] both in order to describe God as the *Celsitudo humilium*, which the latest English translation of the Novus Ordo Missal (2011) renders at one point as the "exaltation of the lowly."[4] The Latin edition of the Novus Ordo retains the Epiphany Collect word for word, but the 2011 English translation underplays the altitudinous dimensions of *celsitudo* and adds the theme of glory: "already by faith, may [we] be brought to behold the beauty of your sublime glory."[5] (And "behold," I tautologically remark, is a less contemplative activity than "contemplate.")

Another difficult word to translate is *species*. Although the word means beauty and can even signify the form or *reality* of something in Patristic and medieval literature,[6] most Catholics know it as the term for the *appearance* of bread or wine that remains after the Consecration. It is unlikely that the author(s) of this Collect had this later, scholastic meaning in mind,[7] but if we apply it nonetheless, the prayer takes on a Eucharistic connotation. The Magi beheld the Holy Face of Jesus, and we contemplate the beauty of that same Face veiled under both sacred species with the hope, as St. Thomas Aquinas puts it in his Prayer before Holy Communion, of forever contemplating that Face unveiled. The petition is asking for the Beatific Vision sometime in the future, but one can't help thinking of the beauty of Our Lord under the species of bread during the act of Adoration that we can contemplate now.

The focus on God's beauty during the Christmas season also brings to mind the specific beauty of the Incarnation. When he was asked to write *Cur Deus Homo* (Why Did God Become

---

3 The Collect after the Fourth Lesson on Holy Saturday and the Collect for the Feast of St. Francis of Paola, April 2.

4 *The Roman Missal*, 3rd ed. (Washington, DC: USCCB Publishing, 2011), 845.

5 *The Roman Missal*, 188.

6 See Augustine, *On the Immortality of the Soul* 8.13.

7 I suspect that the Latin word *species* was only applied to the appearance of a thing after the translation of certain Aristotelian texts into Latin in the twelfth and thirteenth centuries, whereas this Collect, which appears in the Gellone Sacramentary, is at least as old as the eighth century (*Corpus Orationum* 1673).

Man?), St. Anselm of Canterbury hesitated on the grounds that the mystery was simply too beautiful to describe (and the word he uses for "beautiful," incidentally, is *speciosus*, the adjectival version of *species*). "I am afraid that," he wrote, "just as I am invariably annoyed by bad painters when I see the Lord Himself depicted as of ugly appearance, the same fault will be found with me, if I presume to plough through such beautiful subject-matter with an unpolished and contemptible style of writing."[8] The Word becoming flesh makes the invisible visible (see Preface of the Nativity), and yet paradoxically that revelation of the Word is too beautiful for words.

In Dostoyevsky's *The Idiot*, Ippolit cries out: "Is it true, Prince, that you once said the world would be saved by beauty?... What sort of beauty is going to save the world?... Are you a devout Christian?"[9] Prince Myshkin refuses to engage his drunken interlocutor, but inspired by the Epiphany Collect we may hazard a reply. The beauty of God's sublime and Holy Face will save the world. Indeed, It already has.

---

8 *Why God Became Man* 1.1, in *Anselm of Canterbury: The Major Works*, ed. Brian Davies and G. R. Evans (Oxford: Oxford University Press, 2008), 267.
9 Fyodor Dostoevsky, *The Idiot*, trans. Alan Myers (Oxford: Oxford University Press, 1992), III.5, p. 402. I have made slight modifications to the translation.

III

THE TIME
AFTER
EPIPHANY

11

The Collect of the Feast
of the Holy Family

N THE 1962 CALENDAR, THE FEAST OF the Holy Family falls on the Sunday after Epiphany rather than the Sunday after Christmas. One advantage of this arrangement, as Peter Kwasniewski notes, is allowing "the central mystery of the Incarnation of the Eternal Son of the Father to 'breathe' or occupy central stage":

> In terms of the "psychology" of the season, one notes that the more modern feast of the Holy Family is not permitted to "intrude" until the great event of the Nativity in all its facets—including its cluster of special companion saints who, as it were, surround the cradle of the infant King—has been given plenty of room to shine. Our gaze is intently focused on the mystery of the Incarnate Word: Christmas for eight days, the Circumcision when the Redeemer first shed His blood, the Holy Name he was given and by which we are saved, the Epiphany or revelation of God as savior of the Gentiles. Only after this do we turn expressly to the family in which Our Lord grew up, His Baptism in the Jordan, His first miracle at Cana (2nd Sunday after Epiphany), and the start of His preaching and miracles (subsequent Sundays).[1]

Another advantage of the old *ordo* is that it allows the mystery of the Holy Family to breathe as well. Although some of the propers of the feast in the new Missal likewise take up the life of Jesus, Mary, and Joseph in Nazareth, many Catholics find it difficult to think of anything else except the Bethlehem infancy narratives when the feast is celebrated so close to Christmas and prior to the liturgical acknowledgement on January 1 of the Circumcision, the ritual act that formally incorporated Jesus into

---

1   Peter Kwasniewski, "How Different Are the Pre-1955, 1962, and 1969 Calendars from Christmas into Epiphanytide?" *Rorate Caeli*, January 2, 2021, https://rorate-caeli.blogspot.com/2021/01/how-different-are-pre-1955-1962-and.html.

the Holy Family.[2] But when the feast occurs after Epiphany, it is easier to imagine the Holy Family over the long arc of their lives together, from Bethlehem to Egypt and back to Nazareth.

The "big picture" of the Holy Family is also on the mind of the Church when she prays the Collect for this feast:

> *Dómine Jesu Christe, qui Maríæ et Joseph súbditus domésticam vitam ineffabílibus virtútibus consecrásti: fac nos, utriúsque auxílio, Famíliæ sanctæ tuæ exémplis ínstrui; et consórtium cónsequi sempíternum: Qui vivis et regnas.*

Which I translate as:

> O Lord Jesus Christ who, by being subject to Mary and Joseph, didst consecrate domestic life with ineffable virtues: grant that by the assistance of both we may be instructed by the examples of, and gain eternal fellowship with, Thy Holy Family: Who livest and reignest.

It is rare for the Roman Orations to address the Son rather than the Father, and rarer still to address Him by His Holy Name, but by mentioning Jesus, Mary, and Joseph in that order, the Collect ranks the members of the Holy Family according to their degree of sanctity. In the Holy Family, the order of holiness is the opposite of its order of subjection, with Joseph as head, Mary as subject to him, and Jesus subject to both (see the Gospel of the day, Luke 2:42–52). This divinely-ordained discrepancy is worth contemplating. Astonishingly, the omniscient and omnipotent Second Person of the Holy Trinity has voluntarily placed Himself under the authority of two mere mortals; and the holiest mere mortal of all time has chosen to place herself under a carpenter who is less holy than she. Among the lessons to be learned from this mystery is that the Christian concept of subjection does not entail any insinuation that the subordinate person is ontologically or spiritually inferior. There is a difference between value, dignity, and excellence on one hand, and an economy of authority based on role or office on the other.

The Maker of all has placed Himself under the authority of two of His creatures, and in so doing has consecrated (*consecrare*)

---

2 Both the 1962 and 1970 Missals include Luke 2:21 in the Gospel reading on January 1: "And after eight days were accomplished, that the child should be circumcised, his name was called Jesus, which was called by the angel, before he was conceived in the womb."

the home with ineffable virtues. Consecration is literally the act of making something sacred, setting it apart from profane use and dedicating it to God. But in Christian parlance it can also mean to "make holy by means of a sacrament."[3] In the Solemn Nuptial Blessing of the traditional rite of matrimony, the Church prays: "O God, who hast consecrated the conjugal joining (*conjugalis copula*) by so excellent a mystery..." Just as Our Lord took a natural good like marriage and elevated it to the dignity of a sacrament, so too has He done something similar with the family. Thanks to the early life of Jesus Christ, domestic life has a new dignity as a potential channel of grace.

The Collect calls the virtues with which Jesus consecrates domestic life "ineffable." Initially it seems strange to describe virtues as indescribable; after all, can't the virtues be named and defined? (If they can't, then the *Secunda Pars* of St. Thomas Aquinas's *Summa theologiae* is a massive waste of time.)

The adjective "ineffable," it seems to me, serves two purposes. First, it speaks to Christ's sanctification of the home: insofar as the Christian home becomes a channel of grace, it is participating in a supernatural mystery, and insofar as it is participating in a mystery, it is participating in something ineffable. The Church uses a similar logic in the Collect for Friday of the Fourth Week of Lent when she speaks of God as He who "renews the world with ineffable sacraments."

Second, it speaks to the fact that the domestic life of Jesus, Mary, and Joseph was by and large a hidden life. We cannot describe the virtues of the Holy Family as they lived their quotidian lives insofar as we cannot observe them either with our own eyes or through the sacred text.

The Collect does not ask for grace directly from God but for the assistance of Mary and Joseph, and it asks them to do two things for us: help us be instructed by their examples and help us attain eternal fellowship with them. The prayer uses the plural *exempla* rather than the singular *exemplum*. Our attention is directed not to the example of the Holy Family but to their examples, to the different members of the family (each of whom had a different role to play) and to the different chapters of their lives.

---

3   Ellebracht, *Vocabulary of the Ancient Orations*, 145.

Seeking eternal fellowship with the Holy Family, on the other hand, is a reminder of our status as divinely adopted sons.[4] If we are the adopted sons of God the Father, then Jesus is our brother, Mary our mother, and Joseph our foster-father. If we are the adopted sons of God, we have also been adopted into the Holy Family of Nazareth.

Seeking eternal fellowship with the Holy Family also ties into the Postcommunion petition "that at the hour of our death the glorious Virgin Mother and blessed Joseph may run to meet us and that we may be found worthy to be received by Thee into Thy eternal dwellings." Saint Joseph is the patron saint of a happy death because He reputedly died in the arms of Jesus and Mary, and we pray for a similar fate. There is no better way to live or to die than as a beloved member of the Holy Family.

---

4   See chapter 7, "The Orations of the Sunday after Christmas."

12

The Orations of the Second Sunday after Epiphany

HE SECOND SUNDAY AFTER EPIPHANY is one of my favorite "green" Sundays of the year. The Church catches her breath after the grand merrymaking of Christmastide, but she continues the trajectory of Epiphany by contemplating the different ways in which Christ manifested (*epiphainein*) His divinity. After the epiphany to the Magi, the next stop is the epiphany of Christ's divine glory during His first public miracle at the Wedding of Cana. In *Drinking with the Saints*, I recommend going to your wine rack or cellar and pulling out your best bottle of wine for Sunday dinner, because if you are anything like my wife and me, you have been saving such a bottle for a special occasion but you keep forgetting about it, and by the time you remember to use it, it has turned to vinegar. By drinking it now, you pay homage to Christ's making wine so fine that it even impressed the local sommelier (as we imagine the steward in the story to be).

The Orations for this Sunday offer sober sentiments that mix well with this miracle. The Collect is the following:

> *Omnípotens sempitérne Deus, qui cœléstia simul et terréna moderáris: supplicatiónes pópuli tui cleménter exáudi; et pacem tuam nostris concéde tempóribus. Per Dóminum.*

Which I translate as:

> Almighty and everlasting God, who dost moderate things in heaven as well as on earth, mercifully hear the supplications of Thy people, and grant us Thy peace in our times. Through Our Lord.

The use of "supplication" (a public petition) and "in our times" suggests that the peace being sought is a public peace.[1] Hence the Collect carries forth the Christmas theme of peace on earth

---

1 Haessly, *Rhetoric in the Sunday Collects*, 34.

and our New Year's wish for a peaceful civic year but reminds us that the peace we desire can come only from God. "Peace I leave with you, my peace I give unto you: not as the world giveth, do I give unto you" (John 14:27). The theme of peace also anticipates the Epistle reading (Rom. 12:6–16), which portrays the Church in all her ministries united and at peace with herself.

But the Collect also subtly pairs well with the Gospel, for Jesus's transubstantiation of water into wine proves that He too, like His heavenly Father, moderates and has power over the things of heaven and earth. And the use of the verb to moderate or regulate (*moderari*) calls to mind the virtue of moderation, a most important habit to have where wine is concerned: "Wine was created from the beginning to make men joyful, and not to make them drunk," writes the divinely inspired Sirach. "Wine drunken with moderation is the joy of the soul and the heart" (Ecclesiasticus [Sirach] 31:35–36).

The Secret for this Sunday is:

> *Obláta, Dómine, múnera sanctífica: nosque a peccatórum nostrórum máculis emúnda. Per Dóminum.*

Which I translate as:

> Sanctify, O Lord, the offerings, and cleanse us from the stains of our sins. Through Our Lord.

The succinct wording mirrors the Secret for the third Mass of Christmas and thus faintly reconnects us to the Christmas season. And the plea for cleansing forms a subtle contrast with the water in the six stone vases that the Jews used for purification and that Jesus used to make wine. But whereas the Jewish purification only concerned ritual impurity, the Secret prays for purification from moral stain.

Finally, the Postcommunion is:

> *Augeátur in nobis, quǽsumus, Dómine, tuæ virtútis operátio: ut divínis vegetáti sacraméntis, ad eórum promíssa capiénda, tuo múnere præparémur. Per Dóminum.*

Which I translate as:

> May the operation of Thy power be increased within us, we beseech Thee, O Lord: that being quickened by Thy divine sacraments, we may by this gift of Thine be ready

to take possession of that which they promise. Through Our Lord.

The Collect contains an image of restraint (God moderating or regulating the things of Heaven and earth), but the Postcommunion contains images of acceleration: an increase of power and a quickening of soul. Intentionally or not, the prayer again forms an interesting contrast with the Gospel reading. An increase of physical inebriation leads not to a quickening but to a slowing (a decline in motor control and mental alacrity), and it generally renders a person less ready to take possession of something promised. Being filled with the Holy Spirit instead of spirits, however, vivifies and delivers. Even though the lay communicant receives Holy Communion only under the species of bread in the traditional Roman Rite, he should meditate here on the inebriating Precious Blood that is present in the "divine sacraments" he has just received. For if water-made-wine cheers the heart of man (Ps. 103:15), how much more does water-and-wine-made-Christ's-Blood.

13

The Secret for the
Third Sunday after Epiphany

HEN I FIRST CAME ACROSS THE EPISTLE for the Third Sunday after Epiphany as a boy, I thought that this verse—"But if thy enemy be hungry, give him to eat; if he thirst, give him to drink: for doing this, thou shalt heap coals of fire upon his head" (Prov. 25:22; Rom. 12:20)—meant that the best way to deal with an enemy is to be nice to him, because that will really infuriate him. Little did I know that a lit coal is a symbol of purification, and that the Bible is admonishing us to purify our enemy,[1] not tweak him with sanctimonious passive aggression.

Purification is also the theme of the Secret for the Third Sunday after Epiphany:

> *Hæc hóstia, Dómine, quǽsumus, emúndet nostra delícta: et ad sacrifícium celebrándum, subditórum tibi córpora mentésque sanctíficet. Per Dóminum.*

Which I translate as:

> May this offering, O Lord, we pray Thee, cleanse away our offenses, and sanctify the bodies and minds of Thy subjects for the celebration of this sacrifice. Through Our Lord.

Hostia ("offering") is not an easy word to translate. It is a common term for a victim (that which is sacrificed), but it can also refer to an offering or the act of sacrifice itself. It appears 43 times in the Orations of the traditional Roman Missal, always in the Secret. In these prayers *hostia* usually refers to the gifts brought by the faithful but sometimes, as it does here, it also has "a ritual, sacramental character."[2]

Delicta ("offenses") can also be surprisingly slippery. It is usually, and not inaccurately, translated as "sins." But *delictum* is derived from *delinquo*, to fail in one's duty or to fall short.

---

1   See Isaiah 6:7 and the prayer *Munda cor meum* before the Gospel.
2   Ellebracht, *Vocabulary of the Ancient Orations*, 76.

According to a gloss on Ephesians 2:1 with which St. Thomas Aquinas was familiar, *delictum* signifies a sin of omission.[3] On the other hand, St. Jerome uses *delicta* as the genus and sins of thought, word, and deed as the different species.[4] What paradigm the authors of the ancient Roman Orations had in mind is difficult to determine.

Subditi ("subjects") is often translated as "servants," but a more literal rendering is "those who are subject to Thee." As we discuss elsewhere,[5] subjection is not a popular concept in an egalitarian age such as ours, yet the biblical worldview sees only two alternatives: you are either subject to God or subject to the devil (see James 4:7). Subjection to God is paradoxically liberating; the more we are subject to Him, the more we are truly free and truly ourselves.

But a more curious part of this prayer is the second petition to sanctify our bodies and minds. The mind or soul is sanctified by an infusion of sanctifying grace and by a healthy reordering of one's desires. But how is the body sanctified? One answer is through liturgical worship, the kind that takes place during the Holy Sacrifice of the Mass. The main petition draws from Romans 12:1:

> I beseech you therefore, brethren, by the mercy of God, that you present your bodies a living sacrifice, holy, pleasing unto God, your reasonable service.

We will look at "reasonable service" (*logiké latreia*) at another time.[6] For now, it is enough to observe that "reasonable service" is a Logocentric act of worship, and because it is Logocentric, it is Incarnational, and because it is Incarnational, the human body, the kind that Jesus Christ assumed and that we celebrate during

---

3 The verse is "And you, when you were dead in your offences, and sins" (*Et vos, cum essetis mortui delictis et peccatis vestris*). See St. Thomas Aquinas, *Summa theologiae* I-II, Q. 72, art. 6.

4 *Tria sunt generalia delicta quibus humanum subiacet genus, aut enim cogitatione, aut sermone, aut opere peccamus* (*Commentary on Ezechiel* 43.23, as cited by Aquinas in *Summa theologiae* I-II, Q. 72, art. 77, sed contra).

5 See chapter 11, "The Collect of the Feast of the Holy Family," and chapter 75, "The Feisty Orations of the Feast of Christ the King."

6 See chapter 64, "Jew, Gentile, and the Orations of the Reconfigured Third Sunday after Epiphany," and chapter 16, "Reasonable Meditation and the Collect of the Sixth Sunday after Epiphany."

Christmastide, is involved in divine worship. And because it is involved, the body is a vehicle of holiness, one that participates in our spiritual transformation through word and act (bowing, kneeling, standing, responding, etc.). As St. Augustine writes:

> If, then, the body, which, being inferior, the soul uses as a servant or instrument, is a sacrifice when it is used rightly, and with reference to God, how much more does the soul itself become a sacrifice when it offers itself to God, in order that, being inflamed by the fire of His love, it may receive of His beauty and become pleasing to Him, losing the shape of earthly desire, and being remoulded in the image of permanent loveliness?[7]

During this Time after Epiphany, let us be grateful for our bodies, in which Almighty God deigned to participate, in order to appreciate the greater glory of our transformed souls.

---

7 *City of God* 10.6. Translation from *City of God, VIII–XVI*, trans. Gerald G. Walsh and Grace Monahan (Washington, DC: Catholic University of America Press, 1952).

14

The Stormy Orations of the Fourth Sunday after Epiphany

N TODAY'S GOSPEL, OUR LORD MANI-
fests His divinity by commanding the angry sea and
the raging wind, for only the Creator of nature has
complete power over it. The Church Fathers saw more to the
story: the raging wind is a type for the devils whose pride stirs up
waves of persecutions against God's people, and the sea becomes
troubled by the passions and malice of men which, as Dom Gaspar Lefebvre, OSB, puts it, is "the great source of disobedience
to authority and of fraternal strife." In the Church (the ship),
Lefebvre continues:

> The great law of charity prevails, for while in the first three
> commandments the duty of loving God is laid upon us,
> by the remaining seven we are bound, as a natural con-
> sequence, to the love of our neighbor (Epistle). Herein is
> the whole mystery of the Epiphany. Our Lord manifests
> Himself as the Son of God, and all those who acknowledge
> Him as such, and accept Him as their Leader and Head,
> become members of His mystical body. Being one in Christ,
> all Christians should love one another. [1]

The Collect fits the violent image of a storm hand-in-glove:

> *Deus, qui nos in tantis perículis constitútos, pro humána scis
> fragilitáte non posse subsístere: da nobis salútem mentis et
> córporis; ea quæ pro peccátis nostris pátimur, te adjuvánte
> vincámus. Per Dóminum.*

Which I translate as:

> O God, who knowest us to be placed in dangers so great
> that, on account of human frailty, we cannot withstand
> them; grant to us health of mind and body: that those
> things which we suffer on account of our sins we may
> conquer with Thy help. Through Our Lord.

---

1   *Saint Andrew Daily Missal* (1952), 156.

In the prelude (the protasis), we are surrounded by dangers that we are incapable of withstanding because of our frailty or fragility. "Of all the things that breathe and move upon it," Odysseus laments in the *Odyssey*, "Earth nurtures nothing feebler than man."[2] "Man's days are as grass, as the flower of the field so shall he flourish," chants the psalmist. "For the spirit shall pass in him, and he shall not be: and he shall know his place no more" (Ps. 102:15–16). "Man is nothing but a reed, the feeblest thing in nature," Pascal adds. "It is not necessary for the whole universe to arm itself in order to crush him; a vapor, a drop of water, is enough to kill him."[3]

The solution to weakness is strength, and so we pray for health or vitality in both body and soul. It is good to have both: when the spirit is strong but the flesh is weak, we are at a disadvantage. The image of being weak in both body and soul on a ship during a storm calls to my mind the beginning of the *Aeneid*. Caught in a terrible storm designed by the gods to capsize the Trojan fleet, Aeneas loses heart and buckles. Vergil describes the pious hero's limbs growing slack as he wishes in prayer, Job-like, that he had been killed at Troy with his fallen comrades.[4]

The verb *subsistere* ("withstand") is an interesting choice. Again with the Gospel story in mind, the verb can take on two other meanings. *Subsistere* literally means to "remain standing," which is difficult to do when a ship is pitching and rolling. But it also means to "stop," as in Jesus immediately stopping the storm in order to bring a "great calm." Man in his frailty cannot do that.

The petition (apodosis) adds another consideration: our frailty is caused or at least compounded by our sins. And yet despite our feeble, sinful condition, we dare to think that we can prevail with God's help. The strong verb used for "overcome" (*vincere*) makes me hear the cry of "Vincerò!" (I will conquer) in the aria "Nessun dorma" from Puccini's opera *Turandot*.

The Secret also speaks of frailty:

> *Concéde, quǽsumus, omnípotens Deus: ut hujus sacrifícii munus oblátum, fragilitátem nostram ab omni malo purget semper, et múniat. Per Dóminum nostrum.*

---

2   Homer, *Odyssey* 18.138–39, trans. Stanley Lombardo (Indianapolis, IN: Hackett, 2000), 280.

3   Blaise Pascal, *Pensées* (Paris: Georges Crès et Cie, 1919), 147, translation mine.

4   See Vergil, *Aeneid* I.91ff.

Which I translate as:

> Grant, we beseech Thee, almighty God, that the oblation of this sacrifice may ever purify and protect our frailty from all evil. Through Our Lord.

Finally, in the Postcommunion we pray:

> *Múnera tua nos, Deus, a dilectiónibus terrénis expédiant: et cæléstibus semper instáurent aliméntis. Per Dóminum.*

Which I translate as:

> May Thy gifts, O God, set us free us from earthly delights, and ever restore us with heavenly nourishments. Through Our Lord.

Munus (gift, offering) connects us to the Secret, and the prayer for restoration (*instaurare*) connects us to the Collect. We need to be restored in order to be strengthened, and the means of our restoration is the heavenly nourishment of the Eucharist.

Expedio (set us free) literally refers to the foot being set free from a snare, and that brings us back to standing straight despite the ship's destabilizing movements. But it also reminds us what the snares in this life are. Earthly delights are not evil per se, but the Evil One can use them to ensnare us and make us beholden to what is lowest in us rather than what is highest in us. May Christ the Skipper bring calm to the Barque of Peter and help us stand straight and free as His dignified disciples.

15

The Orations of the Fifth Sunday after Epiphany and the Other Holy Family

HE EXPRESSION "HOLY FAMILY" (*SANCTA familia*) was applied to the Church long before it was applied to the relations between Jesus, Mary, and Joseph. One might therefore say that the Fifth Sunday after Epiphany, which coincidentally but suitably follows the Feast of the Holy Family of Nazareth, is about the other Holy Family, the family of believers.[1] Specifically, this Sunday illustrates how this family should comport itself.

The Introit, Psalm 96, verses 7–8 and 1, is joyous:

> Adore God, all you His angels: Sion heard, and was glad: and the daughters of Juda rejoiced. The Lord hath reigned, let the earth rejoice: let many islands be glad. The daughters of Juda rejoice in God and adore Him. For man's joy is to praise God.

Next comes the Collect:

> *Famíliam tuam, quǽsumus, Dómine, contínua pietáte custódi: ut quæ in sola spe grátiæ cæléstis innítitur tua semper protectióne muniátur.*

Which I, following Sr. Mary Gonzaga Haessly, translate as:[2]

> Guard Thy family, we beseech Thee, O Lord, with continual lovingkindness: that, as it leans upon the hope of heavenly grace alone, it may ever be walled about with Thy protection.

Munio is usually translated as "defend," but it literally means to "build a wall." There is a nice pairing of a solid wall of defense and the people leaning on something secure, and the imagery of a wall anticipates the end of the Gospel, when the master in the parable gathers the wheat and puts it into his barn, and thus the wheat is now walled about for its protection. The Collect also resumes

---

1   See Augustine, *Enarratio in Psalmos*, Ps. 118, sermo 2, 1.
2   Haessly, *Rhetoric in the Sunday Collects*, 40.

the joyful tone of the Introit: the adorable God who reigns is the God who will guard His holy family with His lovingkindness.

The Epistle (Col. 3:12–17) describes the ideal Church, a brotherhood of believers united in charity, thankful to God, and abounding in virtues. With our divine adoption still somewhat fresh on our minds (from the Sunday after Christmas and the Feast of the Epiphany), this description offers us a goal towards which to strive as members of this august family as we wait.

Wait for what? The Gospel reading provides the answer. Whereas the Epistle describes the ideal Church, the Gospel (Matt. 13:31–35, the Parable of the Wheat and the Tares) depicts the Church as it actually is in history and will remain for a long time. The parable consists of three main parts: the sowing of grain and weeds, the owner's decision to let them grow up side-by-side, and the harvest. When this Gospel is read for one of the last Sundays after Pentecost, our attention turns to the third part and its warning about the Final Judgment, with the rewards of Heaven and the punishments of Hell. But when it is read for the Fifth Sunday after Epiphany, our attention naturally turns to the second part, Christ's announcement that the members of His Church will be a mixed bag, a fact that we will need to learn to accept as we learn to minister to each other.[3]

Context shapes our praying of the Secret as well. It can be difficult living in a family of wheat and weeds and still confidently praise the right hand of the Lord that strengthens us and lifts us up (see the Offertory verse). With the Lord's right hand still on our minds, the priest prays the Secret:

> *Hóstias tibi, Dómine, placatiónis offérimus: ut et delícta nostra miserátus absólvas, et nutántia corda tu dírigas.*

Which I translate as:

> We offer unto Thee, O Lord, the sacrifices of appeasement, that Thou mayest mercifully absolve our sins, and do Thou Thyself direct our wavering hearts.

Hearts wobble and waver in their dealings with other family members, and invariably they commit sins against their brothers and sisters. And so the Church asks for guidance from God Himself.

---

3 Pius Parsch, *The Church's Year of Grace*, vol. 5, trans. Rev. William G. Heidt, OSB (Collegeville, MN: Liturgical Press, 1958), 124–25.

The verb *dírige*, which I have translated as "direct," forms a good contrast to wavering (*nutans*), for it literally means to set in a straight line (*dis+rego*). Because our hearts are apt to zigzag and not stay within the lines, we need God to steady us and stay the course for the long haul. And there is an emphasis on God's agency with the pronoun *tu* (you yourself). We do not want a representative of God to guide us; we want [the right hand of] God Himself, we insist, to take the tiller of our hearts.

Finally, in the Postcommunion we pray:

> *Quǽsumus, omnípotens Deus: ut illíus salutáris capiámus*
> *efféctum, cujus per hæc mystéria pignus accépimus.*

Which I translate as:

> We beseech Thee, almighty God, that we may take hold of
> the effect of that salvation, the pledge of which we have
> received through these mysteries. Through Our Lord.

Despite proceeding in reverse chronological order, the petition is relatively straightforward. We have a received a pledge of salvation by virtue of the mysteries we have just received in Holy Communion; now we ask to take possession of the effect of that salvation. *Capio* (which I have translated as "take hold") is an aggressive verb that means to seize or grab. There is *almost* a hint of the legend of Proteus, the god whom you must continue to grab despite the various appearances he assumes before he will relent and tell you the truth. In the case of the Eucharist, the appearance of bread and wine "hides" the Truth (who is a Divine Person, the Word made flesh), and it hides a pledge of salvation (those who receive the Eucharist worthily are promised eternal life—see John 6:51-55). We ask to take hold of that salvation, even though our senses cannot detect it.

The Communion verse of the day adds another nuance to the prayer: "All wondered at these things which proceeded from the mouth of God." The verse, Luke 4:22, describes the reaction of the synagogue at Nazareth after Jesus essentially tells them that He is the Messiah. But the next verse is also telling: "Is not this the son of Joseph?" Well, yes and no. Those who hold onto the pledge of salvation, which they have received from the mouth of God and which they continue to marvel at, know that Joseph is Christ's foster-father (and theirs too) and that His true Father is in Heaven. The holy family of God knows the Holy Family of Nazareth.

16

Reasonable Meditation and the Collect of the Sixth Sunday after Epiphany

TILL BASKING IN THE WARMTH OF THE Christmas season, the Time after Epiphany celebrates the good news that God has called all nations and not just the Jewish people into His New Covenant; and it especially dwells on the earthly public ministry of Christ, particularly the manifestations of His Divinity during that three-year span.

Today's Epistle lesson is taken from St. Paul's first letter to the Thessalonians (1 Thess. 1:2–10). Paul himself had "planted" the Church at Thessalonika, having preached both in the synagogue and to the Gentiles. It appears that the majority of converts were Gentiles; when Paul writes about his audience having just "turned to God from idols," we—the faithful of today who probably come from a non-Jewish background—should put ourselves in their shoes and be grateful for our deliverance from the false gods that once beguiled our pre-Christian ancestors. And we can also be grateful for deliverance from our own personal idols, whatever it was that we bowed down to and that was bad for us but no longer has a hold on us.

In today's Gospel (Matt. 13:31–35), St. Matthew alludes to Our Lord's Divine nature by saying that He uttered "things hidden from the foundation of the world"—secrets that could only be known by God Himself. When proclaimed during the Time after Epiphany, the two parables in the Gospel bring to mind the destiny of the new community that Jesus is founding during His earthly ministry. The Parable of the Mustard Seed portrays the small seed of faith turning into a large bush that will house the birds of heaven (angels? converts from around the world?). In any event, like the mustard seed in the parable, the Church, the mystical Body of the God-man, will continue to grow through history until it reaches its preordained size and shelters in its branches all of the Elect. Similarly, the Parable of the Leaven portrays a tiny ingredient (again the Church) having a tremendous, transformative effect on something else (the world). Finally, this pairing of parables reminds us of the equal calling of men and women to this new community. As is the case here, Jesus often gave two parables in a row, the first pitched to men and their traditional occupation and the second geared to women and theirs.

Having turned from idols, having been planted with the seed of Faith, having received the leaven of heavenly love and solid doctrine in our hearts, what do we do next? The Collect provides an instructive answer:

> *Præsta, quǽsumus, omnípotens Deus: ut semper rationabília meditántes, quæ tibi sunt plácita, et dictis exsequámur et factis. Per Dóminum nostrum.*

Which I translate as:

> Grant, we beseech Thee, almighty God, that ever meditating upon reasonable things, we may thoroughly carry out the things that are pleasing to Thee both in words and in deeds. Through Our Lord.

Exsequamur ("we may thoroughly carry out") is a robust verb. *Sequor* means to follow after, chase, or attain, but because the prefix *ex* has a perfective force denoting "completely," "thoroughly," or "to the end," the Church is here petitioning for "a complete and generous 'following out' of those things that belong to God and His service."[1]

But the most intriguing word in the prayer is *rationabilia* ("reasonable things"), for it goes against the grain of our sensibilities. Even though we Catholic Christians maintain that faith and reason are compatible, we tend to put them in two different containers, at least where worship and study are concerned. We act as if "reasonable things" are for the classroom, whereas worship is more for the heart than the mind. And yet here in the midst of our worship is a plea for a constant meditation on reasonable things.

What constitutes the *rationabilia* can be discovered with a little effort. We may infer from the rest of the prayer that at least some of the things found in the category of the reasonable are the

---

1 Haessly, *Rhetoric in the Sunday Collects*, 113.

things that are pleasing to God and are to be carried out, such as we may presume, the double love of God and neighbor or the Ten Commandments. But meditating on reasonable things may involve more than ruminating on things to do like the divine law or works of righteousness. According to some scholars, the term was once synonymous with "spiritual" until its meaning migrated to "reasonable, conformed to the essence of a thing" and *spiritalis* took its place.[2] By this reading, reasonable things would include objects of the speculative intellect (to put it in Thomistic terms) as well as objects of the practical intellect.

It may sound odd to think of "reasonable" and "spiritual" as synonymous until one considers Romans 12:1: "I beseech you therefore, brethren, by the mercy of God, that you present your bodies a living sacrifice, holy, pleasing unto God, your reasonable service." The Greek *logiké latreia* (*rationabile obsequium* or "reasonable service") captures the fact that Christian *latreia* or worship is Logocentric or centered on the Word (*Logos*) that is Christ. As Pope Benedict XVI observes, "the celebration is not only a ritual, it is not only a liturgical game, but is intended to be 'logiké latreia', a transformation of my existence in the direction of the Logos."[3] The last clause is key. Among other things, to be holy or spiritual is to have one's faculty of reason (*ratio*) restored into a likeness of the incarnate Logos. Reasonable things are spiritual things because they renew that spiritual entity known as reason.

Benedict also notes that *rationabile* appears in the Roman Canon, when the faithful pray that God will, as one old translation has it, "bless, approve, ratify, make worthy (*rationabile*) and acceptable this offering" (the 2011 English edition of the new Missal has "make it spiritual and acceptable"). As the pope explains:

> The Church knows that in the Holy Eucharist Christ's gift of Himself, His true sacrifice, becomes present. However, the Church prays that the community celebrating may truly be united with Christ and transformed; she prays that we may become what we cannot be with our

---

2   Ellebracht, *Vocabulary of the Ancient Orations*, 18.
3   Sandro Magister, "Homilies. The Liturgical Year Narrated by Joseph Ratzinger, Pope," http://chiesa.espresso.repubblica.it/articolo/209107bdc4.html?eng=y.

own efforts: a "rational" offering that is acceptable to God. Thus the Eucharistic Prayer interprets St. Paul's words correctly.[4]

By using the term *rationabile* for the Eucharistic offering, observes Peter Kwasniewski,

> the Roman Canon highlights the *rationality* of the Christian faith. The *Logos* became flesh in order to restore man's logos, his reason. We are given the privilege of a rational worship that, on the one hand, still contains the full reality of sacrifice (without which there is no religion, no adoration, no forgiveness of sins), and, on the other hand, is unbloody and spiritual, leading us from the sensible or earthly realm to the intelligible or celestial realm. Protestantism attacked Catholicism as a recrudescence of paganism or a Judaizing cult; modernity attacked Catholicism as irrational superstition and pre-scientific prejudice; postmodernity attacks Catholicism as an avaricious, chauvinistic, omniphobic, intolerant structure of self-serving power; but the Roman Canon serenely bears witness to the luminous rationality of the Faith, the majesty of its God, the excellence of its rites, the lofty aim of its rule of life.[5]

To meditate on God's reasonable things and to make ourselves a rational, spiritual offering are the ways to grow the seed of faith and the leaven of love in our hearts and in our Church and in our world.

---

4   Pope Benedict XVI, "St. Paul: Wednesday General Audience," January 7, 2009, www.vatican.va/content/benedict-xvi/en/audiences/2009/documents/hf_ben-xvi_aud_20090107.html.
5   Peter Kwasniewski, *The Once and Future Roman Rite: Returning to the Traditional Latin Liturgy after Seventy Years of Exile* (Gastonia, NC: TAN Books, 2023), 237.

IV

PRE-LENT

17

The Exilic Collect of
Septuagesima Sunday

PRE-LENT OR SEPTUAGESIMA (THE roughly seventieth day before Easter)—a fascinating season that lasts two and a half weeks—acts as a bridge between the jubilance of the Christmas cycle and the austerity of Lent. Violet vestments are worn and the Gloria and Alleluia are suppressed, but there is no mandatory fasting; indeed, the old custom of voluntarily finishing off foods forbidden during Lent ironically led to the excesses of Carnival.

The propers for Septuagesima serve as a perfect primer on how to approach the Lent-Easter cycle. During Matins of this Sunday, the Church contemplates the fall of Adam, that fateful act which, as we will hear during the *Exultet* on Holy Saturday, is a *felix culpa* that precipitates our redemption through the suffering, death, and resurrection of Jesus Christ.

The Collect for Septuagesima Sunday is likewise instructive:

> *Preces pópuli tui, quæsumus, Dómine, cleménter exáudi: ut, qui juste pro peccátis nostris afflígimur, pro tui nóminis glória misericórditer liberémur. Per Dóminum.*

Which I translate as:

> Graciously hear, we beseech Thee, O Lord, the prayers of Thy people: that we who are justly afflicted for our sins, may be mercifully delivered for the glory of Thy name. Through Our Lord.

Just as Lent recalls the forty years that the Hebrews spent in the wilderness, Septuagesima recalls the seventy years of the Babylonian Exile, when the Chosen People were so homesick that they could not sing a song of Zion (see Ps. 136:3-4).[1] Septuagesima

---

1 The suppression of the word "Alleluia" during Septuagesima and Lent is an apt imitation of the Hebrews refusing to sing by the rivers of Babylon, for Alleluia is the song on the lips of the angels and saints in our true home of Heaven.

and Lent are sober reminders of our status as wayfarers living east of Eden, "justly afflicted for our sins"[2] in a valley of tears.

But even though we are afflicted justly, we pray that God may "graciously hear" our prayers. The plea *clementer exaudi*, which occurs three times in the Roman Orations, is somewhat difficult to translate. *Audi* means to hear and *ex-audi* means to hear clearly, to heed or grant, even to obey. *Clementer* is the adverbial form of *clemens*, from which derives *clementia* or clemency. In both Latin and English, *clementia* has a juridical ring to it, as when a judge shows clemency in sentencing; and one of the titles of the Roman Emperors was *Clementia tua* or "Your Grace." Through this Collect we are essentially acknowledging that we are guilty but begging for clemency nonetheless.

Why would God the Supreme Judge show clemency to miserable sinners such as us? Because, the Collect states, it will give glory to His name. Perhaps it is the people who, delivered from their sins, will give God glory, or perhaps the act of clemency itself counts as a glorious act. Either way, the petitioner's hope is that God will be incentivized to action by the glory of His name. That hope, which is an echo of Psalm 78:9,[3] is present at every Mass in the *Suscipiat*, when the faithful pray that God will accept this Eucharistic sacrifice for the praise and glory of His name.

But in the Old Testament the glory of YHWH (*Kebod Jahweh*) is also an actual "physical phenomenon indicative of the divine presence" that appeared on Mount Sinai, in the Tabernacle, and in the Temple, and that often manifested itself as some form of brightness.[4] The Church's Easter prayers apply this brightness to the glory of the Resurrection, and so when the Septuagesima Collect prays for deliverance for the glory of God's name, it is already looking ahead to the Light at the end of the penitential tunnel into which we are now entering, giving us hope that our mortifications will meet with a happy result.

---

2   This phrase is absent in the new Missal. Its closest counterpart may be found in the Postcommunion Prayer in option C for a Votive Mass *In Quacumque Necessitate*: *Tribulationem nostram, quæsumus, Domine, propitius respice, et iram tuæ indignationis, quam pro peccatis nostris juste meremur, per passionem Filii tui, propitiatus averte. Per Christum.*

3   *Adjuva nos, Deus, salutaris noster; et propter gloriam nominis tui, Domine, libera nos.*

4   Ellebracht, *Vocabulary of the Ancient Orations*, 32–33.

18

The Pauline Collect of
Sexagesima Sunday

TATION CHURCHES ARE AN INTRIGUING
part of the traditional Missal. For eighty-nine Masses
on eighty-six days of the year, the 1962 Roman Missal
mentions a station, the church in Rome to which the pope and
the faithful would process and where he would celebrate Mass
that day. Station churches were sometimes chosen to reflect the
liturgical occasion (such as the church of the Holy Cross "in
Jerusalem" on Good Friday), but they could also influence the
liturgy itself. The Collect of the Thursday of the Third Week of
Lent, for example, mentions Saints Cosmas and Damian because
the station church for the day is named after them.

The Roman custom of station churches explains some of the
elements of Sexagesima Sunday.[1] Because the station of this
Sunday is St. Paul-Outside-the-Walls, one of the four great basilicas of Rome, the Epistle is 2 Corinthians 11:19–33 and 12:1–9, in
which Paul recounts his many sufferings as an apostle of Christ.
The Collect is likewise noteworthy:

> *Deus, qui cónspicis, quia ex nulla nostra actióne confídimus:*
> *concéde propítius; ut contra advérsa ómnia, Doctóris géntium*
> *protectióne muniámur. Per Dóminum.*

Which I translate as:

> O God, who seest that we put not our trust in anything
> that we do; mercifully grant that by the protection of the
> Doctor of the Gentiles we may be defended against all
> adverse things. Through Our Lord.

The prayer is a succinct reflection of Pauline theology. Like Saint
Paul, the Doctor of the Gentiles, we should not trust our own
ability to act morally, but should glory in our infirmities, that the

---

1   See Gregory DiPippo, "The Station Churches of Septuagesima,"
New Liturgical Movement, February 9, 2020, www.newliturgicalmovement.
org/2020/02/the-station-churches-of-septuagesima.html.

power of Christ may dwell in us (see the Epistle reading). The Epistle includes a long list of adversities that Paul encountered, and it is from all adverse things that we pray to be protected.

The verb for defending (*munire*) is an appropriate choice, for it is a military image. The Collects of the Septuagesima season are concerned with affliction and adversity. We recognize that during Lent, we will be following Jesus into the desert to be tempted by the devil, and we have enough self-knowledge to know that we cannot survive this struggle alone. We also know that the danger of failure is real, for as the Gospel of the day (the Parable of the Sower) teaches, only a minority of seeds make it to fruition (Luke 18:31–43). We therefore beg for protection in the conflict.

But there is another reason that *munire* is an appropriate choice. This verb for defending and protecting literally means to "fortify with a wall." Did the author of this Collect have this meaning in mind as he contemplated the location of St. Paul-Outside-the-Walls? After all, the walls outside of which the basilica stands are the walls of the city, put there for protection. Perhaps that is why the Secret for Sexagesima Sunday uses *munire*.

When a liturgy develops organically, it absorbs the local tastes and flavors of the ages through which it passes. Joseph Ratzinger describes his wonder as a boy upon discovering this fact:

> It was becoming more and more clear to me that here I was encountering a reality that no one had simply thought up, a reality that no official authority or great individual had created. This mysterious fabric of texts and actions had grown from the faith of the Church over the centuries. It bore the whole weight of history within itself, and yet, at the same time, it was much more than the product of human history.[2]

Sexagesima Sunday is a good example of Ratzinger's point. Its fabric was woven in part from the particular history of the Church in the city of Rome, yet its particularity opens up to a greater universal reality to which all are summoned. In that respect, the traditional Roman liturgy is not unlike St. Paul himself, the co-founder of the Church in Rome and yet the Apostle to all the gentile nations, that is, to us goys.

---

2 *Milestones: Memoirs 1927–1977*, trans. Erasmo Leiva-Merikakis (San Francisco: Ignatius Press, 1998), 20.

19

The Shrovish Collect of Quinquagesima Sunday

HE FINAL SUNDAY OF THE SEASON OF pre-Lent or Septuagesimatide is Quinquagesima, so-called because it occurs approximately fifty days before Easter. In former ages, Christians would gradually begin abstaining from meat and dairy products on a voluntary basis in preparation for the mandatory fast of Lent. During the previous two weeks, the faithful in the Latin West would have begun abstaining from cheese and other dairy products; around this time they would now begin abstaining from flesh meat. Hence this Sunday is also known in Italian as "Dominica di Carnevale," *carnevale* coming from the Latin for "removal of meat" (*carnem levare*) the origin of our word "carnival."

The propers for Quinquagesima Sunday offer excellent instruction on how to approach the imminent season of Lent. The Gospel (Luke 18:31–43) proclaims the approach of Christ's Passion and the importance of faith as the key to being "made whole" by Our Lord's suffering and death. The verse of the Introit proclaims confidence in God and declares, "In Thee, O Lord, have I hoped" (Ps. 30:2).

The Epistle (1 Cor. 13:1–13) forcibly reminds us that all of our asceticism, like the kind we will soon be practicing for forty days, is worthless if it is not infused by the signature Christian virtue of charity. Ultimately, the purpose of our Lenten mortification is an increase of the theological virtues of faith, hope, and love.

But bringing in more good also requires driving out more bad; hence the Sunday Collect:

> *Preces nostras, quǽsumus, Dómine, cleménter exáudi: atque a peccatórum vínculis absolútos, ab omni nos adversitáte custódi. Per Dóminum nostrum.*

Which I translate as:

We beseech Thee, O Lord, mercifully hear our prayers: and having loosed us from the bonds of [our] sins, keep us from all adversity. Through Our Lord.

The Collect bears a resemblance to the other two Collects of Pre-Lent. The protasis (first half) is almost identical to that of Septuagesima Sunday, and the apodosis (second half) likewise mentions deliverance from our sins. The plea for protection from adversity (*adversitas*) echoes the plea from the Sexagesima Sunday Collect for protection from all adverse things (*adversa omnia*).

The Collect, however, does not explicitly pray for deliverance from our sins but from the "bonds of sins." No doubt the "our" is implied by the use of "us" in the prayer, but as Sr. Mary Gonzaga Haessly notes, the author may have wanted "sins" to be taken in a wider sense as everything contaminated by original sin.[1] Even the Blessed Virgin Mary could pray for deliverance from sins, insofar as she would want to be free of the entangling effects of sin all around her and to remain free from all sin.

The apodosis has a particular order in mind: God absolves us of sin, then He keeps us from all adversity (or, to be kept from every other kind of adversity besides sin, since the Latin *omnis* can mean "the rest" as well as "all"). In Mark 2:5, Our Lord freed the paralytic from sin before He freed him from paralysis. Our worst adversary is sin.

Finally, intentionally or not, the Collect's petition for absolution ties in nicely with the origins of "Shrovetide," the three-day period of Quinquagesima Sunday, Shrove Monday, and Shrove Tuesday. Although popularly seen as a last-chance shot at merriment and mayhem before Ash Wednesday, Shrovetide's name betrays its purpose: "to shrive" is to administer or receive the sacrament of confession.[2] Apparently our forebears thought it a good idea to be loosed from the bonds of their sins before entering into the arena of the desert fast where, like Christ, they might meet the devil in combat. Better to have less for him to grab onto.

---

1   Haessly, *Rhetoric in the Sunday Collects*, 45–46.
2   See "Shrive, v." *Oxford English Dictionary*, 3rd ed. (Oxford: Oxford University Press, 2023), OED online.

V

LENT

20

The Mortifying Oration
of Ash Wednesday

SH WEDNESDAY, WHICH INAUGURATES
the sacred season of Lent, is one of the most memorable days of the liturgical year. In the traditional
rite, the four blessings of the ashes along with the antiphons
emphasize the need for our repentance and God's infinite mercy.
Blessed by God through the mediation of one of His angels, the
ashes become not only a token of our lowliness and mortality
but a wholesome and forgiving remedy to all those who are truly
contrite and who call upon the name of the Lord. One of the
prayers reminds us of the example of the Ninevites, who were
told by the prophet Jonah that they would be punished by God
for their sins. Although they were heathen, the Ninevites listened
to this Jewish prophet; repenting in sackcloth and ashes, they
were spared. There is hope for us all.

The prayers and readings of the Mass likewise stress the importance of fasting and other ascetical practices so long as they
are done in the right spirit. Mourn and weep, we are told, but
do not be sad; that is, do not make an empty show of external
observances but use them as a means of effecting an interior
transformation. Lent is traditionally inseparable from the forty-
day fast that begins today, and this fast should be kept in order
to aid us in our conversion or "rending of heart" (Lesson). The
Lenten Preface explains how. By mortifying our appetites, bodily
fasting helps curb our vices; by curbing our vices, fasting helps
elevate our minds, liberating them from the mire of our disordered desires; and by elevating our minds, fasting helps confer
virtue and reward, reinstituting righteous habits and restoring
a capacity to do and enjoy the good.

The Collect for Ash Wednesday is:

> *Præsta, Dómine, fidélibus tuis: ut jejuniórum veneránda*
> *solémnia, et cóngrua pietáte suscípiant, et secúra devotióne*
> *percúrrant. Per Dóminum.*

Which I translate as:

> Grant, O Lord, to Thy faithful ones that they may take
> up with fitting piety the solemnities of fasting which
> should be venerated, and persevere with steadfast devo-
> tion. Through Our Lord.

Fasting is not a cure-all: to be spiritually efficacious, it requires
"fitting piety," the right spirit. Lenten fasting is not private, even
though it involves a regulation of one's private body: it is (or
rather was for most of her history) part of the *solemnia*, the solemn observances of the Church. And these solemnities "should
be venerated," held in reverence, not as an onerous duty but as a
part of the exercise of one's baptismal priesthood. And we pray to
"persevere" with a secure devotion. *Curro* means to run, and *per-
curro* means to persevere to the end. Our goal is not to slow down
during Lent but to speed up and hang in there. We are in training.

The Secret is:

> *Fac nos, quæsumus, Dómine, his munéribus offeréndis con-
> veniénter aptári: quibus ipsíus venerábilis sacraménti cele-
> brámus exórdium. Per Dóminum.*

Which I translate as:

> Make us, we beseech Thee, O Lord, to be fittingly adapted
> to these gifts which are to be offered, by which we cele-
> brate the beginning of this venerable Mystery. Through
> Our Lord.

Liturgical fasting is not about forty days to becoming a thinner,
sexier You: it is about becoming adapted, molded, and configured
to the Messiah, who emptied Himself to become a slave like us.
At the beginning of Lent, we pray to have the right disposition to
our fasts, and we do so in the name of the offerings by which we
celebrate the beginning of this venerable mystery. "Mystery" is a
loaded term: it means both "mystery" and "sacrament." When we
begin the season of the Passion of the Christ, we enter into the
Paschal Mystery, which is also the sacrament of our redemption.

The Postcommunion is:

> *Percépta nobis, Dómine, præbeant sacraménta subsídium: ut
> tibi grata sint nostra jejúnia, et nobis profíciant ad medélam.
> Per Dóminum.*

Which I translate as:

> May the Sacraments that we have received, O Lord, provide us help: that our fasts may be acceptable to Thee and profitable unto us for healing. Through Our Lord.

Fasting, dieting, etc., are nothing without God. They only become an aid to healing when they are fed (paradoxically) by the Sacraments of the Body and Blood of the Eucharist. We mortify the flesh to heal the spirit, and we heal the spirit only through the Food that is Christ Himself. If we thin ourselves during Lent (and we should), it is only to become spiritually fat with the help of the nourishing flesh of the Lamb.

21

Fasting and the Orations
of the First Sunday of Lent

HE GREATEST DIFFERENCE BETWEEN
the seasons of Lent in the 1962 and 1969 calendars
is on the subject of fasting. The 1962 calendar presupposes that the faithful will be keeping the ancient forty-day
Lenten fast, and it orders its prayers and readings accordingly.
One can even go so far as to say that the Lenten propers in the
old Missal are geared towards the sanctification of the person
through fasting and abstinence since they mention, explain, and
pray for a successful fast on every day of Lent prior to Holy Week.
The 1970 Missal, on the other hand, was issued in the wake of
Pope Paul VI's 1966 Apostolic Constitution *Pænitemini*,[1] which
made the Lenten fast optional. The new Missal retains several
references to fasting on Ash Wednesday (still a mandatory fast
day), but there are only two required references to the fasts of
the faithful for the rest of the season.[2] Consequently, with the
exception of Ash Wednesday, the new Missal offers very little
guidance on fasting and almost no prayers for its success.[3] "The
practice of penance," Vatican II's *Sacrosanctum Concilium* states,
"should be fostered" (5.110). But if one wants regular instruction
on the nature and meaning of fasting, and if, moreover, one
wants priests and congregations daily praying and offering up
the Holy Sacrifice for the efficacy of one's fasts, one is better

---

1 Pope Paul VI, *Paenitemini*, www.vatican.va/content/paul-vi/en/apost_
constitutions/documents/hf_p-vi_apc_19660217_paenitemini.html.
2 The Collect for the Third Sunday of Lent and the Prayer over Offerings for Saturday in the Fifth Week of Lent. I say "required" because the
traditional Preface for Lent was retained in the new Missal as Preface IV
but made optional. I also stipulate fasts of the faithful because the new
Mass's First Sunday of Lent refers to Christ's fast in the desert, but there
is no reference to, let alone prayer for, our imitating His action.
3 See Lauren Pristas, "The Post-Vatican II Revision of the Lenten Collects," in *Ever Directed towards the Lord*, ed. Uwe Michael Lang (London:
Bloomsbury T&T Clark, 2007), 62–89; see also Lauren Pristas, *The Collects
of the Roman Missals* (London: Bloomsbury T&T Clark, 2013), 113–58.

off turning to the Missal used during Vatican II rather than the one created after it.

The traditional Orations for the First Sunday of Lent, for example, both pray for a successful fast and explain why the practice is important. The Collect is:

> *Deus, qui Ecclésiam tuam ánnua quadragesimáli observatióne puríficas: præsta famíliæ tuæ: ut, quod a te obtinére abstinéndo nítitur, hoc bonis opéribus exsequátur. Per Dóminum.*

Which I translate as:

> O God, who dost purify Thy Church by the yearly observance of Lent: grant to Thy household that what it strives to obtain from Thee by abstaining, it may secure by good works. Through Our Lord.

Some Church Fathers claimed that the Great Fast of Lent was begun by the Apostles, but even if it is a third- or fourth-century invention, the Collect claims that it is God who uses this season of fasting to purify His Church. Religious fasting is different from medical fasting or what we are tempted to call cosmetic fasting (dieting for the sake of looking good). The goal of religious fasting is to purify the soul, but since the soul cannot purify itself (pace neo-Platonic philosophers and Pelagian heretics), successful religious fasting depends entirely on God's grace. (Similarly, the Postcommunion Prayer of the day prays for a purification "from the old.")

The Collect then petitions God to obtain by good works what cannot be obtained by abstaining. The Collect does not stipulate what exactly the household of God is trying to obtain by either abstinence or good works, but the Postcommunion does: fellowship in the mystery of salvation. The operative logic is similar but not identical to "out with the bad, in with the good"—the food from which we abstain is not bad, although the activity of abstaining is designed to correct an unhealthy attachment to food.

The Secret puts it nicely: "refraining from flesh at our meals" helps us "refrain from harmful pleasures." And once we have rid ourselves of harmful or vicious pleasures, we should fill the vacuum with the good. One is reminded of the upcoming Gospel for the Third Sunday of Lent (Luke 11:14–28), which speaks of the unclean spirit who, after being exorcized, returns to a clean but empty house with seven of his fiendish friends. Fill the house with good things, in other words, before the bad returns.

Fasting, then, is an important activity, but it is not a cure-all. Our Lord mentions that some demons can be exorcized only by fasting *and* prayer (Matt. 17:21): the two must go together. In the Collect, good works supplement the shortcomings of fasting or abstinence. And good works are supposed to be an integral part of Lent. Several Church Fathers taught that the money saved by fasting should go to the less fortunate. As Pope Saint Leo the Great put it: "May the abstinence of the fasters be the refreshment of the poor" (Sermon 13). Or in the words of the beautiful Maronite liturgy: "How splendid is fasting that is adorned with charity. Break your bread generously with one who is hungry; otherwise, yours is not fasting but saving!"[4]

Today's Gospel tells us that "Jesus was led by the Spirit into the desert, to be tempted by the devil" for forty days and forty nights (Matt. 4:1). Let us, then, follow the Spirit of the liturgy into the desert and confront our demons through fasting, prayer, and good works.

---

4   Vespers Hymn for the Tuesdays of Lent.

The Transformative Collect
of the Second Sunday of Lent

HE COLLECT FOR THE SECOND SUNDAY
of Lent is:

*Deus, qui cónspicis omni nos virtúte destítui: intérius
exteriúsque custódi; ut ab ómnibus adversitátibus muniámur
in córpore, et a pravis cogitatiónibus mundémur in mente.
Per Dóminum.*

Which I translate as:

O God, who seest that we are bereft of all virtue, guard us
inside and out: that we may be defended from all adversities to our bodies and cleansed from all perverse thoughts
in our minds. Through Our Lord.

The noun *virtus* is not easy to translate. Although it can mean
moral virtue, as we have rendered it here, in the Roman Orations
it is generally used in reference to God's supernatural power,
especially His power to make man's cultic act divine. And when
it is used in reference to man himself, it is usually as a divinely-
infused, superhuman power like the courage of the martyrs.[1]
Declaring that man is bereft of all *virtus*, then, is not an endorse-
ment of the doctrine of total depravity; it is an assertion that
holiness is impossible without God.

Those Christians who believe in man's total depravity also
tend to subscribe to a doctrine of "imputed righteousness," the
idea that God does not really transform fallen man, but throws a
cloak of justice over him which enables him to enter Heaven, like
a blanket of snow upon a pile of dung. The Collect, by contrast,
presupposes that salvation and holiness thoroughly transform the
human person both inside and out. We first want to be protected
from bodily adversity, which can disturb our inner peace and
strain our trust in God, as it did to Job. Once protected, we ask

---

1 Ellebracht, *Vocabulary of the Ancient Orations*, 127–29.

God to clean out our perverse or crooked thoughts. Cleansing is an important theme of Lent: all our mortifications are meant to have a purgative value. But cleansing our thoughts is especially difficult. It is easier to control our actions than the promptings and musings of our mind, and therefore even the best of men can be plagued with the worst of thoughts. The difference between a saint and the average man is not that the saint has only pure thoughts, but that he trains his mind to reject, calmly yet firmly, bad thoughts as soon as they arise. And should they persist, he refuses to let them lead him to discouragement but throws himself all the more passionately on the mercy of God. Perverse thoughts are a stubborn, many-headed hydra, yet we are confident that God can conquer them.

On a linguistic note, there is a pleasing juxtaposition between "defended" and "cleansed," since there is a slight pun on the words *muniamur* and *mundemur*. It is also difficult to express in English the tight contrast between *in corpore* and *in mente*.

Body, soul, and holiness are also the subjects of the Sunday readings. In the Epistle from 1 Thessalonians, St. Paul reminds us that God does not call us to uncleanness (*immunditia* is related to the Collect's *mundemur*). Rather, He wills our sanctification, and that involves knowing how to possess our vessels (bodies) in honor. The Gospel reading for the Second Sunday of Lent, on the other hand, is Matthew's account of the Transfiguration (17:1–9), when Jesus is transfigured on (presumably) Mount Tabor as Saints Peter, James, and John look on. The traditional interpretation of this event is that Our Lord was preparing these three Princes of the Apostles for the brutal and demoralizing spectacle of the crucifixion by giving them a foreshadowing of His glorious resurrection. (They are the same three Apostles who will be called to witness Christ's agony in the garden.) And similarly, in order to inspire the faithful during the penitential season of Lent, the Church on this Sunday anticipates the glory of Easter by calling to mind Christ's transfiguration.[2]

But we can also think of the Transfiguration as the goal to which the Collect aspires. Jesus's glorified, transfigured body is free from bodily adversity, and His soul is free of perverse

---

2 See also chapter 72, "The Orations of the Feast of the Transfiguration, August 6."

thoughts. Romano Guardini once defined a beautiful work of art as one in which "the external phenomenon is at all points the perfect expression of the inner essence."[3] The brilliant clothes and face of Jesus Christ during the Transfiguration are the perfect expression of His inner beauty, a beauty we adore, strive to imitate, and, God willing, will someday resemble.

---

3 Romano Guardini, *The Spirit of the Liturgy*, trans. Ada Lane (New York: Sheed & Ward, 1935), 49.

23

The Succinct Collect of
the Third Sunday of Lent

N THE SURFACE, THE COLLECT FOR THE
Third Sunday of Lent is about as simple as it gets:

*Quǽsumus, omnípotens Deus, vota humílium réspice: atque
ad defensiónem nostram, déxteram tuæ majestátis exténde.
Per Dóminum.*

Which I translate as:

We beseech Thee, almighty God, look back on the petitions
of Thy humble ones, and stretch forth the right hand of
Thy majesty to be our defense. Through Our Lord.

The Collect is a good example of why Pierre Maranget characterized the Roman Orations as "remarkable for their simplicity, grav-
ity, clarity, strength, and conciseness, as well as for the elevation
of thought and the abundance and accuracy of their theological
teaching."[1] Most Collects have three parts (not including the
conclusion): the address, a statement of fact, and a petition.[2]
The address is directed to God, the statement of fact is about
Him ("Thou who dost X, Y, and Z"), and the petition is for us.
This Sunday's Collect substitutes a statement of fact for a double
petition, giving it a somewhat rushed urgency.

It also finds ways of describing God without a separate statement of fact. "Almighty," "right hand," and "majesty" all emphasize
divine power. For 90% of the world's population, the right hand is
the stronger and more capable of the two, and in the Psalms, God's
right hand is synonymous with His might. There is also a hint of
the Christological in the petition for the Father to extend His right
hand, for it is the Son who sits at the right hand of the Father.

"Majesty" also connotes supernatural power. According to Sr.
Mary Pierre Ellebracht, the Hebrew *Kebod Yahweh* (the Glory

---

1 See Haessly, *Rhetoric in the Sunday Collects*, quoted in front matter.
2 Haessly, 14; see also the Introduction.

of God) signifies both God's power and His luminosity. Early Christians translated the latter with *claritas* and the former with *majestas*.[3]

All this focus on divine power is to muster it for our protection. The Collect prays that God's capacity for offense will make for us the best defense. Power is also the theme of this Sunday's Gospel (Luke 11:14–28). When the Jews who were watching Jesus perform an exorcism accuse Him of having demonic power, He reminds them that a house divided against itself cannot stand and that a strong man is strong only until a stronger man comes, overpowers him, takes away his armor, and distributes his spoils. Jesus then tells the story of a demon who is exorcized and returns with seven spirits more wicked than he to repossess the man. In asking God to protect us with His power, the Collect is asking Him to protect us from the strong man.

And we ask Him to protect us because we know we are weak. The first petition of the Collect is *vota humilium respice*. *Respicere* is the Latin verb that is typically used for "have regard for" or "provide for," but I have translated it according to its more primitive meaning of looking back or looking again. The Introit for this Sunday begins with the declaration, "My eyes are always on the Lord: for He shall pluck my feet out of the snare: Look back (*respice*) upon me, and have mercy on me."

The fact that we are always looking at the Lord indicates that we are suppliant servants, for "As the eyes of the servants are on the hands of their masters, as the eyes of the handmaid are on the hands of her mistress: so are our eyes unto the Lord our God, until he have mercy on us" (Ps. 122:2).

And so as we look upon God, we ask Him, both in the Introit and Collect, to look upon us, to turn around, so to speak, notice our lowliness, and take pity on us. And we are clearly lowly because in the Collet we call ourselves *humiles*, a word that in classical Latin is a term of reproach for the lowly and insignificant, but in ecclesiastical Latin becomes an honest confession of our status.

More specifically, we ask God to look upon the *vota* of us lowly creatures. *Votum*, which we have translated as "petition," has a rich history. The word was used in pagan times to signify

---

3   Ellebracht, *Vocabulary of the Ancient Orations*, 40.

a solemn promise made to a deity, a vow. It then came to signify *what* was being promised and was thus tied to sacrificial offerings. It also came to mean any wish or desire, which is probably why our word "vote" is derived from it, since voting is an act of stating your political preferences. In ecclesiastical Latin, *vota* are public prayers or desires, sometimes the prayers of the liturgical act that we are celebrating right now.

Lent is a time to cast out those demons in our lives that can be cast out only by prayer and fasting (see Matt. 17:21). Our petitions (*vota*) are our prayers, and our fasting makes us aware of our weakness. And perhaps that, too, is another tie-in to the Gospel. Some have speculated that Jesus's Parable of the Strong Man is an allusion to Isaiah 49:24–25:

> Shall the prey be taken from the strong? Or can that which was taken by the mighty be delivered? For thus saith the Lord: "Yea verily, even the captivity shall be taken away from the strong: and that which was taken by the mighty, shall be delivered. But I will judge those that have judged thee, and thy children I will save."

In other words, the devil is the strong man who has taken us captive and made us his prey. Deliver us, then, O Lord, from the mighty, and save Thy children.

24

The Consoling Collect
of Laetare Sunday

VERYONE KNOWS THAT LAETARE SUN-
day is one of the two "pink" (or rather, rose) Sundays
of the year, and that it is a somewhat joyful interlude
during the austerity of Lent, one meant to afford a short breather,
so to speak, during a six-week marathon. But what precisely are
we rejoicing about? The Collect affords us a clue:

> *Concéde, quǽsumus, omnípotens Deus: ut qui ex mérito nostræ
> actiónis affligimur, tuæ grátiæ consolatióne respirémus. Per
> Dóminum.*

Which I translate as:

> Grant, we beseech Thee, almighty God: that we, who by
> the merit of our actions are crushed down, may by the
> consolation of Thy grace breathe again. Through Our Lord.

Most hand missals translate *affligimur* as "afflicted," and they
are correct. But since *affligere* is ultimately derived from a root
that means "to crush," it forms a natural contrast with *respirare*,
to breathe again or to revive. One recalls the terrible torture
inflicted on St. Margaret Clitherow who was crushed to death
while pregnant by large stones under the reign of Queen Elizabeth
I on Good Friday for refusing to renounce the Catholic Faith. In
this Collect, we acknowledge that our own actions bring with
them the heavy weight of death, and we pray to have the weight
lifted and breathe again. Breathing again also reinforces the idea of
Laetare Sunday as a breather in the midst of the ardors of Lent.

Further, we pray to breathe again or be revived by the consolation of God's grace. The appeal to consolation brings us back
to the Introit of the day:

> Rejoice, O Jerusalem: and come together all you that love
> her: rejoice with joy, you that have been in sorrow: that
> you may exult, and be filled from the breasts of your con-
> solation. Ps. 121:2. I rejoiced at the things that were said

to me: "We shall go into the house of the Lord." Glory
be to the Father.

What brings consolation are the breasts of Jerusalem. The traditional Roman Rite is wonderfully concrete: if Jerusalem is a
mother (and she is, as the Epistle reading confirms), then she
has breasts that console us like a mother quieting her crying
infant. But what precisely are the breasts of our heavenly mother,
the Church? The Gospel answers the question. In the Miracle
of the Loaves and Fishes, we are given a type for the Eucharist,
the Bread of Life that defies the laws of space, time, and matter
by mystically multiplying our spiritual food. It is this sensibility
that led Blessed Julian of Norwich to compare the "sweet open
side" of Christ's crucified body, from which His Precious Blood
and water poured, to a mother's breast. [1]

In England, Laetare Sunday is "Mothering Sunday," the original
Mother's Day. In medieval times, schoolboys and apprentices were
allowed to visit their "mother church," the church in which they
were baptized. And since they were visiting home, they visited
their earthly mothers and brought them gifts. Simnel cakes are
a tasty vestige of this ancient tradition. [2]

The rejoicing of Laetare Sunday, in other words, is the joy
of knowing that our Holy Mother the Church, despite whatever
scandals or corruptions may rock her, still has the breasts of
Eucharistic consolation that feed and nourish us. And how appropriate is Holy Communion when it is done kneeling and on the
tongue. Granted, it is not the exact position of an infant being
nursed, but it betokens an attitude of supplication, helplessness,
and receptivity. And as Blessed Julian explains, Jesus wants us
to have the trusting and dependent nature of a child. [3]

---

1 *Revelations of Divine Love* 60, trans. Grace Warrack (London: Methuen
and Company, 1901), 150–51.
2 Rev. Francis X. Weiser, SJ, *Handbook of Christian Feasts and Customs:
The Year of the Lord in Liturgy and Folklore* (New York: Harcourt, Brace,
and Company, 1958), 177–79.
3 *Revelations of Divine Love*, 61, 152–55.

25
The Secret for Passion Sunday

N THE 1962 ROMAN CALENDAR, THE last two weeks of Lent constitute a season within a season. Passiontide, which begins with Passion Sunday, is a heightened anticipation of, and preparation for, the Paschal mystery of Our Lord's death, resurrection and ascension. Whereas the earlier weeks of Lent focus more on the penance and mortification of the faithful, Passiontide focuses more on, well, the Passion of the Christ. During this time, sacred images in the church are covered as a sign of sorrow, as a way of enlivening our sense of unworthiness, and in order to direct our attention to the mystery of the season. Similarly, the "Judica me" and the "Glory be to the Father" are omitted from the Mass on Sundays and regular weekdays.

The Secret of Passion Sunday ties into these themes in a subtle way:

> *Hæc múnera, quǽsumus, Dómine, et víncula nostræ pravitátis absólvant, et tuæ nobis misericórdiæ dona concílient. Per Dóminum.*

Which I translate as:

> May these offerings, we beseech Thee, O Lord, dissolve the chains of our depravity, and conciliate for us the gifts of Thy mercy. Through Our Lord.

We have seen "depravity" during the season of Lent before: on the Second Sunday, the Collect prays for deliverance from *pravæ cogitationes*. Here, we pray that the chains of depravity may be dissolved. But how? Through the conciliation of the gifts of God's mercy. *Concilio* is a difficult verb to translate. It literally means to "cry out together," to be of one voice in clamoring to God. It has the connotation of reconciliation, of coordinating our pleas to God with one voice and making peace with our God, against whom we have sinned. But how to coordinate? The question brings us to the Sunday's Epistle reading. In Hebrews 9:11–15, we are confronted with the reality of Christ the High Priest, who in His humanity enters into the Holies with His own Blood, obtaining eternal redemption for those who whose "transgressions . . . were under the former testament," so that "they that are called may receive the promise of eternal inheritance, in Christ Jesus Our Lord."

As we enter into the final phase of Lent, we pray that Christ the High Priest may act as Mediator between God and man, who in His suffering, death, and resurrection reconciles us to the Father and dissolves the chains of death and sin that keep us from Him.

26

The Collect of Palm Sunday

ALM SUNDAY IN THE TRADITIONAL CAL-
endar does three things: it continues the Passiontide
theme of the Cross that began a week before; it inaugurates Holy Week; and it looks ahead with hope to Easter Sunday,
our light at the end of the Lenten tunnel. All of this is evident
in the Collect of the Mass:

> *Omnípotens sempitérne Deus, qui humáno géneri ad imitán-
> dum humilitátis exémplum, Salvatórem nostrum carnem
> súmere et crucem subíre fecísti: concéde propítius; ut et
> patiéntiæ ipsíus habére documénta et resurrectiónis consórtia
> mereámur. Per eúndem Dóminum nostrum.*

Which I translate as:

> Almighty and everlasting God, who, so that the human
> race might have an example of humility, hast made our
> Savior to take our flesh and undergo the Cross; graciously
> grant that we may deserve to have both the lessons of His
> patience and the fellowship of His resurrection. Through
> the same Our Lord.

The Collect is an excellent example of what we call in the Introduction "spiritual eructation."[1] Debates about the so-called two
forms of the Roman Rite often involve a quantitative analysis of
how much of the Bible is explicitly included, the assumption being
that the more biblical passages there are in a liturgical event, the
better. Historically, however, apostolic liturgies developed along
a different set of priorities. Obviously, Sacred Scripture is cited
in the Introit, readings, etc., but in addition to the sacred liturgy
proclaiming or chanting biblical passages in order to give us
instruction or channel our emotions and *cause* prayer, the liturgy
includes prayers that are the *effects* of having appropriated Scripture. Psalm 44:2 in the Douay Rheims translation is "My heart
hath uttered a good word," but a more literal translation is "My
heart hath belched [*eructavit*] a good word." The idea is that in

---

1   See p. xx.

hearing and keeping the Word of God, we appropriate it (which literally means to make it our own) and, after having properly digested these verbal victuals from above, we release our own good words in life, prayer, or preaching. Saint Augustine writes:

> You eat when you hear, you belch forth when you preach, and yet you belch forth what you have eaten. That most eager feaster John, for whom the very table of the Lord was not enough unless he leaned on the Lord's breast and drank in divine secrets from His hidden [heart]; what did he belch out? "In the beginning was the Word, and the Word was with God" (John 1:1).[2]

Just as the Bible is the product of a good "eating" and "belching" of divine revelation, so too are the prayers of the sacred liturgy the product of a good eating and belching of the Bible. We see this principle in action in the Palm Sunday Collect, which appropriates and rearticulates the New Testament teaching on Jesus Christ, especially two verses: "He humbled [*humiliavit*] Himself, becoming obedient unto death, even to the death of the Cross (Phil. 2:8)," and "Christ also suffered for us, leaving you an example [*exemplum*], that you should follow His steps" (1 Pet. 2:21).

Both allusions also foreshadow future worship: the first verse is used prominently during the Divine Office of the Triduum, and the second appears in the Epistle for the Second Sunday after Easter.

Another spiritual eructation occurs in the Collect's synonym or complement of *exemplum*, the rather curious *documenta*, which we have translated as "lessons." Christ is our Teacher precisely because of His humility: "Learn of Me, because I am meek and humble of heart" (Matt. 11:29). And we have His lessons of humility thanks to the documents of the New Testament.

Imitation is critical to Christian life: we imitate our *exemplum* Jesus Christ, and we imitate those who imitate Him, that is, the Saints (see 1 Cor. 4:6, 11:1; Phil. 3:17; 1 Thess. 1:6, 2:14). "The imitation of Christ," writes St. Basil the Great,

> is necessary for the perfection of life, not only in His living example of humility, patience, and freedom from anger, but also in that of His very death. As Paul, the imitator of Christ, says, "I am conformed to His death,

---

2 *Enarratio in Psalmum* 145.7.9, translation mine.

that I may somehow obtain the resurrection from the dead" (Phil. 3:10–11).[3]

The theme of imitation therefore highlights our part in the drama of the Passion: we too must take up our cross and follow Him in order to complete the sufferings of Christ (see Col. 1:24). It is especially appropriate to recall this aspect of our faith at this moment of the liturgical year, and at this moment on Palm Sunday. Presumably, when the priest prays this oration, he and the faithful have just finished participating in the blessing of palms and the procession that literally imitates Our Lord's humble entry into Jerusalem, humble because He rode in on a donkey rather than on a horse like a triumphant war-king.

The word *fecisti*, which we have translated as "hast made," sounds a little strong; it could give the impression that the Father forced the Son to undergo these humiliations. But understood in the right theological framework, the wording is sound. The Preface of the Cross used for this Mass includes the line:

> Father almighty and everlasting God, who didst set [*constituisti*] the salvation of mankind upon the tree of the Cross, so that whence came death, thence life might rise again; and that he who overcame by a tree might be overcome by a tree.

"Making" and "setting" up the Son, however, does not happen without the Son's full consent and cooperation. As we sing during the Passiontide hymn for Lauds,

> *Se volénte natus ad hoc*
> *Passióni déditus.*[4]

That is:

> Of His free choice He goeth
> To a death of bitter pain.

Finally, the Collect is elegantly constructed. Together, the double description of our Savior's activity and our double petition to the Father form a chiasm, an ABBA pattern:

---

3   *On the Holy Spirit* 15.35, trans. Stephen M. Hildebrand (Yonkers, NY: St. Vladimir's Press, 2011).
4   From the original wording of the hymn *Pange lingua* by Venantius Fortunatus.

The Savior taking our [mortal] flesh (A)
The Savior enduring the Cross (B)
Our learning from His endurance (B)
Our fellowship with His risen flesh [His resurrection] (A)

We can imagine this chiasm as a V of descent and ascent. Christ descends first with His Incarnation and then even lower with His humiliating death. We meet Him at the bottom of the V by imitating Him, and hence participating in His Passion (wiping His brow like Veronica and carrying His Cross like Simon of Cyrene) and are thus able to ascend with Him in His Resurrection. We pray that just as art imitates life, our life may imitate this beautiful oration.

VII
EASTERTIDE

27

The Collect of Easter Sunday

HE COLLECT FOR THE GREATEST SUN-
day of the year is:

*Deus, qui hodiérna die per Unigénitum tuum æternitátis nobis
áditum devícta morte reserásti: vota nostra, quæ præveniéndo
aspíras, étiam adjuvándo proséquere. Per eúndem Dóminum.*

Which I translate as:

O God, who on this [special] day through Thine Only-
Begotten has conquered death and opened up for us the
gate of eternity; just as you inspire our prayers by coming
before them, follow up on them by helping us. Through
the same Our Lord.

In Latin, the word "day" (*dies*) has two genders. When it is
masculine it is an ordinary day, and when it is feminine it is
a special day. In this Collect, *dies* is feminine, for a Man rising
from the grave three days after His brutal execution and opening
up Heaven is indeed a special day. The usage also ties into the
Gradual: "This is the day (*dies*, feminine) which the Lord hath
made; let us rejoice and be glad therein."

The Collect has two antonomasias, a literary device that substitutes a proper name for a characteristic. Instead of "Jesus Christ,"
"Thine Only-Begotten" is used, and instead of "everlasting life"
or "everlasting happiness" or "Heaven," "eternity" is used.[1] In
context, it seems to me that these devices imbue the prayer with
a certain playfulness or perhaps intimacy, as if the Church is
excitedly saying: "We don't need to spell this out, O Lord: You
obviously know what we are talking about."

Devicta morte, which we have translated as "conquered death,"
is a succinct but powerful ablative absolute. *Vinco* is to defeat or
conquer, and *devinco* (used here) is to utterly and thoroughly defeat
or conquer. Christ did not just win the battle, but the war. O death,
where is thy victory now? You are through! The sentiment echoes

---

1   See Haessly, *Rhetoric in the Sunday Collects*, 59.

95

several other texts, such as the Preface for Easter, "Who by dying destroyed our death and by rising again restored our life," and the opening stanza of the sequence for the day, the beautiful *Victimæ Paschali Laudes* (see Appendix 1), as well as the stirring Paschaltide refrain in the Byzantine liturgy, "Christ is risen from the dead, conquering death by death. And to those in the tomb, He granted life."

Reserasti, which we have translated as "opened up," can also mean to unseal or unbar. It appears here in syncopated form— that is, the full word *reseravisti* has been contracted to *reserasti*. It is a nice poetic touch. Technically, Christ did not open the gates of eternity on the day that He rose from the dead but on the day that He ascended to Heaven. Still, the Church cannot but think of eternity on this day. To my mind, the image of unbarring also betokens the icon of the Resurrection, which depicts Christ breaking the chains of death and unsealing the coffins of Adam and Eve as the first step to their lives of eternal happiness.

The petition or apodosis is a masterpiece of tight rhetoric. There is a juxtaposition between "following up" and "coming before." There is an alliteration of *prœveniendo* and *prosequere*, and of *aspiras* (*ad-spiras*) and *adjuvando*, and these alliterations are arranged chiastically: *prœveniendo* (A) *aspiras* (B), *etiam adjuvando* (B) *prosequere* (A).[2] There is assonance between *prœveniendo* and *adjuvando*, and their arrangement in the same order constitutes an anaphora.[3]

Together, the diction and devices create a memorable image. God comes before our prayers (*vota* can also mean desires) and inspires them. *Aspiras* literally means to breathe at, and it is reminiscent of Jesus appearing to the Apostles on that first Easter Sunday and breathing the Holy Spirit onto them (see John 20:22). But *aspiro* also means to be favorable to or to assist, because it conjures up the image of a fair breeze.[4] In the *Aeneid*, Vergil uses the verb for Juno creating favorable winds and for Venus breathing "divine love" into her words.[5] In this Collect, the breath of God has put wind in our sails, and so we now ask that He follow up on His initial gust and help us reach the port, or rather the gate, of everlasting happiness.

---

2 The Collect of Palm Sunday also has a nice chiasm, as we saw last chapter.
3 Haessly, *Rhetoric in the Sunday Collects*, 59.
4 See "Aspiro," def. 2, *Lewis and Short*, 176.
5 *Aeneid* 5.607 and 8.373, respectively.

28

The Orations of Low Sunday

OBODY LIKES IT WHEN A GOOD PARTY is over, even when the party stretches out for eight days. But all good things (this side of the grave) must come to an end, and so the Orations for the Sunday after Easter, which concludes a glorious octave, beg that the joys of the Resurrection may continue even though the main celebration has come to a close.

The Secret for Low Sunday is:

> Súscipe múnera, Dómine, quǽsumus, exsultántis Ecclésiæ: et cui causam tanti gáudii præstitísti, perpétuæ fructum concéde lætítiæ. Per Dóminum.

Which I translate as:

> Receive, we beseech Thee, O Lord, the offerings of Thy exultant Church, and grant to her, to whom Thou hast given cause for such great joy, the fruit of perpetual gladness. Through Our Lord.

Similarly, the Postcommunion Prayer is:

> Quǽsumus, Dómine Deus noster: ut sacrosáncta mystéria, quæ pro reparatiónis nostræ munímine contulísti; et præsens nobis remédium esse fácias, et futúrum. Per Dóminum.

Which I translate as:

> We beseech Thee, O Lord our God, to make the sacrosanct mysteries, which Thou hast bestowed as a fortification of our reparation, a remedy for us both now and in the future. Through Our Lord.

"Sacrosanct" is the perfect word for the mysteries (i.e., sacraments) that God has bestowed upon us, for they are both "sacred"—set apart for divine use—and "holy" (*sanctus*)—infused with the life-giving breath of the Holy Spirit. The sacrament of our reparation is, I suspect, Baptism, which repairs our relationship with God and which the neophytes received last week during the Easter Vigil. But the sacrament that fortifies our repaired life is the Eucharist, which we have just received at this point in the Mass.

It is the Collect that I find particularly fetching:

> *Præsta, quǽsumus, omnípotens Deus: ut, qui paschália festa perégimus; hæc, te largiénte, móribus et vita teneámus. Per Dóminum.*

Which I translate as:

> Grant, we beseech Thee, almighty God, that we who have finished the Paschal feasts may, by Thy bounty, hold onto them in our practices and in our life. Through Our Lord.

Ago is the Latin verb for doing or making, and *per-ago* (which I have translated as "have finished") is the verb for thoroughly doing, for carrying an action through to its end. We will, of course, continue to celebrate the Easter season all the way up to Pentecost, but on this Octave Sunday we complete the celebration of Easter Day.

The petition of the Collect subtly traces a movement from outer to inner. The external observance of ritual and ceremony (the "Paschal feasts") conditions our other "practices" or habits outside the liturgy. These habits, in turn, become so internalized that they reconstitute our very "life," changing our character and our destiny. In some respects, the Collect reflects the moral anthropology of Aristotle's *Nicomachean Ethics* but with one key difference: the movement from outer observance to inner transformation cannot succeed without God's bounty. *Te largiente* literally means "with You giving lavishly." God not only has to give, but He has to give lavishly, to make the joys of Easter stick to our being and change it forever. So please, God: give lavishly.

29

The Freefall Collect of
Good Shepherd Sunday

HE COLLECT FOR THE SECOND SUNDAY
after Easter, also commonly known as "Good Shepherd
Sunday," is brief but striking:

> *Deus, qui in Filii tui humilitáte jacéntem mundum erexísti,*
> *fidélibus tuis perpétuam concéde lætítiam: ut, quos perpétuæ*
> *mortis eripuísti cásibus, gáudiis fácias pérfrui sempitérnis. Per*
> *eúndem Dóminum nostrum.*

Which I translate as:

> O God, who by the humility of Thy Son hast raised up
> a falling world, grant to Thy faithful perpetual gladness:
> that those whom Thou hast delivered from the dangers of
> perpetual death Thou mayest cause to thoroughly enjoy
> endless joys. Through the same.

Sr. Mary Haessly uses this Collect as an example of "antithetical
chiasm," that is a chiastic or V-like structure (ABCCBA) marked
by antitheses or contrasts. The statement of fact about God ("O
God, who...") is dominated by the language of descent: the
world is not simply fallen but *still* falling, spiraling downward
to Hell.[1] God the Father responds by the humility of His Son,
who, we can imagine, humbly races down from Heaven to catch
us before we perish. The Son not only stops our fall but raises
us up, lifting us higher. In the Latin, "raised up" (*erexísti*) is the
last word in the phrase, keeping the focus on the sinful descent
of man and the saving descent of God until the last moment. It is
an apt characterization of the Paschal mystery that we continue
to celebrate during this season, for Holy Week likewise characterizes salvation in terms of Jesus Christ's humility.[2]

The petition, on the other hand, is replete with references to
eternity: we ask for perpetual gladness, thank God for deliverance

---

1 See Haessly, *Rhetoric in the Sunday Collects*, 19.
2 See chapter 26, "The Collect of Palm Sunday."

from perpetual death, and ask to revel in sempiternal joys. The emphasis underscores why the Paschal mystery—that is, the Crucifixion, Resurrection, and Ascension of Jesus Christ—is so important. It is not just a matter of life and death; it is a matter of eternal life and eternal death. Mentioning the terrors of eternal death also sets into sharp relief, and helps us be all the more grateful for, the joys of eternal life.

More specifically, we thank God for deliverance from the *dangers* of perpetual death. It is a good reminder, especially for an age such as ours that values long life and physical health, that the greatest dangers that man faces on earth concern not temporal death but eternal. "And fear ye not them that kill the body and are not able to kill the soul," Our Lord commands, "but rather fear him that can destroy both soul and body in hell" (Matt. 10:28). Finally, the author has chosen the perfect word for "dangers," for the Latin word *casus* also means a fall, and thus it chiastically echoes the "falling world" mentioned earlier. Perhaps we should translate *casus* as "pitfalls."

Although the imagery of the Collect is not explicitly pastoral or bucolic, it nevertheless contributes to the theme of Good Shepherd Sunday. Christ is the Good Shepherd who strikes with lightning speed at the wolves, saving His flock from the dangers of ravenous predators who wish to drag us down to perpetual death. And Christ strikes with His humility and total self-offering, leaving us an example to follow, as the Epistle reading from 1 Peter 2 attests. We also suspect that humility is another difference between the Good Shepherd and the hireling mentioned in the Gospel (John 10:11–16). The hireling "hath no care for the sheep," probably because he cares only about his wages or position. In other words, he is filled with self-regard and self-interest rather than self-emptying humility. May Jesus Christ, the shepherd and bishop of our souls (1 Pet. 2:25), dive down to save us from both wolves and hirelings and carry us up to eternal joys.

30

The Joyful Orations of the Third Sunday after Easter

URING THE FORTY DAYS BETWEEN EAS-ter and Ascension Thursday, the Church exults in the sheer joy of the Resurrection, a joy likened to the euphoria of a mother holding her baby in her arms for the first time.[1] "A woman, when she is in labour, hath sorrow, because her hour is come," says Our Lord in the Gospel for the day, "but when she hath brought forth the child, she remembereth no more the anguish, for joy that a man is born into the world" (John 16:21).

But the Church is also mindful of the neophytes who were given new life during the Easter Vigil, and she continues to pray for them and instruct them. In the Epistle (1 Pet. 2:11–19), St. Peter tells us not to use our newly-gained liberty as a cloak for malice, but to think of ourselves as pilgrims passing through this world on our way to the eternal joy which our earthly Easter celebrations betoken. Such admonitions, of course, are equally applicable to all Christians, whether their Baptism occurred weeks ago or years.

The Orations for the Third Sunday after Easter are similarly well-suited to Christians both new and old. The Collect is:

> *Deus, qui errántibus, ut in viam possint redíre justítiœ, veritá-tis tuœ lumen osténdis: da cunctis qui Christiána professióne censéntur, et illa respúere, quœ huic inimíca sunt nómini; et ea quœ sunt apta sectári. Per Dóminum.*

Which I translate as:

---

1 Forty days in the traditional rite is the unit of time between Easter Sunday and Ascension Thursday that corresponds to the time when the risen Christ walked on the earth and visited His disciples. It is symbolized by the Paschal candle, which is lit on the Easter Vigil and extinguished after the proclamation of the Gospel on Ascension Thursday. The Easter season in the 1962 Missal, however, lasts 55 2/3 days, for it ends on Ember Saturday afternoon of Pentecost (after the Office of None, to be precise).

O God, who dost show to them that go astray the light of
Thy truth so that they may return to the path of justice;
grant to all those who are marked by their profession of
the Christian faith to reject those things which are hostile to this name, and to follow those things that befit it.
Through Our Lord.

The author plays upon the double meaning of *errare*, which in
Latin can mean either "go astray" or "err." Mankind does both,
which is why it needs the light of truth to correct its errors and
someone to put it back on the right path. Both the intellectual
(light of truth) and the moral (path of justice) thus appear in the
Collect's protasis or first part. And so does our risen Lord, who
is the Light of the World, the Truth, and the Way (*via*, which we
have translated as "path," can also mean "way"). I also wonder if
the idea of people going astray is a faint echo of Good Shepherd
Sunday, for it evokes the image of sheep going astray that need
a Good Shepherd to reign them back in (see Is. 53:6).

The apodosis or second half of the Collect may have the neophytes in mind when it refers to the faithful as "those marked
by their Christian profession," for they had to make a profession of faith when they were received into the Church on Holy
Saturday. But the Collect is clearly praying for all who claim
to be Christian, that they may live up to their calling: first, by
driving out the bad (literally, "spitting out" whatever is hostile
to the Christian faith), and second, by following after what is
fitting for the Faith. The use of the word "Christian" is rare in
the Sunday Orations (while "Catholic" makes no appearance at
all). Usually, reference to the Church or her members is made
with terms like "Thy faithful" or "Thy household." Here, we
see the name "Christian" come to the fore as an indication of
the Christian vocation to which the neophytes are called and of
which veteran Catholics are reminded.

The Secret, in turn, discloses more about living out this Christian faith:

*His nobis, Dómine, mystériis conferátur, quo terréna desidéria
mitigántes, discámus amáre cæléstia. Per Dóminum.*

Which I translate as:

> Grant, O Lord, that by these mysteries it may be conferred
> upon us to mitigate our worldly desires and to learn to
> love the heavenly. Through Our Lord.

Contemptus mundi, or disdain of the world, is not a virtue much
talked about these days, but it is essential to the Christian life.
For it is only when we see through the false allures of this world
(and reduce our desires for them accordingly) that we get our
priorities straight and learn to love what is above us. Note that
it is not a question of quashing our desires, but of finding their
true source of satisfaction, of heightening our desires for what
is truly satisfying (the heavenly). The Secret calls not for a
contraction of our desires but their expansion.

The Postcommunion Prayer, on the other hand, guards against
a Gnostic interpretation of the contrast between the worldly and
the heavenly:

> *Sacraménta quæ súmpsimus, quǽsumus, Dómine, et spiri-*
> *tuálibus nos instáurent aliméntis, et corporálibus tueántur*
> *auxíliis. Per Dóminum.*

Which I translate as:

> May the sacraments that we have received, we beseech
> Thee, O Lord, restore us with spiritual nourishment and
> protect us with bodily aids. Through Our Lord.

Instaurare, which we have translated as "restore," is the same verb
used in Ephesians 1:10, "to restore all things in Christ," or as the
Douay Rheims puts it, "to re-establish all things in Christ." We
can only restore or re-establish all things in Christ once we have
been restored by the saving mysteries of Christ. And we also
pray, in a subsidiary way, that we may be protected from bodily
harm, so that we may do the work of restoring all in Christ. The
spiritual comes first, but it is not opposed to the bodily, for we
were put on this earth as embodied beings to integrate the two
and sanctify our material existence. And what better reminder of
this happy integration is there than the figure of the risen Christ,
whose broken body is restored and walks among us during the
forty days of Easter?

31

The School of Love in the Collect of the Fourth Sunday after Easter

F THE EUCHARIST IS, AS POPE BENEDICT XVI calls it, the "great school of love,"[1] then it is fitting that the prayers of the Eucharistic liturgy should at least on occasion attempt to school our desires. The Collect of the Fourth Sunday after Easter is a fine example of this effort:

> *Deus, qui fidélium mentes uníus éfficis voluntátis, da pópulis tuis id amáre quod præcipis, id desideráre quod promíttis: ut inter mundánas varietátes ibi nostra fixa sint corda, ubi vera sunt gáudia. Per Dóminum.*

Which I translate as:

> O God, who makest the minds of the faithful to be of one purpose, grant to Thy people to love that which Thou dost command, to desire that which Thou dost promise; so that, amidst the changing things of this world, our hearts may be there fixed where joys are true. Through Our Lord.

Although neither the Resurrection nor the Ascension is mentioned, the Collect indirectly echoes the themes of the season. God is described as He who makes the minds of the faithful to be of one will. This statement of fact offers a pleasing juxtaposition of intellect (*mens*) and will (*voluntas*), but it also hearkens to the Easter Vigil, when some of the children of wrath and discord were baptized and became adopted members of one harmonious family. Similarly, the apodosis's eloquent contrast between the changing things of this world and the place "where joys are true" anticipates the Epistle reading's characterization of the "gifts from above" coming from a God in "whom there is no change nor shadow of alteration" (James 1:17), while the petition to fix our hearts where joys are true foreshadows the Collect of the Ascension, which prays that our minds may dwell amidst heavenly things.

---

1 "Message of the Holy Father Benedict XVI to the Youth of the World on the Occasion of the 22nd World Youth Day, 2007."

The final petition regarding our hearts is also the culmination of the Collect's initial double petition for love of what God commands and for desire of what He promises. The importance of this twofold petition is highlighted by asyndeton, the deliberate omission of the conjunction "and" between the two separate requests. Asyndeton also quickens the pace, lending to the prayer a certain breathless urgency.

Each request is noteworthy. It is not enough to do what God commands; one must love His commandments as well. A citizen who obeys the law merely out of fear of punishment is not truly just, and a believer who avoids sin merely to avoid Hell is not truly holy. As Aristotle reminds us, the happy life consists of knowing the good, doing the good, and *loving* the good. And God's commandments are surely good.

The petition to desire what God promises is also important but perhaps a little puzzling. One can understand the need to pray for a deeper love of God's commandments. How many people, for example, truly love the command to be moderate? I may appreciate moderation because of all the benefits that it brings me (better health and appearance, longer life, no DUIs, etc.), but it is difficult to get *excited* about the virtue of temperance, that is, to love it for its own sake. The things that God promises to His elect, however, should be things that are easy to desire. Who would not be thrilled about eternal bliss, about seeing God and the Saints face to face, about the resurrection of our bodies and their transfiguration into super "spiritual bodies"? (1 Cor. 15:44). And yet human frailty being what it is, even these things can be viewed apathetically, and even by believers. Original sin and the allures of this world are such a powerful combination that even the people of God need divine help in getting excited about Heaven.

That said, it is significant that the Collect does not ask for an escape from the changing things of this world but for an Archimedean point from which to remain unaffected by them. I recently heard a dreadful sermon by a member of a new order who implied that it was all but impossible to be saved unless one entered the cloister. Apparently the good friar has never read the words of St. Francis de Sales: "It is an error, or rather a heresy, to say that devotion is incompatible with the life of a soldier, a tradesman, a prince, or a married woman."[2]

Saint Francis also has a delightful extended metaphor that I believe illustrates the Collect's final petition and on which I end:

> Just as the pearl oyster lives in the sea without ever taking in a drop of salt water, and just as by the Chelidonian Islands springs of fresh water may be found in the midst of the sea, and just as the firefly passes through the flames without burning its wings, so also can a vigorous and resolute soul live in the world without being infected by worldly ways, can discover sweet springs of piety amid its salt waters, and can fly through the flames of earthly lusts without burning the wings of the holy desire for a devout life.[3]

Thanks be to God, once schooled in love, there is no place that a Christian heart cannot thrive.

---

2 St. Francis de Sales, *Introduction to the Devout Life* 1.3 (Point Roberts, WA: Eremitical Press, 2009).
3 St. Francis de Sales, *Introduction*, Preface.

32

The School of Love in the Orations of the Fifth Sunday after Easter

AST WEEK, WE SAW HOW THE COLLECT for the Fourth Sunday after Easter carries out the task of schooling our desires in service to the "great school of love" that is the Eucharist. This week we observe a similar pedagogy at work in the Orations of the Fifth Sunday after Easter. We begin with the Collect:

> *Deus, a quo bona cuncta procédunt, largíre supplicíbus tuis: ut cogitémus, te inspiránte, quæ recta sunt; et, te gubernánte, éadem faciámus. Per Dóminum nostrum.*

Which I translate as:

> O God, from whom all good things proceed, grant unto Thy suppliants that, with Thou inspiring them, they may think the things that are right and, with Thou guiding them, they may do the very same. Through Our Lord.

It is a Collect filled with flowing motion. All things proceed from God, God's Spirit moves His suppliants to think right things, and His guidance moves them to do right things. The pairing of inspiration/thinking and guiding/doing is well done. To inspire (*inspiro*) is literally to put the breath or spirit into someone, where thoughts reside, while to guide (*guberno*) is literally to pilot a ship or to steer from without, where actions reside. One wonders if the image as a whole is not meant to be nautical: God breathes into the sails (inspires) and takes the helm (guides). In any event, the final petition to do what is right aligns with the central theme of the Epistle (Jas. 1:22–27) that we must be doers of the Word.

The Collect, in turn, is supplemented by the Postcommunion:

> *Tríbue nobis, Dómine, cæléstis mensæ virtúte satiátis, et desideráre quæ recta sunt, et desideráta percípere. Per Dóminum nostrum.*

Which I translate as:

Grant to us, O Lord, that having been satiated by the power of this heavenly table, we may both desire the things that are right and obtain the things we desire. Through Our Lord.

A not infrequent paradox in the Roman Postcommunions is how the Eucharist is a food that increases our hunger. Here we see a contrast between satiation and desire: filled with the Eucharist, we ask to be made hungry for the good.

The petition also adds to our schooling in how to approach the things that are right. In the Collect we asked for the ability to think on right things and to do them; here we ask for a desire of right things and to obtain them. Not just our minds and our deeds must be corrected, but our hearts must fall in love with what is right in order to achieve the good life. It is a recurring temptation to think of happiness as simply getting what one wants; if I want a nice house, a fancy car, and a plump bank account and get them, I will be happy. But this view overlooks one crucial factor. As Cicero writes: "To want what is not decent is itself the very worst misery. And not obtaining what you want is not so miserable as wanting to obtain what is not right, for depravity of the will brings more evil than fortune brings good to anyone."[1] Or as St. Monica succinctly puts it after her son St. Augustine asks her if everyone who has what he wants is happy: "If he wants good things and has them, he is happy; but if he wants bad things, he is unhappy, even if he has them."[2]

Incidentally, a lesson in what and what not to want is timely, for immediately after the Fifth Sunday after Easter, the Church observes Rogationtide for three days in a row, when the faithful petition for a multitude of blessings and protections from God. But as the old saying has it, be careful what you ask for.

As for the Secret, it does not speak explicitly of desire or of the things that are right, but it does speak of both the means and the result of wanting and getting what is right.

Súscipe, Dómine, fidélium preces cum oblatiónibus hostiárum: ut per hæc piæ devotiónis offícia, ad cæléstem glóriam transeámus. Per Dóminum nostrum.

---

1 *Hortensius,* frg. 39 (Muller), translation mine.
2 Augustine, *On the Happy Life* 2.10, translation mine.

Which I translate as:

> Receive, O Lord, the prayers of the faithful along with
> the oblations of their sacrificial offerings: that by these
> offices of loving devotion we may cross over to heavenly
> glory. Through Our Lord.

The prayer has a rich concentration of sacrificial language: the
word *preces* (prayers) has a sacrificial connotation,[3] and obviously so do *oblatio* and *hostia* (sacrificial offering, victim, etc.).
Officium or office is essentially the Latin word for *leitourgia*, a
public service offered on behalf of the people.[4] The Secret links
the earthly sacrificial liturgy we are performing to the glory of
the Heavenly Liturgy. And the petition "may we cross over to
heavenly glory" can be read as an anticipation of the upcoming
feast of the Ascension, which celebrates Our Lord's passing over
into heavenly glory. Heavenly glory is what we too wish to attain.
Glory is the reward for thinking, desiring, and doing what is right,
and heavenly glory is the reward for thinking, desiring, and doing
what is right in the eyes of God. We pray that this liturgical office
or school of "loving devotion" will make it so for us.

---

3   Ellebracht, *Vocabulary of the Ancient Orations*, 141.
4   See Peter Kwasniewski, "Refuting the Commonplace that 'Liturgy'
Means 'Work of the People,'" *New Liturgical Movement*, May 9, 2022,
www.newliturgicalmovement.org/2022/05/refuting-commonplace-that-lit-
urgy-means.html.

33

The Elevating Collect
of Ascension Thursday

HE COLLECT OF ASCENSION THURSDAY is:

> *Concéde, quǽsumus, omnípotens Deus: ut, qui hodiérna die Unigénitum tuum Redemptórem nostrum ad cælos ascendísse crédimus, ipsi quoque mente in cæléstibus habitémus. Per eúndem Dóminum.*

Which I translate as:

> Grant, we beseech Thee, almighty God, that we who believe Thine only-begotten Son, our Redeemer, to have this day ascended into Heaven, may ourselves dwell in mind amidst heavenly things. Through the same Our Lord.

It is the petition that I find particularly interesting. The Collect draws a natural parallel between Our Lord's rising up to Heaven and our own mental dwelling in heavenly things. But it also seems to be a rejection of the reprimand in the Epistle reading of the day, when two angels gently rebuke the disciples for staring up to Heaven after Jesus ascended into a cloud: "Ye men of Galilee, why stand you looking up to heaven? This Jesus, who is taken up from you into heaven, shall so come, as you have seen Him going into heaven" (Acts 1:10).

The tension is resolved by attending to the qualifier *in mente*. The sense is that we do not need to wait until the other side of the grave to get to the "heavenly things." We can dwell among them right now, even in the midst of this valley of tears and labors. Where? In our minds. We cannot have a total immersion in heavenly things until we get to Heaven, but we can have mental peace and mental nourishment, thanks be to God, despite everything else. This beautiful sentiment foreshadows the Golden Sequence that we will hear/sing on Pentecost (see Appendix 2), when the Holy Spirit is addressed with the following: "In labor, you are rest." The Holy Spirit is not rest *after* labor, but rest *in the midst of* labor, a cool breeze during hard, sweltering work. God is consoling us right now, not taking away all our woes, but providing refreshment as they happen. While we work through the entanglements of this world, we remain free, dwelling with the Most High and enjoying a foretaste of the total bliss which is to come.

And so, even though there is no profit to be gained from staring at an empty sky, there is much profit to be gained from ruminating on a higher realm filled with meaning. Understandably, then, Sacred Scripture exhorts us to seek the things that are above (see Col. 3:1–2), for our "citizenship" (*politeuma*) is in the Heavens (see Phil 3:20).

Our sacred authors are not the only ones to see the value of dwelling amidst the heavenly. After concluding that the just city is impossible on earth, Plato's *Republic* adds a note of hope from the mouth of Socrates: "But in heaven, perhaps a pattern is laid up for the man who wants to see and found a city within himself on the basis of what he sees. It doesn't make any difference whether it is or will be somewhere. For he would mind the things of this city alone, and of no other."[1]

For Socrates, it does not matter whether the heavenly archetype exists or not, so long as it inspires the proper instantiation of justice in one's life. Politically, the just city can exist only "in words" (*en logois*), but personally, perhaps it can exist in one's soul. The Gospels, on the other hand, boldly proclaim that the *logos* is not just a word but the Word made flesh. When St. Paul writes that our citizenship is in the heavens, could it be that he had the *Republic* in mind? Perhaps, but either way the key takeaway is that we participate, here and now, in a real City of God, and that we should keep our minds oriented accordingly. And the Logos Jesus Christ, who on this day triumphantly returned to this City and sits now at His Father's right, can cause that to happen within us.

---

1 *Republic* IX.592b, trans. Allan Bloom (New York: Basic Books, 1968).

34

The Contextual Orations of the Sunday after Ascension

HE SUNDAY AFTER ASCENSION WAS once known as *Dominica de Rosis* or "Sunday of the Roses." It is said that some churches in the Middle Ages strewed roses on the pavement in honor of Christ's triumphant entry into Heaven. But the epithet probably comes from a Roman custom. The station church of the day is *Sancta Maria ad Martyres* (Latin) or *Santa Maria Rotonda* (Italian), better known as the former Pantheon. During the papal Mass—and in order to anticipate the feast of Pentecost—red rose petals symbolizing the tongues of flame that descended upon the disciples were showered onto the people from the central opening in the roof known as the oculus. Today, *la pioggia di petali di rose* ("the rain of rose petals") takes place on Pentecost itself (after the 10:30 a.m. Mass) with the help of local firemen who scale the building and release tens of thousands of petals into the interior.

The 1962 Missal's Sunday after Ascension both celebrates Our Lord's consummation of His earthly ministry (see the first Alleluia and Offertory verse) and eagerly awaits the fulfillment of His promise: to send to His disciples the Holy Spirit, "the Spirit of truth, who proceedeth from the Father" (Second Alleluia and Gospel). It is in expectation of the Paraclete that we are admonished to be vigilant in prayer (Epistle).

The Orations of the Sunday, on the other hand, make no mention of either the Ascension or of Pentecost; indeed, they could effortlessly appear anywhere in the liturgical year. But their placement on this Sunday is a good example of the power of context, of how things viewed vis-à-vis several other things appear differently than when they are viewed on their own. This phenomenon is common with colors, but it is also true in literature and liturgy.

In the Secret, for example, the Church prays that these spotless sacrifices may purify us and grant to our minds the vigor of heavenly grace (*Sacrificia nos, Domine, immaculata purificent: et mentibus nostris supernæ gratiæ dent vigorem*). The phrase *gratia superna*, which is commonly translated as "heavenly grace," literally means "grace from above." There is, of course, no ontological difference between the two, but the connotation is different. Four days ago, the Apostles looked up to Him who was ascending above them, and next Sunday they will look up to the Spirit descending upon them. *Gratia superna*, even if unintentionally, puts us in mind of the events we are commemorating.

Similarly, the Postcommunion is:

> *Repléti, Dómine, munéribus sacris: da, quǽsumus: ut in gratiárum semper actióne maneámus. Per Dóminum.*

Which I translate as:

> Grant, we beseech Thee, O Lord, that being replenished with sacred offerings, we may ever remain in thanksgiving. Through Our Lord.

It is a perfectly versatile prayer, but placed after the Communion verse, it is the answer to a question. In the Communion verse (John 17:12–13 & 15), Jesus prays that His disciples not be taken out of the world but kept from evil, but nothing is said about how the disciples can remain in the world without being contaminated by it. The Postcommunion provides an answer: fed on the Eucharist, we remain in a state of thanksgiving, and as long as our hearts are filled with gratitude to God, evil will not affect our relationship to Him.

But it is the Collect that has the most contextual potential:

> *Omnípotens sempitérne Deus: fac nos tibi semper et devótam gérere voluntátem: et majestáti tuæ sincéro corde servíre. Per Dóminum.*

Which I translate as:

> Almighty and eternal God, grant us always to bear a will devoted to Thee and to serve Thy majesty with a sincere heart. Through Our Lord.

On its own, this prayer could be used every day without alteration, but placed after the Ascension, it takes on new meaning. Praying for a sincere heart keeps the Paschal mystery in mind, for on Easter Sunday, we were admonished by St. Paul to feast "not with the old leaven nor with the leaven of malice and wickedness, but with the unleavened bread of sincerity and truth" (1 Cor. 5:8). And the petition for a devoted will foreshadows the Epistle's admonition to have charity (1 Pet. 4:8), for as St. Francis de Sales teaches, devotion is "a certain degree of excellent charity."[1]

Further, the verb *gerere*, which I have translated as "to bear," can also mean "to carry on," while in the Roman Orations God's majesty (*majestas*) is usually in reference to His strength.[2] If we picture ourselves as the original Apostles who have recently witnessed Jesus ascending into Heaven, for what would we pray? Perhaps it would be to carry on with a will devoted to the God who has just manifested His strength through the Ascension of His Son. The association of majesty and the Ascension is reinforced by Hebrews 1:3, where the ascended Christ is described as sitting "on the right hand of the majesty on high." And to my mind at least, "majesty" also evokes a certain awe, which I imagine is the feeling a person gets from seeing the gifts of the Holy Spirit descend upon him and his friends like tongues of flame, or for that matter, of standing in an architectural wonder and watching rose petals rain down from an opening fourteen stories above. May the external stimuli of sacred liturgy and its internal, supernal graces keep our wills on fire for our Paschal Lamb and Savior and attuned to His majesty.

---

1   St. Francis de Sales, *Introduction* 1.1.
2   Ellebracht, *Vocabulary of the Ancient Orations*, 40–41.

35
The Orations of the Feast of Pentecost

EAR THE END OF THIS VOLUME, I COM-
ment on the magnificent sequence *Veni Sancte Spiritus*,
but here, I focus on the rich diction of the three Mass
Orations for the feast dedicated to the Holy Spirit.

The Collect for Pentecost is:

> *Deus, qui hodiérna die corda fidélium Sancti Spíritus illus-*
> *tratióne docuísti: da nobis in eódem Spíritu recta sápere, et de*
> *ejus semper consolatióne gaudére. Per Dóminum… in unitáte*
> *ejúsdem Spíritus Sancti.*

Which I translate as:

> O God, who on this day didst teach the hearts of the
> faithful by the illumination of the Holy Spirit, grant us
> by the same Spirit to understand what is right and ever
> to rejoice in His consolation. Through Our Lord … in the
> unity of the same Holy Spirit.

Illustratio is usually translated as "light," but that is not quite
right, for this noun is not a thing but an activity. The Holy Spirit
is on the go, enlightening the hearts of Christ's disciples. We want
that same Spirit to be actively working on us, and in two specific
ways: to understand what is right and to rejoice in His consolation.

The double petition may be inspired by John 14:16–17, when
Jesus calls the Holy Spirit both "Comforter" (Paraclete) and
"Spirit of Truth." But leaving it at that is not so simple. If there
is any word in the Latin liturgical tradition that justifies a book
like *Lost in Translation*, it is *sapere*. Although I have translated it
as "understand," *sapio/sapere* can also mean:

- to taste
- to have a taste for, to savor
- to resemble
- to be well acquainted with the true value of things, to be
wise (hence the Latin word for wisdom, *sapientia*)

When translating, one has to make a choice. Blessed Ildefonso
Schuster favors the meaning of savoring: he translates *recta sapere*

as "to relish what is right," and writes that the first petition is to "have that desire for the things of God which denotes a certain spiritual well-being, and is the result of the interior life maintained by the Paraclete in our souls."[1] Seen in this light, the Collect ties into the schooling of love that we have been exploring.[2] Pius Parsch, on the other hand, claims that the Collect "begs God for right understanding."[3] Both, of course, are right. *Recta sapere* is wonderfully polyvalent, asking for much in only two words.

The Secret for Pentecost is:

> *Múnera quǽsumus, Dómine, obláta sanctífica: et corda nostra Sancti Spíritus illustratióne emúnda. Per Dóminum ... in unitáte ejúsdem Spíritus Sancti.*

Which I translate as:

> Sanctify, we beseech Thee, O Lord, the gifts offered, and purify our hearts by the illumination of the Holy Spirit. Through Our Lord ... in the unity of the same Holy Spirit.

The Collect understandably associates the illuminating activity of the Holy Spirit with teaching, for "shedding light" on a subject allows one to learn a subject. In the Secret, on the other hand, the illumination of the Holy Spirit cleanses hearts rather than instructs them. Whereas *mundo*, which appears in the Postcommunion below, means to clean, *emundo*, which is used here, means to clean thoroughly. Further, in the Vulgate *emundo* has the additional meaning of cleansing from sin or purifying (see Hebr. 9:14).

But can light purify? It can if it is sunlight. Heliotherapy, the treatment of disease with sunshine, was practiced by the ancient Greeks in the Old World and by the Incans in the New. Depending on who you talk to, sunbathing can rid the body of insomnia, depression, autoimmune problems, vitamin D deficiency, obesity, and tuberculosis. By analogy we pray that the radiation of the Holy Spirit will have a similar effect on our spiritual diseases.

The Postcommunion is:

---

1   Bl. Ildefonso Schuster, *The Sacramentary*, vol. 2, trans. Arthur Levelis-Marke (London: Burns, Oates & Washbourne, 1925; repr. Waterloo, ON: Arouca Press, 2020), 390.
2   See chapters 31, "The School of Love in the Collect of the Fourth Sunday after Easter," and chapter 32, "The School of Love in the Orations of the Fifth Sunday after Easter."
3   Parsch, *The Church's Year of Grace*, 5:212.

Sancti Spíritus, Dómine, corda nostra mundet infúsio: et sui roris íntima aspersióne fœcúndet. Per Dóminum . . . in unitáte ejúsdem Spíritus Sancti.

Which I translate as:

> May the outpouring of the Holy Spirit clean our hearts, O Lord, and by the inward sprinkling of His own dew may they be made fruitful. Through Our Lord . . . in the unity of the same Holy Spirit.

Whereas the Collect and Secret characterize the Holy Spirit in terms of light, the Postcommunion describes the Holy Spirit in terms of water. Both images have Scriptural precedents (for the latter, see 1 Cor. 12:13). In fact, the biblical description of the Holy Spirit in liquid and even alcoholic terms is the reason why hard liquor is called "spirits."[4]

The first petition—that the outpouring of the Holy Spirit clean our hearts—uses an imagery of gushing, while the second—that the sprinkling of His dew fecundate our hearts—uses an imagery of misting. It is an intelligent pairing. The best way to clean a tree (assuming you would ever want to do such a thing) is to blast the hose on it; the best way to water a tree is to put the hose on a trickle. A heavy rain washes away valuable topsoil while a gentle rain nourishes the plants and fills the aquifer below. And the Latin word *ros*, which I have translated as "dew," can also refer to a light rain.

Finally, both waterings are internal. *Infusio*, which I have translated as "outpouring," literally means "pouring into." The petition is evocative of Romans 5:5, "the charity of God is poured forth in our hearts by the Holy Spirit who is given to us." Here, however, we ask for more than the infused virtue of charity; we ask for the indwelling of the Holy Spirit Himself. Similarly, we ask for the "inward sprinkling" not of His dew, but of "His own dew," that is, His very self. *Intima*, which I have translated as "inward," can also mean "most intimate." Seen in this light, the second petition is almost risqué, beautifully affirming the feminine receptivity of every believer's heart, male or female. May God plant the seed in our hearts and make it grow.

---

4   See Michael P. Foley, "Drunk Catholic History: Spirits and the Holy Spirit," *OnePeterFive*, August 18, 2015, https://onepeterfive.com/ drunk-catholic-history-spirits-and-the-holy-spirit/.

36

The Curious Conventions Regarding the Holy Spirit in the Roman Orations

N THE ROMAN RITE, THE TYPICAL FOR-
mulation of the Collects, Secrets, Postcommunions,
and Prayers over the People is *to* the Father *through* the
Son *in* the Holy Spirit. It is a venerable arrangement, one that is
biblically inspired (see Ephesians 2:18). In the fourth century, St.
Basil the Great already treats the convention as well-established
(though he also used "to the Father with the Son along with the
Holy Spirit").[1] The Orations in our oldest liturgical manuals (the
so-called Verona and Gelasian Sacramentaries) presuppose this
formula, and indeed both sacred liturgy and the Christian life
as a whole can be defined as a sacrificial offering to the Father
through the Son in the Holy Spirit.

Beginning in the second millennium, the Latin liturgical tradition came to include several Orations addressed to the Son
rather than to the Father. Modern liturgical purists found these
additions abhorrent (and some still do), and so the 1970 Missal
greatly reduced their number. In a post and a book chapter, Peter
Kwasniewski defended the Christocentric Orations in the 1962
Missal, describing them in one response to a commenter as "a rare
species in an ecosystem."[2] I too think of the universal Church's
different liturgies as so many ecosystems, and during this Octave
of Pentecost, we have the opportunity to reflect further on the
peculiarities of the Roman ecosystem. For Whitsuntide includes
another exotic creature: Orations that refer to the Holy Spirit.

Orations *addressing* the Holy Spirit are not rare in the Roman
Rite (new or old): they are nonexistent. Although the priest prays

---

1   *On the Holy Spirit* 1.3.
2   Peter Kwasniewski, "Patricentric Purism and the Elimination of Liturgical Prayer Addressed to Christ," *New Liturgical Movement*, April 12,
2021, www.newliturgicalmovement.org/2021/04/patricentric-purism-and-
elimination-of.html; idem, *Resurgent in the Midst of Crisis: Sacred Liturgy,
the Traditional Latin Mass, and Renewal in the Church* (Kettering, OH:
Angelico Press, 2014), 79–93.

to the Holy Spirit at every Mass with the Offertory rite's *Veni Sanctificator*; although he says or sings almost every morning during Terce *Nunc Sancte nobis Spiritus*; and although the Church on Pentecost and throughout its octave addresses the Holy Spirit in the Mass sequence *Veni Sancte Spiritus* and in the Office hymn *Veni Creator Spiritus*—nevertheless, there is not a single Roman Collect, Secret, or Postcommunion Prayer that uses the vocative for the Third Person of the Blessed Trinity.

The closest that the Roman liturgy comes to an orational address of the Paraclete is what we see on the Vigil of Pentecost, the feast itself, and throughout its Octave—namely, prayers directed to the Father that mention the Holy Spirit and end with "in the unity of the *same* Holy Spirit, God, forever and ever. Amen." Even then, not every oration within these seven special days mentions the Holy Spirit.

As for the rest of the year, the Temporal Cycle includes a Collect (*pro aliquibus locis*) for Our Lady, Queen of the Apostles (Saturday after Ascension) and a Postcommunion for the Friday after Ash Wednesday that follow the formula of addressing the Father and mentioning the Spirit, while the Sanctoral cycle has similar Orations for St. Philip Neri (May 26, Secret), St. John Mary Vianney (August 8, Secret), St. Joan Frances de Chantal (August 21, Postcommunion), and St. Josaphat (November 14, Collect). Not surprisingly, the Saint most commonly linked to the Holy Spirit is the Blessed Virgin Mary: the Collects for the Immaculate Heart (August 22) and Presentation (November 21) have references to her as His dwelling place. Even the Votive Mass of the Holy Spirit and the Votive Mass for seeking the grace of the Holy Spirit never pray *to* the Holy Spirit, although all their Orations likewise mention Him.

Perhaps all this sounds unfair to the Holy Spirit, but before we start an equity-in-prayer movement, it is meet to consider two points:

1. The Church's prayers to the Holy Spirit elsewhere counterbalance any apparent slight to the equal dignity or divinity or personhood of the Holy Spirit in the Orations. Indeed, the Trinitarian ending of the Orations, which makes all prayer *in* the Holy Spirit, affirms the Spirit's importance. When the Church references the Trinity in prayer, it is usually with a

"coordinating" or a "mediatorial" pattern. Coordinating patterns, such as "Glory be to the Father *and* to the Son *and* to the Holy Spirit" lay stress on the equality of Persons, while mediatorial patterns, such as we see in the conclusions to the Orations, make "clear the order of the divine persons in the economy of salvation."[3] This economic order, however, is not a denial of ontological equality.

2. The Orations' manner of speaking about the Holy Spirit rather than to Him reinforces, to my mind at least, a certain ineluctable aura surrounding Him. The Collects of Advent ingeniously omit the Holy Name of Jesus (even though they talk about and sometimes even address the Son of God) as a way of dramatizing the concept of waiting for the yet unnamed Messiah. Similarly, refraining from addressing the Holy Spirit dramatizes a certain *je ne sais quoi* of Pneumatology; the last Person in the Holy Trinity to be revealed is in some respects the Person about Whom we know the least. For St. Gregory of Nazianzus, the Old Testament clearly proclaims the Father and less clearly proclaims the Son, while the New Testament clearly proclaims the Son but only gives us a glimpse of the Holy Spirit.[4] Historically, the Spirit was revealed gradually and only after the mysteries of Father and Son came into better focus. One way to think about the Roman Orations' conventions regarding the Holy Spirit is as an instantiation of Gregory's advice that we should follow God's pattern of neither revealing His doctrine suddenly nor of concealing it to the last.[5]

None of this is to say that the composers of these prayers had these points in mind. They may have simply acted within the parameters of a liturgical-literary style and nothing more until, in the second millennium, the rules were relaxed enough to allow a few prayers to the Son. The result is a heritage of prayers with most addressed to the Father, some to the Son, and none to the Spirit. As Kwasniewski points out, there are providential reasons to be grateful for the Orations to the Son

---

3 Gilles Emery, OP, *The Trinity*, trans. Matthew Levering (Washington, DC: Catholic University of America Press, 2011), 7.
4 *Oration* 31.26. See *On God and Christ: The Five Theological Orations and Two Letters to Cledonius*, trans. Frederick Williams and Lionel Wickham (Yonkers, NY: St. Vladimir's Seminary Press, 2002).
5 *Oration* 31.27.

(for example, as an antidote to Arianism[6]), and there may well be providential reasons to be grateful for an *absence* of Orations to the Spirit, even on His feast day or during His octave. For perhaps that is precisely how the Holy Spirit, under Whose guidance the liturgical treasures of the Church were formed, wants it. Perhaps the One who enlightens our hearts wishes to stay out of this particular limelight.

---

6   Kwasniewski, "Patricentic Purism."

VII

THE TIME AFTER PENTECOST

37

The Confessional Collect
of Trinity Sunday

HE COLLECT FOR THE FEAST OF THE
Most Holy Trinity is:

Omnípotens sempitérne Deus, qui dedisti fámulis tuis in con-
fessióne veræ fidei, ætérnæ Trinitátis glóriam agnóscere, et in
poténtia majestátis adoráre unitátem: quǽsumus, ut, ejúsdem
fidei firmitáte, ab ómnibus semper muniámur advérsis. Per
Dóminum.

Which I translate as:

Almighty and eternal God, who didst grant to Thy servants,
in the confession of the true Faith to acknowledge the
glory of the eternal Trinity, and in the power of Majesty
to adore Its Unity: we beseech Thee, that by steadfastness
in the same Faith, we may ever be defended from all who
are opposed to us. Through Our Lord.

In theme and wording, the Collect echoes the Preface of the Most
Holy Trinity, which is used on this feast and throughout the Time
after Pentecost: confession of the true God, Trinity and unity, the
glory of the Divine Persons, adoration and Majesty. Reading the
two prayers back-to-back is a profitable exercise.

The statement of fact ("O God, who....") declares that God
has given His servants two gifts: a confession of the true Faith,
which enables them to acknowledge the glory of the Trinity; and
the power of His Majesty, which enables them to adore the unity
of the Trinity. Once a rich and polyvalent term, the current concept
of confession is a mere shadow of its former self. Whereas now
confession refers only to a self-disclosure of sin, in the Bible and
in the early and medieval Church it referred to three things: praise
of God, accusation of self, and profession of faith. A "confessor"
is the term for a saint who has not been martyred, but the early
martyrs were also called confessors because of their brave confession of faith: to this day, the space below the altar in some early

basilicas that contains the relics of a martyr is called a *confessio*.

Confession of the true Faith is powerful. In the Postcommunion Prayer of this feast, we dare to list it with Holy Eucharist as something that can grant wellness to both body and soul.[1] Here in the Collect, confession of the Faith is identified as something that gives us the ability to be cognizant of the glory of the Trinity. *Agnoscere* means "acknowledge," and as Catholics we acknowledge the Trinity's glory often—for example, every time we say the minor doxology "Glory be to the Father and to the Son and to the Holy Spirit." But *agnoscere* can also mean to know or recognize,[2] and I suspect that these meanings are at play as well. Does not our Christian Faith enable us to recognize God's glory, to see the ways in which, as Gerard Manley Hopkins puts it, "the world is charged with the grandeur of God"? It is a privilege to have this power of recognition, and it is a privilege to know the great mystery that there are three Persons in one God.

It is also a privilege to be able to love God's unity, for this power comes not from our own native willpower but from His supervening Majesty. In the Roman Orations, "glory" is something that belongs *primarily* to God, while "majesty" (*majestas*) belongs *exclusively* to Him. The martyrs, for instance, have glory, but only God has majesty, for it is virtually synonymous with His essence. His Majesty does, however, empower us to love His unity. To my mind at least, there is a subtle compare-and-contrast between *in confessione veræ fidei* and *in potentia majestatis*.[3] Both are powerful, but confessing the true faith is an example of cooperative grace, in which both man and God have agency, while the love that comes from God's power is an example of operative grace, which God works in us without us—like the infused virtue of charity.[4]

---

1 *Proficiat nobis ad salutem corporis et animæ, Domine, Deus noster, hujus sacramenti susceptio: et sempiternæ sanctitatis Trinitatis ejusdemque individuæ Unitatis confessio. Per Dominum.* Which I translate as: "O Lord, our God, may our reception of this sacrament and our confession of the eternal and holy Trinity and Its undivided Unity bring about health of body and of soul. Through Our Lord."

2 See the Vulgate translation of Matthew 12:33—*ex fructu arbor agnoscitur*.

3 See Ellebracht, *Vocabulary of the Ancient Orations*, 40.

4 The theological virtue of faith is infused in us without us (see St. Thomas Aquinas, *Summa theologiæ* I-II, Q. 55, art. 4), but I wonder if the *confessing* of the Faith is a more cooperative act.

The petition, on the other hand, asks for protection from adverse things or persons. I have translated *adversa* or *adversi* as "all who are opposed to us" because the word *ad-versus* literally refers to someone who is turned to face you (in this case, aggressively) and is thus both opposite of you and opposed to you. The three hand missals I consulted—*St. Andrew Daily*, *St. Joseph*, and Baronius Press—translate the word as "adversities," but I think they are missing the point. First, there is a Latin word for adversity and it is *adversitas*, not *adversus*. The Roman Collects sometimes pray for deliverance from *adversitas*, but here I believe that the author has in mind the *people* who war against our confession of the true Faith, like those who persecute Christians: there is, in other words, an implicit juxtaposition of the three Persons who are confessed in the true Faith and the persons who are opposed to that confession. Firmness in the Faith is difficult precisely because the Faith has enemies both visible and invisible.

But we do not pray for the destruction of these enemies. Others have turned against us, but we do not turn against them. Instead, we pray that firmness in the Faith may provide a defense against their assaults. The image is mildly militaristic: *muniamur* literally means to "be fortified with a wall." We are asking that our steadfastness in the Faith will act as a wall to keep us safe, perhaps to buy us enough time to convert our (mortal) enemies into making the same confession.

The 2002 Roman Missal, incidentally, has an altered version of this prayer for its Solemnity of the Most Holy Trinity:

> *Deus Pater, qui, Verbum veritátis et Spíritum sanctificatiónis mittens in mundum, admirábile mystérium tuum homínibus declarásti, da nobis, in confessióne veræ fidei, ætérnæ glóriam Trinitátis agnóscere, et Unitátem adoráre in poténtia maiestátis. Per Dóminum.*

Which I translate as:

> God the Father, who by sending into the world the Word of truth and the Spirit of sanctification revealed a wonderful mystery to men: grant to us that in the confession of the true Faith we may acknowledge the glory of the eternal Trinity and in the power of Majesty we may adore Its Unity. Through Our Lord.

The petition for steadfastness in the Faith and protection from our adversaries has been omitted, and the original statement of fact about God has been turned into a petition. Whereas the original Collect presupposes that the faithful have been acknowledging the Trinity's glory and loving Its unity, the new Collect asks for them now.

But the real puzzle is the 2011 official English translation:

> God our Father, who by sending into the world the Word of truth and the Spirit of sanctification made known to the human race your wondrous mystery, grant us, we pray, that in professing the true faith, we may acknowledge the Trinity of eternal glory and adore your Unity, powerful in majesty. Through Our Lord.

There are, in my opinion, four peculiarities in the English translation.

1. It reverses what we acknowledge. Before we acknowledged the glory of the Trinity; now we acknowledge the "Trinity of glory." The latter is theologically ambivalent, and it weakens the allusion to our doxological practices. One wonders why this change was made.

2. It destroys the pairing of [the power of] confession and the power of divine Majesty.

3. It changes the power of Majesty from the cause of adoration to an attribute of divine unity. Our love of God is no longer seen as something that can only exist when it is sustained by divine power.

4. Finally—and this returns us to our main theme—it translates *confessio* as "profession." As we noted earlier, one of the meanings of confession is a profession of faith, and so the translators have by no means erred. But the decision, in my opinion, is nonetheless somewhat unfortunate. The only way we will be able to retrieve or maintain our rich Christian vocabulary is by using it. When we avoid terminology because it is no longer readily intelligible or because an easier word comes to mind, we collaborate in the emaciation of our own theological patrimony. Better to confess the true Faith in our own hallowed words, whether that confession is in season or out.

38

The Rare Collect of the First Sunday after Pentecost

NLESS YOU HAVE ACCESS TO A TRADI-
tional Latin Mass on weekdays or are about 700 years
old, you have never assisted at a Mass where all the
propers of the First Sunday after Pentecost were used. The Mass
was replaced by the Feast of the Holy Trinity in 1334, although
it continues to be celebrated on the ferial days between Trinity
Sunday and the Second Sunday after Pentecost. For centuries
its Orations were commemorated on Trinity Sunday, but this
practice was abolished in the 1962 Missal.

'Tis a shame, for the Collect in particular is striking:

> *Deus, in te sperántium fortitúdo, adésto propítius invocatióni-*
> *bus nostris: et, quia sine te nihil potest mortális infírmitas,*
> *præsta auxílium grátiæ tuæ; ut, in exsequéndis mandátis*
> *tuis, et voluntáte tibi et actióne placeámus. Per Dóminum.*

Which I translate as:

> O God, the strength of all who hope in Thee, kindly
> be present to our invocations; and because our mortal
> weakness can do nothing without Thee, bestow the help
> of Thy grace: that in carrying out Thy commandments,
> we may be pleasing to Thee in will and action. Through
> Our Lord.

The phrase in *te sperantium fortitudo* is found in only one other
place in the Missal, the Collect for the Feast of Pope St. Gregory VII on May 5, but *in te sperantium* is used again in the
Collect for the Third Sunday after Pentecost, this time paired
with *protector*. God is strength itself, but only for those who
hope in Him; He is not the strength, for example, of those who
despise Him or are fleeing Him.[1] And even though the prayer
is addressed to the Father, the use of *fortitudo* so soon after
Pentecost also calls to mind fortitude as one of the seven gifts

---

1   Haessly, *Rhetoric in the Sunday Collects*, 73.

of the Holy Spirit. Perhaps God the Father is the strength for those who hope in Him by His sending the Holy Spirit to us with His seven gifts.

The Collect makes two petitions.

First, it asks God to be present to our invocations. One can translate *invocationes* as "prayers," but I chose "invocations" because the word is rather rare in the liturgy. (Other terms for prayer, such as *deprecatio*, *oratio*, and *preces* are more common.) Even rarer, indeed unique, is the use of *invocatio* in the plural. The other two times that *invocatio* appears in the Roman Orations, the word is in the singular and is used in a more conventional way, namely, to call upon the name of the Lord.[2] This is a rare Collect with rare diction.

Second, the prayer asks for the help of God's grace and explains why: "because our mortal weakness can do nothing without Thee." I defer to the moral theologians, but it seems to me that by virtue of free will a person can do a simple good act without the benefit of sanctifying grace: an unrepentant murderer, for example, can leave a generous tip at a restaurant. Nevertheless, the murderer's random act of kindness would not be meritorious or conducive to his salvation. (And even his ability to be generous is a gift from God.) To use our free will *consistently* well, which is what a saint does, we are utterly dependent on the help of God's grace. The Collect refers to the two saintly habits of doing the good and loving the good habitually as fulfilling the Lord's commandments in both will and deed, and it is this fulfilment that constitutes the prayer's ultimate goal. If, as St. Paul writes, love is the fulfilment of the law (Rom 13.10), then we must truly love God and our neighbor and not just be do-gooders.

Providentially, the love of God and neighbor is the theme of the biblical readings of this Sunday. In the Epistle (1 Jn 4:8–21), St. John teaches that God is love (*caritas*) and that we must love both Him and our neighbor. The Gospel (Luke 6:36–42) develops this teaching with the famous passage "Judge not, lest ye be judged" and the Parable of the Mote and the Beam. Love of one's neighbor entails, among other things, being far more critical of oneself than of him.

---

2   Ellebracht, *Vocabulary of the Ancient Orations*, 116–17.

39

The Wonderful Collect of Corpus Christi

ESPITE OCCASIONAL ASSERTIONS TO the contrary, the Mass formulary and Office for the feast of Corpus Christi were almost certainly composed by St. Thomas Aquinas (1225–1274) at the behest of Pope Urban IV.[1] That includes the Collect for the feast:

> *Deus, qui nobis sub Sacraménto mirábili passiónis tuæ memóriam reliquísti: tríbue, quæsumus, ita nos Córporis et Sánguinis tui sacra mystéria venerári, ut redemptiónis tuæ fructum in nobis júgiter sentiámus: Qui vivis et regnas.*

Which I translate as:

> O God, who in this wonderful Sacrament hast left us a memorial of Thy passion: grant us, we beseech, to venerate the sacred mysteries of Thy body and blood in such a way that we may ever sense within us the fruit of Thy redemption. Who livest and reignest.

The prayer, which is inspired by biblical passages such as Luke 22:19 and 1 Corinthians 11:24–26 that describe Jesus instituting the Eucharist during the Last Supper, is noteworthy as an early example of an oration addressed to Jesus Christ.[2]

Further, the Collect is a useful reminder of various Catholic doctrines concerning the Eucharist.

First, the Blessed Sacrament—and the Mass that confects it— is not a reenactment of the Last Supper but a re-presencing of the suffering, death, resurrection, and ascension of Jesus Christ. As the Epistle reading for the feast reminds us, "For as often as you shall eat this bread, and drink the chalice, you shall shew the death of the Lord, until He come" (1 Cor. 11:26).

Second, by mentioning the sacred mysteries of Christ's body *and* blood during a feast dedicated only to the Lord's body, the

---

1 See Donald Prudlo, "The Anniversary of the Feast of Corpus Christi," *New Liturgical Movement*, August 11, 2020, www.newliturgicalmovement. org/2020/08/the-anniversary-of-feast-of-corpus.html.
2 See chapter 36, "The Curious Conventions Regarding the Holy Spirit in the Roman Orations."

Collect indirectly calls our attention to the doctrine of concomitance, the belief that even the smallest particle of the Host contains not only the whole of Christ's body, but also His blood, soul, and divinity as well. The Resurrection of Jesus Christ from the dead means that what was separated on Good Friday (blood, body, and soul) has been reunited. And His Ascension into Heaven, where He sits in glory at the right hand of the Father, means that the reunion shall last forever: never again is Christ's blood to be separate from His body, not even in the different species of His sacrament. As Aquinas writes in his magnificent sequence for the Mass, *Lauda Sion Salvatorem*:

> *Caro cibus, sanguis potus:*
> *Manet tamen Christus totus*
> *Sub utráque specie.*
> *A suménte non concísus,*
> *Non confráctus, non divísus:*
> *Integer accípitur.*

Which I translate as:

> Flesh as food, blood as drink,
> Yet the whole Christ remains
> Under either kind.
> By being consumed
> He is not cut up, broken, or divided:
> He is received in His entirety.

In other words—and this brings us to our third point—the Blessed Sacrament is truly wonderful. Our current bodies are marvelous things, a source of artistic and scientific amazement, but St. Paul tells us that they are a mere acorn in comparison to the tree that will be our glorified bodies, the kind that Jesus Christ currently has thanks to the Resurrection. His risen body is an object of far greater wonder because it defies the laws of space, time, and matter as we know them. It is that marvelous risen body that we receive in the Eucharist, and it is one of the reasons why we will never fully understand this sacrament. Again in the words of the Sequence:

> *Quod non capis, quod non vides,*
> *Animósa firmat fides,*
> *Præter rerum órdinem.*

Which I translate as:

> What you do not grasp, what you do not see,
> An ardent Faith confirms
> Outside the order of things.

Finally, the petition asks that veneration of the Eucharist will lead not simply to the fruit of redemption but to our *feeling* this fruit. Salvation, friendship with God, and *theosis* (which I take to be among the fruits of redemption) are great and wonderful things, but the only thing better than having them is knowing that you have them and feeling their effects. Indeed, we may view the feast of Corpus Christi as an attempt to make this wish come true. By exciting our love for the Lord in His Blessed Sacrament, the feast aspires to fill us with a holy joy. For as we sing in the Sequence about this feast:

> *Sit laus plena, sit sonóra,*
> *Sit jucúnda, sit decóra*
> *Mentis jubilátio.*

Which I translate as:

> Let our praise be full, let it resound,
> Let our heart's jubilation
> Be sweet and charming.

40

Heavenly Life on Earth: The Secret of the Second Sunday after Pentecost

ECAUSE OF AN INDULT FROM 1885, THE Second Sunday after Pentecost in the United States is usually replaced by the feast of Corpus Christi. Even then, the propers for this Sunday are used during the ferial days of the week that follows. One of those propers, the Secret, is particularly arresting:

> *Oblátio nos, Dómine, tuo nómini dicánda puríficet: et de die in diem ad cœléstis vitæ tránsferat actiónem. Per Dóminum nostrum.*

One edition of the *St. Andrew's Missal* translates this prayer as:

> May this sacrifice to be offered in Thy name, O Lord, cleanse us from sin, that by its virtue our daily life on earth may become likened unto that of Heaven. Through Our Lord.[1]

Another edition of the *St. Andrew's Missal* has:

> Lord, may we be cleansed by this sacrifice, which is to be offered in Your name; so that every day our life on earth may become more like the life of heaven. Through.[2]

These are beautiful sentiments and entirely in keeping with Catholic thought. St. Philip Neri, for example, used to say, "In this life there is no Purgatory; it is either all hell or all paradise; for he who suffers tribulations with patience enjoys paradise, and he who does not suffers hell."

And yet, however noble the thought, it is not quite an accurate translation of the Secret. The *St. Joseph's Missal* is a bit warmer:

---

1   *The Saint Andrew Daily Missal* (1952), 731.
2   G. Lefebvre, *The Saint Andrew Daily Missal* (Bruges, Belgium: Liturgical Apostolate, 1959), 641.

> May the offering about to be dedicated to Thy name purify
> us, O Lord, so that from day to day it may carry us on
> to the reality of heavenly life. Through. [3]

The first half is spot on. *Oblatio* is an offering, not a sacrifice. In pre-Christian times, a sacrifice was an oblation that is altered when it is given to God, e.g., by being immolated or consumed in fire. An oblation or offering, on the other hand, can be given to God without undergoing change, as when bread and wine are offered to God but then given to the Levitical priests for their use. That said, you could reasonably pray during the Offertory rite for the sacrifice that is about to be dedicated to God, for surely the bread and wine will be soon altered during the sacrificial act of consecration.

The second half of the prayer is also well translated, except perhaps for one word. The translator uses "reality" to translate the Latin *actio*, which obviously means "action" but also "performance." The prayer is not so much asking for the reality of a heavenly paradigm to inform our lives on earth as it is for us to perform this reality on earth, to enact it or act it out. Whereas the Collect on the feast of the Ascension prays that our minds may dwell amidst heavenly things here on earth,[4] this Secret focuses not on a transformation of our minds but of our deeds. Be ye doers of the Word, it is saying.

Consequently, it also makes sense to think of the "heavenly life" mentioned here as "heavenly living" or even (I suggest with some hesitation) "heavenly lifestyle." For the focus is not on the attainment of a permanent condition (like eternal life) but on a pattern of behavior that will last for the rest of our lives.

And speaking of which, did you notice that the author of this Secret has the hutzpah to ask that this one Mass that we are celebrating affect us for the rest of our lives, "from day to day"? Talk about the power of a single Mass!

Here, then, is my revised translation:

> May the offering about to be dedicated to Thy name purify
> us, O Lord, and from day to day may it carry us on to
> the performance of a heavenly life. Through...

---

3 The *Saint Joseph Daily Missal*, ed. Rev. Hugo H. Hoever, O.Cist. (New York: Catholic Book Publishing Co., 1953).
4 See chapter 33, "The Elevating Collect of Ascension Thursday."

Amen to that. And it ties in nicely with the Parable of the Great Banquet, which is the Gospel reading for today's Mass. A great lord invites many to his supper, but they are all too busy: one has just bought a farm, another has bought five yoke of oxen, and another has just gotten married. Hot with anger, the lord commands that the poor, feeble, blind, and lame be invited in their stead. And when there is still room, he tells his servant:

> Go out into the highways and hedges, and compel them
> to come in, that my house may be filled. But I say unto
> you, that none of these men that were invited shall taste
> of my supper.

The message is clear: if you do not translate the word of the Lord into action, you shall not enjoy the banquet. May the banquet of the Mass effect that translation, that we may enjoy the Great Banquet.

41

The Heart-Warming Orations of the Feast of the Sacred Heart of Jesus

EVOTION TO THE SACRED HEART OF Jesus takes its biblical inspiration from the account of our crucified Lord, His heart pierced by the soldier's lance and yielding blood and water, signs of the Eucharist and Baptism that mark the birth of the Church, the purveyor of those sacraments (see John 19:34). Devotion to the Sacred Heart existed privately in the early Church and among medieval doctors such as St. Bonaventure, but it was not until the seventeenth century that it became part of the Church's public liturgy, when dour heresies such as Jansenism tended to deny God's sweet and gentle love for all mankind and when secular indifference threatened to ignore it entirely.

In response to these distortions, Divine Providence inspired St. John Eudes in 1672 to compose a Mass of the Sacred Heart for the religious order he had founded. But it was St. Margaret Mary Alacoque who is chiefly remembered for the spread of this devotion. In 1675 Our Lord appeared to her on the Friday following the octave of Corpus Christi and asked her to work for a feast of the Sacred Heart on this day. The feast was fixed on the universal calendar in 1856, and in 1929 an Act of Reparation to the Sacred Heart, with a plenary indulgence attached to its public recital, was added.

The Feast of the Sacred Heart is an example of the principle of "liturgical recapitulation," when a particular mystery is revisited later in the year but viewed under a different aspect.[1] In a sense, the original feast honoring Jesus's Sacred Heart is Good Friday, but our hearts are too filled with sorrow on that day to

---

1 For more on this topic, see Michael P. Foley, "Divine Do-Overs: The Secret of Recapitulation in the Traditional Calendar," *The Latin Mass* 19.2 (Spring 2010): 46–49, republished on June 3, 2022 at www.newliturgicalmovement.org/2022/06/divine-do-overs-secret-of.html; idem, "The Reform of the Calendar and the Reduction of Liturgical Recapitulation," in *Liturgy in the Twenty-First Century: Contemporary Issues and Perspectives*, ed. Alcuin Reid (London: Bloomsbury T&T Clark, 2016), 321–41.

appreciate the joyful mercy of His own. A second feast is more than warranted for meditating on the mystery of Our Lord's Sacred Heart in a more jubilant key.

The Collect for the feast is:

> *Deus, qui nobis in Corde Fílii tui, nostris vulneráto peccátis, infinítos dilectiónis thesáuros misericórditer largíri dignáris: concéde, quǽsumus; ut, illi devótum pietátis nostræ præstántes obséquium, dignæ quoque satisfactiónis exhibeámus officium. Per eúndem Dóminum nostrum.*

Which I translate as:

> O God, who in the Heart of Thy Son, wounded by our sins, dost mercifully deign to bestow upon us the infinite treasures of Thy love: grant, we beseech Thee, that we who render to It the service of our devotion and piety may also fulfill our duty of worthy satisfaction. Through the same Our Lord.

The Collect teaches that God plans to give us the infinite treasures of His love not through His Son's Heart but *in* it. The Sacred Heart of Jesus *contains* us; we are not just close to His Heart or dear to His Heart but in His Heart, and it is there that God the Father will inundate us with love.

The Collect also has a subtle word play to boot. God deigns (*dignare*) to bless us with His treasures, and we pray that we may offer worthy (*dignus*) satisfaction through our devotion to His Son's Sacred Heart, despite the fact that that Heart was wounded by our very sins. How merciful is God the Father, to reward us through our sins in such a way!

The Secret, which builds upon this theme, is:

> *Réspice, quǽsumus, Dómine, ad ineffábilem Cordis dilécti Fílii tui caritátem: ut quod offérimus sit tibi munus accéptum et nostrórum expiátio delictórum. Per eúndem Dóminum.*

Which I translate as:

> Look upon, we beseech Thee, O Lord, the inexpressible charity of the Heart of Thy beloved Son: so that what we are offering may be a gift acceptable to Thee and an expiation of our offenses. Through the same Our Lord.

Let us not forget that when God the Father looks at the Heart of His Son, He is looking at a Heart with an enormous gash in it. If forensic evidence from the Shroud of Turin is to be taken into account, the Roman soldier pierced Our Lord's Heart with so much force that the spear point passed completely through and pierced the skin of His back. Nor did the Resurrection close this wound, which is why St. Thomas was told by Jesus to put his (entire) hand into His side. And so, when the Father gazes at His Son sitting at His right hand for all eternity, He sees in His Son's Sacred Heart vivid proof of a love to which no words can do justice.

We want the Father to look at His Son's Heart to remind Him not of what scoundrels we are for being complicit in His Son's death but of His Son's great love for us and how much He suffered for our sake. "Christ shows without ceasing the marks of His wounds to His Father for us," writes Blessed Columba Marmion. "He causes all His merits to be of avail to us: and because He is always worthy of being heard by His Father, *His prayer is always granted.*" [2] We therefore approach the Father with hope that our petition will be granted, namely, that our offenses may be expiated ("purged by sacrifice") by this Sacrifice of the Mass.

The Postcommunion is:

> *Prǽbeant nobis, Dómine Jesu, divínum tua sancta fervórem: quo dulcíssimi Cordis tui suavitáte percépta, discámus terréna despícere, et amáre cœléstia: Qui vivis et regnas.*

Which I translate as:

> May Thy holy mysteries, O Lord Jesus, impart to us divine fervor: whereby having tasted the sweetness of Thy most loving Heart, we may learn to despise earthly things and to love what is heavenly: Who livest and reignest.

This is a powerful prayer. It boldly equates the act of Holy Communion with *tasting* the Heart of Jesus. The prayer is especially powerful when one recalls the Eucharistic miracles in which consecrated Hosts miraculously turned to flesh. Such miracles have taken place in Lanciano, Italy in the eighth century (where the Host-Flesh is intact to this day), Buenos Aires in 1996, Tixtla, Mexico in 2006, Sokolka, Poland in 2008, and Legnica, Poland in 2013. In each case, histopathological studies or related analyses have revealed that the flesh is the heart tissue of a living person

---

2 Marmion, *Christ the Life of the Soul,* 70, emphasis added.

with AB (the universal) blood-type suffering great trauma.[3] Every time we receive Holy Communion, we are getting a Heart transplant and a Blood transfusion from Christ on the Cross.[4]

And should our hearts be one with Jesus's, and should His blood course through our veins, what kind of lover would we become? The petition of the Postcommunion answers: a lover who loves what is heavenly and looks down on what is earthly. It is a love that dare not speak its name in the new Missal, which has all but eliminated this reference to our Catholic patrimony.[5] Nevertheless, an essential component of being holy is being a lover whose subjective loves are perfectly aligned with the objective order of lovable things.[6] And as we will see in several of the Orations in this Part, "despising the earthly" does not mean hating God's creation or having a contempt for the people and things around us but simply assessing temporal goods accurately and not getting too attached to them.[7] Paradoxically, this reality-oriented approach makes one a better lover of those goods. It is to see with the eyes of God and to love with His Heart.

---

3 Franco Serafini, *A Cardiologist Examines Jesus: The Stunning Science Behind Eucharistic Miracles* (Manchester, NH: Sophia Institute Press, 2021).
4 This line is from Fr. Leo Patalinghug.
5 See Michael P. Foley, "Renewing Respect for Christian Despisal," *The Latin Mass* 27.1 (Winter/Spring 2018): 36–40, republished on April 7, 2023 at www.newliturgicalmovement.org/2023/04/renewing-respect-for-christian-despisal.html; cf. Kwasniewski, "Should We 'Despise Earthly Goods and Love Heavenly Ones'?"
6 See Augustine, *On Christian Doctrine* 1.27.28.
7 See also chapter 2, "The Heartfelt Collect of the Second Sunday of Advent."

42

The Merciful Orations of the Third Sunday after Pentecost

HE TRADITIONAL ROMAN RITE observes at this point of the calendar the "Time After Pentecost." Extending over almost half of the year, it is the great season of the Holy Spirit, the age between the first Whitsunday and the Last Judgment. While Advent commemorates the world before the Incarnation, and the Christmas and Easter cycles recall Christ's earthly life, the Time after Pentecost corresponds to the age, broadly speaking, in which we currently live. The Preface of the Holy Trinity reminds us of the ongoing work of the Father, Son, and Holy Spirit in our lives, while the green vestments betoken our hope in God, the Giver of life and growth, while we await the Second Coming.

Each Sunday of the Time after Pentecost equips us with the graces and lessons we need in order to remain faithful disciples in this post-apostolic age. While reminding us of the "day of visitation" at the end of time (Epistle), today's Sunday recalls Our Lord's infinite mercy and love for us and the immense value of penance: "There shall be joy before the angels of God upon one sinner doing penance," proclaims today's Gospel (Luke 15:1–10). We should therefore cast our cares upon the Lord with confidence and hope (Epistle & Gradual).

The Collect is:

> *Protéctor in te sperántium, Deus, sine quo nihil est válidum, nihil sanctum: multíplica super nos misericórdiam tuam, ut, te rectóre, te duce, sic transeámus per bona temporália, ut non amittámus ætérna. Per Dóminum.*

Which I translate as:

> O God, the Protector of all who hope in Thee, without whom nothing is strong, nothing holy, multiply upon us Thy mercy; that with Thee as our ruler, Thee as our guide, we may so pass through temporal goods in such a way that we not lose those which are eternal. Through Our Lord.

We have already seen the phrase *in te sperantium* in the Collect for the First Sunday after Pentecost, where it was paired with *fortitudo* instead of *protector*.[1] And the word order was different. In the Collect for the First Sunday, *fortitudo* was last: *Deus, in te sperantium fortitudo*. Placing the noun at the end has a powerful, suspenseful effect, and it contrasts nicely with our *infirmitas* or weakness mentioned in that prayer, which likewise occurs at the end of a clause. Latin syntax, miserable schoolboys are taught, doesn't matter—until it does.

Here, *Protector* hits the hearer like a punch in the face, right out of the gate. Indeed, God is the gate, the One who establishes the boundaries and erects the fences and protects the flock within. And the flock is not everyone on the planet but only those who hope in Him. And once God has set the bounds, He can multiply His mercy upon those within the bounds.

The rest of the prayer is notable for its elegance. The protasis (first part) of this Collect, Sr. Mary Haessly writes,

> is unusually elaborate, consisting of the Address, the Appositional phrase, and the Statement of Fact. The Appositional phrase presents the positive aspect, the relative the negative: God is the Protector of those who hope in Him, and without His protection, nothing is strong; God is strength, everything else weakness. The antithesis imparts vigor to the thought.[2]

The Collect is also notable for its double use of asyndeton, that is, the omission of "and" when you would expect it. "Without whom nothing is strong, nothing is holy" is thus subtly contrasted with "Thee as our ruler, Thee as our guide," and the omission of a conjunction gives the prayer a certain poetic flair as well as a kind of urgency.

The word that I translate as "strong" is *validus*, which appears nowhere else in the Roman Orations of the 1962 Missal. *Validus* is different from mere strength insofar as it refers to something that is potent, powerful, robust, or efficacious. To give an anachronistic example of the meaning of *validus*: the Vatican's lexicon for new Latin defines gin as *valida potio junipera*, "strong

---

1 See chapter 38, "The Rare Collect of the First Sunday after Pentecost."
2 Haessly, *Rhetoric in the Sunday Collects*, 78.

juniper-based beverage."[3] This concept of strength is evocative of Ogden Nash's cheeky poem "A Drink with Something in It," where in each stanza the "something" in a cocktail that creates the desired effect on the quaffer is the main alcoholic ingredient. The prayer, then, is declaring that without God, nothing has a kick to it, nothing has verve, vim, or vigor.

But lest we seek that kick in a bottle and only a bottle, let us heed the Collect's main petition. "May we so pass through temporal goods that we may not lose goods eternal." Temporal goods are not to be rejected per se but made use of in such a way that we can enjoy the eternal. The Collect calls to mind St. Augustine's classic distinction between *uti* and *frui* in *On Christian Doctrine*, making good use of a thing versus resting in the delight of the thing. God gave us temporal goods for our benefit, but they are flagstones on the way to true happiness, so long as we don't get stalled on those flagstones. For the well-ordered Christian soul, we can have our cake and eat it too, savoring the temporal and reveling in the eternal, provided we remember which is which.

The Secret builds upon these themes:

> *Réspice, Dómine, múnera supplicántis Ecclésiæ: et salúti credéntium perpétua sanctificatióne suménda concéde. Per Dóminum.*

Which I translate as:

> Look upon, O Lord, the offerings of Thy suppliant Church, and grant to Those believing in Thee, who are about to receive them, salvation through perpetual sanctification. Through Our Lord.

"Perpetual sanctification" anticipates the petition of the Postcommunion, and it also underlines the Catholic notion of salvation. *Pace* Martin Luther, we are not lumps of dung blanketed with snow even in Heaven. Rather, our salvation goes beyond a mere external or forensic justification to an internal transformation that renders us shiny clean little icons of Christ.

The choice of *credentium* also forms a nice supplement to the *sperantium* in the Collect. We hope in the Lord, and we believe in the Lord.

---

3 *Lexicon Recentis Latinitatis* (Vatican City: Libraria Editoria Vaticana, 2003), 344.

Finally, *respice*, from which our word "respect" is derived, literally means to look back on, to do a double take. After God has protected us by setting up the boundaries in the Collect, we ask that He keep an eye on what He has established.

The Postcommunion is:

> *Sancta tua nos, Dómine, sumpta vivíficent: et misericórdiæ sempitérnæ prǽparent expiátos. Per Dóminum.*

Which I translate as:

> May Thy holy things which we have received quicken us,
> O Lord: and may they prepare us who have been expiated
> for a sempiternal mercy. Through Our Lord.

The Postcommunion resumes the theme of mercy, but instead of asking for mercy now, it asks that we be prepared for sempiternal mercy. I don't know why "sempiternal" was chosen instead of "eternal" or "perpetual" (different ecclesiastical authors have different definitions of these words), but the point remains the same: God not only shows mercy to us now, but for His elect He shows mercy forever. In Heaven, we will be just as dependent on His mercy as we are on earth.

Expiatos is not an easy word to translate. I tentatively suggest the clunky "us who have been expiated," for it keeps the original Latin sense of purification or purgation. The verb *pio*, from which "piety" is derived, means to appease.[4] On the other hand, with the perfective force of *ex*, *expio* means to appease thoroughly, to make amends fully or to purify anything defiled by a crime.[5]

The *St. Andrew's Missal* translates *expiatos* as "atoning for our sins." "Atonement," it has been said, is the only English word that has contributed to Catholic theology: At-one-ment rightly expresses the effects of the Paschal Mystery, which makes us one with God. Whether the ancient Latin author of this prayer had this in mind, God only knows. But it is worth contemplating as we pray for God's abundant mercy during this Time after Pentecost, for surely, Christ's expiation and the Holy Spirit's sanctification unite us with Him whom we have offended.

---

4 See "Pio," *Lewis and Short*, 1379.
5 See "Expio," *Lewis and Short*, 695.

43

Rebel Wills and the Secret of the Fourth Sunday after Pentecost

HE SECRET FOR THE FOURTH SUNDAY after Pentecost is:

Oblatiónibus nostris, quǽsumus, Dómine, placáre suscéptis: et ad te nostras étiam rebélles compélle propítius voluntátes. Per Dóminum.

Which I translate as:

Be pleased, we beseech Thee, O Lord, with our offerings, which have been received [by Thee], and graciously force our wills [back] to Thee, even when they are rebellious. Through our Lord.

At this point of the Mass, the priest has more or less completed the Offertory rite and has offered bread, wine, himself, and all of us as an oblation to God. Understandably, he now implores God to be pleased with these offerings.

There is a subtle word play between *rebelles* and *compelle* in the second half of prayer: "even when we rebel, [don't forget to] compel." It is a marvelous petition. During every "Our Father" we pray "Thy will be done," but how often do we mean it without reservation? It is easy to pray: "Thy will be done, as long Thy will doesn't include for me cancer, bankruptcy, a bad cup of coffee, etc." It is far more difficult to echo Job's response to misfortune—"If we have received good things at the hand of God, why should we not receive evil?" (Job 2:10)—or to say with Our Lord in the Garden of Gethsemane, "My Father, if this chalice may not pass away, but I must drink it, Thy will be done" (Matt. 26:42).

So even though we are good Christians who go to Mass, such as Mass on the Fourth Sunday after Pentecost, our wills still recoil at the idea of total acquiescence to the will of God. We continue to rebel even after our Baptism. How fitting that this Secret is prayed during the Mass that has as its Gospel Luke 5:1–11, the story of Jesus ordering Peter to "launch out into the deep and let down" his nets. When Peter obeys and takes in an enormous haul of fish, he poignantly says, "Depart from me, for I am a sinful man, O Lord." To which Our Lord replies, "Fear not, from henceforth thou shalt catch men." Peter acknowledges Jesus as Lord and yet tells Him to go away. Clearly, he fears that he will not be up to whatever task Jesus may call him to, for he knows that his will is rebellious. But Jesus instead not only keeps him but makes him a fisher of other rebellious wills, a fisher of men.

The Church Fathers were quick to point out that the great difference between fishing for men and fishing for fish is that when you are fishing for men, you are fishing something out of the sea *that does not belong there* and will die without being rescued. Even so, drowning victims are infamous for often taking their would-be rescuers down with them: you might say that even though folks who are drowning want nothing more than to be saved, their wills are rebellious, or at least not fully cooperating. It is a terrible and self-destructive reflex, and yet we sinners do it all the time as well.

And so we pray, Almighty God: drag us, kicking and screaming if you have to, into a conformity with Your will while there is still time, for we know that as a Gentleman who respects our final decisions, You drag no one kicking and screaming into Heaven.

44

The Loving Collect of the Fifth Sunday after Pentecost

ECAUSE OF THEIR USUAL PROXIMITY to the feast of Saints Peter and Paul on June 29, the Fourth and Fifth Sundays after Pentecost make some allusion to the first Vicar of Christ: the Gospel of last Sunday concerned the Barque of Peter, and the Epistle of this Sunday is taken from St. Peter's First Letter (3:8–15). Today's Epistle and Gospel both stress the importance of being a "lover of the brotherhood," a person who, like St. Peter, truly loves his brothers and sisters in Christ in spite of everything. Indeed, our offerings to God are suspect if they are tainted by coldness or indifference to our fellow Christians (see the Gospel reading). Today's Collect, a brief but breathtakingly eloquent prayer, explains why: it is by having a God-given and well-ordered love of the people and things around us that we reach the divine goods that God has promised us, goods that surpass all human desire:

> *Deus, qui diligéntibus te bona invisibília præparásti: infúnde córdibus nostris tui amóris afféctum: ut te in ómnibus et super ómnia diligéntes, promissiónes tuas, quæ omne desidérium súperant, consequámur. Per Dóminum.*

Which I translate as:

> O God, who hast prepared invisible goods for those who love Thee: pour forth into our hearts the affect of Thy love: that loving Thee in all things and above all things, we may obtain Thy promises, which exceed every desire. Through Our Lord.

There is a classical distinction between *intellectus* and *affectus* that is difficult to translate. *Intellectus* is an understanding of what is good, whereas *affectus* is the heart's appropriation of what is good. It is a feeling but also more than that: it is a disposition, a condition, a state of being. In this Collect the Church asks God for a love that changes our disposition, to make us better lovers.

And the Collect answers what and how we shall love. The Catholic tradition rightly speaks of the virtue of *contemptus mundi*, of disdaining the world. But disdain is not hate: it is looking down on things that are low, but it is also seeing their true value. That is why St. Hildegard of Bingen defines *contemptus mundi* as "the radiance of life."[1] How can disdain be radiant? By seeing through the false allures of the world, we can affirm what truly makes life worth living and start living that life. In seeing through the false, we begin to truly live.

But seeing through the false allures of the world does not mean hating all things. As the Collect lays out, the trick is to love all things as the fingerprints of God, and to love Him as superior to what He has created. The prayer reminds me of a quote from the Irish author William Macken:

> I will tell you this. There is no use looking and admiring beauty, unless you see what is behind it. Any man will become bored looking at beautiful things if he is just looking at them for themselves. In themselves they are poor things. It is in what they are a reflection of that their true beauty lies. You see a reflection of a wood and a mountain in a still pool. That is good. But look beyond the reflection at the real thing and the reflection pales in your eyes.[2]

Finally, the goal of loving God in all things and above all things is to attain something that exceeds our every desire. Our current age is beset with lusts, desires, and unreal aspirations. The temptation is to recoil from this pornographic, polyamorous, consumerist cesspool and become Stoic—numb, immune to desire, unfeeling. But the Collect corrects this impulse. The problem with us is not that that we desire too much, but that we desire too little. Our Catholic Faith does not reduce our desires but increases them: it makes us, in the true sense of the word, more erotic. And yet, even so, God will reward us above and beyond these heightened, heavenly desires. The Collect beautifully channels what we already know from 1 Corinthians 2:9: "That eye hath not seen, nor ear heard, neither hath it entered into the heart of man, what things God hath prepared for them that love Him."

---

1 Saint Hildegard of Bingen, *Ordo Virtutum*, 2.114, translation mine.
2 Walter Macken, "God Made Sunday," in *God Made Sunday and Other Stories* (London: Pan Books, 1962), 41.

45

The Palpably Agricultural and Mildly Pugnacious Collect of the Sixth Sunday after Pentecost

HE CHURCH GAVE TWO SACRAMENTS to her catechumens at Easter or Pentecost: Baptism and the Holy Eucharist. Those two sacraments, and their effects on our souls, remain on her mind on the Sixth Sunday after Pentecost. In the Epistle reading of the Mass, St. Paul speaks of our life in the risen Christ as baptized members of His Body (Rom. 6:3-11); in the Gospel, the Multiplication of the Loaves foreshadows the miracle of the Eucharist, in which Christ's Body victoriously transcends the laws of space, time, and matter (Mark 8:1-9).

The Collect of this Sunday hearkens to these themes, but in a key all its own:

> *Deus virtútum, cujus est totum quod est óptimum: ínsere pectóribus nostris amórem tui nóminis, et præsta in nobis religiónis augméntum; ut, quæ sunt bona, nutrías, ac pietátis stúdio, quæ sunt nutríta, custódias. Per Dóminum.*

Which I translate as:

> O God of hosts, to whom all that is best doth belong, plant in our chests a love of Thy name and grant within us an increase of religion: that Thou mayest nourish what is good and, with the zeal of Thy mercy, protect what is nourished. Through Our Lord.

Looking only at the nonreflexive verbs, the imagery that emerges is agricultural. Planting, increasing, nourishing, and protecting: not only is there an echo of 1 Corinthians 3:6, but these meta-phors gingerly anticipate the readings of the day. In the Epistle, St. Paul writes: "For if we have been planted together in the likeness of His death, we shall also be in the likeness of His resurrection," while the Gospel speaks of Christ nourishing His followers in the desert, lest they faint along the way. Summer is the season of growth, both botanically and spiritually. And the same goes for the liturgical season. Religion was planted in the hearts of our catechumens on Holy Saturday and watered during the Easter season. Now, during this Time after Pentecost, we ask for continued progress in religion for both them and us.

The agricultural motif may also explain some of the unusual wording. Normally the Roman Orations follow the verb *præsta* (grant) with a noun or pronoun in the dative case: Grant *to* us, grant *to* Thy family, etc. Here, however, *præsta* is followed by *in nobis*, which is in the ablative case and which I have translated as "within us." Sr. Mary Haessly explains:

> The Petition opens with 'insere', a metaphor borrowed from agriculture, to be continued with 'præsta'. Just as the husbandman does not leave the seed exposed on the surface of the ground, but plants it securely within the earth, so God plants the seed of grace securely within the soul.[1]

The wording is distinctive in other ways as well. *Pectus* means breast or breastbone in Latin, but it is often used figuratively for the heart, soul, or mind. The safe translation of *pectus* in this Collect is "heart," since the heart is where love is planted and grows. I have chosen, however, to translate the word as "chests" because I believe that there is a soupçon of spiritedness or feistiness in this prayer. The Lord, for example, is called the God of hosts or armies, and there is an implicit praise of zeal—which, incidentally, is delightfully ambivalent. Because *pietatis studio* does not have a possessive pronoun, the zeal in question can belong either to God or to man. If it is God's, *pietas* means mercy and the phrase becomes an ablative of manner: we ask God to protect with the zeal of His mercy. If it is man's, *pietas* means piety and the phrase becomes an ablative of means: we ask God to protect by means of our zeal for piety.[2] Either way, zeal is a good thing. It is therefore my opinion that when we ask God for a love of His name in this Collect, we are not asking for the tender love of a mother for her child while nursing but the fiery love of Blessed Miguel Pro shouting *¡Viva Cristo Rey!*

---

1 Haessly, *Rhetoric in the Sunday Collects*, 149.
2 Haessly, 84–85. For the peculiar use of *pietas* in the Roman Orations, see chapter 50, "God Has Piety? The Collect of the Eleventh Sunday after Pentecost."

Similarly, we ask for an increase of religion. Religion takes guts; it takes commitment. Today those who like to say that they are "spiritual but not religious" have become so numerous that they have earned their own abbreviation (SBNR) and a rather fulsome entry on Wikipedia, with affirmations from feminism, Wicca, and other forms of neo-paganism. No doubt some SBNRs are sincere in this belief, but for others, I suspect, the statement is little more than a cloak to hide the gaping cavity below their Adam's apple, for they are, as C. S. Lewis puts it, men without chests.[3] The Reverend Lillian Daniel addresses SBNRs in the following way:

> You are now comfortably in the norm for self-centered American culture, right smack in the bland majority of people who find ancient religions dull but find themselves uniquely fascinating.... Any idiot can find God alone in the sunset. It takes a certain maturity to find God in the person sitting next to you who not only voted for the wrong political party but has a baby who is crying while you're trying to listen to the sermon. Community is where the religious rubber meets the road.[4]

If this is true in the eyes of Reverend Daniel (who has described herself as the pastor "of a large liberal Protestant church"), how much truer should it be for Catholics, who presumably have a thicker and more robust definition of religion?

Finally, the Collect bears a remarkable similarity to Psalm 79:14–16, which likewise combines the agricultural and combative:

> The boar out of the wood hath laid [God's vineyard, Israel] waste: and a singular wild beast hath devoured it. Turn again, O God of hosts, look down from heaven, and see, and visit this vineyard. And perfect the same which Thy right hand hath planted: and upon the son of man whom Thou hast [strengthened] for Thyself.

"God of hosts" (*Deus virtutum*) is a common title for the Lord in the Psalms and hence it appears several times in the Introits and Graduals of the 1962 Roman Missal. But it is a rarity in the

---

3 "Men without Chests" is the name of the first chapter of Lewis's *Abolition of Man* (Oxford: Oxford University Press, 1943).
4 Lillian Daniel, https://religionnews.com/2013/08/13/answering-the-spiritual-but-religious-an-interview-with-lillian-daniel/.

Roman Orations: besides this Collect, its only other appearance is in the Secret for the Feast of the Precious Blood on July 1. I do not know if the author intentionally chose this divine title to allude to Psalm 79, but the parallelism works either way. It takes a God of armies to take down the fiendish boar, that singular wild beast: we pray that with a love of God's Holy Name, an increase of religion, and the zeal of mercy or piety we may have the chests to stand by Him when the hunt begins.

46

Fruit, Free Will, and Providence: The Collect of the Seventh Sunday after Pentecost

T IS TEMPTING TO CALL THE SEVENTH Sunday after Pentecost "Fruit Sunday" because both the Epistle and the Gospel use fruit as an important metaphor. In the Gospel, Our Lord warns of false prophets and tells us how to recognize these wolves in sheep's clothing: "By their fruits you shall know them." In the Epistle, St. Paul speaks to the "infirm" Romans (newly converted and not yet fully formed?) in plain and simple language. When you worshiped idols, he tells them, the effect or fruit was death. When you serve God, the fruit is holiness and everlasting life.

Paul is also ironic to the point of sarcasm when he writes, "When you were the servants of sin, you were free from justice." Talk about an empty liberty. It reminds one of Psalm 87:5–6: "I am become . . . free among the dead, like the slain sleeping in the sepulchres, whom Thou rememberest no more."

The Collect of the day does not mention either fruit or free will, but its subject provides a framework for understanding these two themes: Divine Providence.

> *Deus, cujus providéntia in sui dispositióne non fállitur: te súpplices exorámus; ut nóxia cuncta submóveas, et ómnia nobis profutúra concédas. Per Dóminum.*

Which I translate as:

> O God, whose providence in its ordering never fails; we humbly beg Thee to put away from us all harmful things and to hand over all those things which are profitable to us. Through Our Lord.

In sui dispositione is not easy to translate. In post-classical Latin, *dispositio* refers to ordering, management, or direction. God's providence does not fail insofar as God is able to arrange everything to have a providential end; He is able to move the pieces of the cosmic chessboard around, so to speak, to bring about His plan of salvation. God can even use evils providentially despite the fact that He does not cause or will evils, but only allows them to arise. Finally, He is able to do all these things without violating our free will. Indeed, because God knows past, present, and future as present, He is able to take advantage of man's freely made decisions to bring about a providential end. Rather than providence and free will being antithetical, the Christian notion of providence incorporates or subsumes the free will of men and angels.

And because the Church knows these things, she prays on this Sunday that God in His providence will take away all harmful things and give us all helpful things. There is a nice contrast here between *noxia* (noxious, harmful, criminal, guilty) and *pro-futura* (useful, profitable, advantageous, beneficial). *Profutura* was often used to describe medicine, and so it also ties in well with today's Postcommunion, which refers to the reception of Holy Communion as God's "medicinal act" (*medicinalis operatio*). And the contrast between harmful and helpful things is reinforced by the verb *submovere*, which I have translated as "put away" but could also be rendered "make room" or "make way," for it is the word used to describe what lictors (body-guards for magistrates) did to clear a room or get the crowd out of the way.

The Collect also has a distinctive verb for giving, which we have translated as "hand over." *Concedere* means to concede or relinquish and has an edge to it in a way in which *dare*, the most common verb for giving, does not. It is as if the author were saying, "Come on, Heavenly Father, don't hold out on us! Hand over the good stuff!"

And why do we not want our Father to hold out? Because we know that we can bear good fruit only with God's grace. We want our "wages" to be holiness and eternal life rather than death. We want to be frugiferous, not barren.

47

What the...? The Eighth Sunday after Pentecost and Its Collect

ACH YEAR, THE GOSPEL FOR THE Eighth Sunday after Pentecost hits me like a slap in the face and makes want to say at the end of its proclamation "What the...?" instead of *Laus tibi Christe*. (Kudos to the ancient architects of the Roman liturgy for including one of the "hard sayings" of the Gospels.) The Gospel is perplexing because it appears to approve the injustice of a corrupt employee. The master in the Parable of the Unjust Steward (Luke 16:1–9) praises his assistant as one worldling admiring the clever maneuvering of another; Our Lord, on the other hand, commends the man's foresight in providing for his future. It is also possible that by reducing the amount which his master's debtors owed, the unjust steward took out his own unjustly added commission and thereby became, in his actions if not his intentions, more just.

Christ's command in the Gospel to "make yourself friends with the mammon of iniquity" is not a call to worldly compromise but an admonition to use riches in such a way that we are worthy of eternal life, fit to be received into our Father's everlasting dwellings. For as St. Paul explains in this Sunday's Epistle (Rom. 8:12–17), we are to live not by the light of temporal goods but according to the Spirit, mortifying the deeds of the flesh.

It is in light of these readings that the Collect seems almost ironic:

> *Largíre nobis, quǽsumus, Dómine, semper spíritum cogitándi quæ recta sunt, propítius et agéndi: ut, qui sine te esse non póssumus, secúndum te vívere valeámus. Per Dóminum.*

Which I translate as:

> Graciously grant to us, O Lord, we beseech Thee, the spirit to think and do always the things that are right; that we who cannot be without Thee may be able to live according to Thee. Through Our Lord.

I say "almost" because there is no contradiction between the Collect and the biblical readings. Indeed, the Collect functions as a hermeneutic or lens by which to interpret them. Of course, God wants us always to think and do what is right, but that does not mean carrying on like babes in the woods or deer in the headlights. Rather, as Our Lord says elsewhere, "Be as prudent as serpents and as innocent as doves" (Matthew 10:16). In *Theology for Beginners* Frank Sheed observes that "prudence" is often misconstrued as timidity or playing it safe, but it simply means the virtue of seeing "the world as it actually is and our relation to it as it should be."[1] There are therefore circumstances in which it is prudent to be subtle and clever, and there are circumstances in which it is prudent to be martyred, for as Sheed points out, "there is no gain in avoiding martyrdom at the loss of one's eternal soul."[2] Live, then, prudently, like St. Thomas More. It is a good lesson to keep in mind at all times but especially in an age such as ours.

But the Collect is even more specific than that: it does not ask for the ability to think and do what is right but for the *spirit* to think and do what is right. The petition ties into the Epistle's call to live according to the Holy Spirit, who makes us the adopted children of God, transposing us into a supernatural state of intimacy with, and participation in, our Maker; it also reminds us of a spirit world of good and evil. During Rogationtide and other litanies we pray for deliverance from the "spirit of fornication"; here we pray for the infusion of a better spirit. "Spirit" is breath, and we want to be filled with and breathe the good in order to think it and do it.

Finally, the petition for the spirit to think and do what is right is subordinate to the main petition of the prayer: to be able to live according to God. What a wonderful life that would be. The verb used for "to be able" is *valeo/valere*, which also means to "have the strength to do" (*Vale*, for example, means "Wax strong" or "Fare well" in Latin and is used to say goodbye). We want God to infuse a spirit of right thinking and right action not for its own sake but to have the strength to live in total conformity with His will, which we cannot accomplish on our own. For if we can't exist without God, we certainly can't live consistently as a perfect reflection of His will without Him as well.

---

1 Frank Sheed, *Theology for Beginners* (Ann Arbor, MI: Servant Books, 1981), 136.
2 Sheed, 136.

48

Weeping over Jerusalem: The Ninth Sunday after Pentecost and Two of Its Prayers

HIS SUNDAY IS UNIQUE. IT IS, AS FAR as I can tell, the only time that the Catholic liturgical year commemorates a Jewish event or feast that happens after the birth of the Church. It is one thing for a Christian calendar to incorporate Jewish feasts like the Passover (Good Friday) or *Shavuot* (Pentecost) that Jesus of Nazareth Himself kept, or that the Holy Spirit sanctified, but the Ninth Sunday after Pentecost hearkens to the Ninth of the Month of Av or *Tisha B'av*, the saddest day in the Jewish calendar. On this day—which like the Ninth Sunday after Pentecost falls sometime in July or August—pious Jews remember the destruction of the first Holy Temple by Nebuchadnezzar in 587 BC, and the destruction of the second by the Romans in AD 70. Observances include a twenty-five-hour period in which all eating and drinking, washing and bathing, application of creams and oils, wearing of (leather) shoes, and marital relations are forbidden.

In the Gospel for this Sunday (Luke 19:41–47), Our Lord sheds tears over Jerusalem's fate after coming from the Mount of Olives where, more than thirty years later, the Roman legions would commence their horrific and devastating campaign against the Holy City. (Readers interested in learning more about this terrible event can read Josephus's harrowing account of it, or Dom Guéranger's entry for this Sunday in *The Liturgical Year*.) The destruction of the Temple is a stern reminder of divine chastisement and the need for our repentance and conversion. As St. Paul teaches in the day's Epistle (1 Cor. 10:6–13), we must never think we stand on our own, lest we fall.

The Collect and Secret offer two aids to our conversion and staying on the right side of divine justice. The Collect reads:

*Páteant aures misericórdiæ tuæ, Dómine, précibus supplicán-
tium: et ut peténtibus desideráta concédas; fac eos, quæ tibi
sunt plácita, postuláre. Per Dóminum.*

Which I translate as:

> Let the ears of Thy mercy, O Lord, be open to the prayers
> of the suppliant; and so that Thou wilt grant the things
> desired by the petitioners, make them to ask for the things
> that are pleasing to Thee. Through Our Lord.

The function of a Collect is to collect the individual prayers of
the congregation into a unified whole to present to God, but
this Collect keeps a rather aloof tone. Rather than speak of "Thy
people" or "Thy family" as other Collects do, it generically mentions suppliant petitioners (of course, in Latin the possessive
pronoun is often implied, so the Collect is not disowning these
supplicants either). The aloofness, as I am calling it, creates
a rhetorical space that puts an onus on the listener or reader
to do what the Collect prays for, namely, to submit only good
petitions. Even though the Collect is beseeching God to make us
ask for things that are pleasing to Him, it is clearly pressuring
us (in a good way, of course) to start thinking in these terms
so that we are part of those Elect supplicants. And what are
those terms? Not simply to ask for things that are pleasing to
God, but to desire them. The early Collects for the Time after
Pentecost (the Fifth through the Thirteenth Sundays) tend to
focus—as we will see in the coming chapters—on retooling and
heightening our desires.

How far is this schooling of desire from the gussied-up mate-
rialism of "the Prayer of Jabez" fad,[1] in which Christians were
encouraged to pray for the trinkets of this life as if they had no
eternal longings at all! The Roman Rite, by contrast, aims both
to expand and to reorder our desires so that higher goods take
priority over lower ones, and then, once all goods are reordered,
one may transcend even them for God.

The Secret for the Ninth Sunday after Pentecost also implies
an internal transformation, for it prays that we may frequent the
mysteries of the Mass worthily:

---

1   Bruce Wilkinson, *The Prayer of Jabez: Breaking Through to the Blessed
Life* (New York: Multnomah Books, 2000).

> *Concéde nobis, quǽsumus, Dómine, hæc digne frequentáre mystéria: quia, quóties hujus hóstiæ commemorátio celebrátur, opus nostræ redemptiónis exercétur. Per Dóminum nostrum.*

Which I translate as:

> Grant us, we beseech Thee, O Lord, to frequent these mysteries: for as often as the memory of this sacrifice is celebrated, the work of our redemption is performed. Through Our Lord.[2]

The Secret, the meaning of which was once the subject of much debate in twentieth-century liturgical studies, abounds in references to the Eucharist. *Hujus hostiæ commemoratio*, which I have translated as "the memory of this sacrifice," is an example of a *genitivus inversus*, that is, an abstract noun that is accompanied by another noun in the genitive case and more or less functions as an adjective. Therefore, the phrase can also be translated as "this memorial sacrifice." Translating *opus nostræ redemptionis exercetur* also presents challenges. A very literal translation is "the work of our redemption is exercised." As Sr. Mary Ellebracht argues, *redemptio* in the Roman Orations is *not* "the historical Sacrifice of the Cross extended and made numerically present in the Eucharistic Sacrifice," but rather "the sacramental effect of the cultic action" of the Mass itself. She continues: "What we, in more abstract terminology, would call the 'graces which flow from the Work of Redemption,' the liturgy expresses with its characteristic concreteness as *redemptio*."[3] We need the graces that flow from the work of redemption in order to be worthy of receiving the Eucharist; if we are worthy of the Eucharist, we are persons who desire and ask for the things that are pleasing to God. Finally, we need to desire and ask for the things that are pleasing to God to avoid being like the unhappy earthly Jerusalem, over which the Chosen People, like Our Lord, still weep.

---

2   This ancient oration, which first appears in the Leonine Sacramentary, is quoted in Vatican II's *Sacrosanctum Concilium* 2. The 2011 English translation is: "Grant us, O Lord, we pray, that we may participate worthily in these mysteries, for whenever the memorial of this sacrifice is celebrated the work of our redemption is accomplished. Through."

3   Ellebracht, *Vocabulary of the Ancient Orations*, 53.

49

Running Humble: The Tenth Sunday after Pentecost

HE TENTH SUNDAY AFTER PENTECOST teaches us much about Christian humility. The Introit urges us to cast our care upon the Lord (Ps. 54:23), and the Offertory verse speaks of trusting in God rather than ourselves (Ps. 24:1–3). Trust in God is needed in order to have humility, the subject of both the Epistle and the Gospel. Jesus tells the Parable of the Pharisee and the Publican (Luke 18:9–14) to correct those who "trusted in themselves as just and despised others." The hero of the story, a humble Publican, is justified by God while the proud Pharisee is not, for "every one that exalteth himself shall be humbled, and he that humbleth himself shall be exalted." In the Epistle, St. Paul's admonitions to the Corinthians are an implicit call to humility. Don't get cocky, he is basically saying: you were once all as dumb as the idols you worshiped, and if you have the ability now to recognize Jesus as Lord, it is only by virtue of the Holy Spirit. Further, if you have any special talents or position within the Church, those too are a gift from God and have nothing to do with your innate merit (1 Cor. 12:2–11).

All of which makes the Collect somewhat puzzling, thanks especially to one word:

> *Deus, qui omnipoténtiam tuam parcéndo máxime et miserándo maniféstas: multíplica super nos misericórdiam tuam; ut ad tua promíssa curréntes, cæléstium bonórum fácias esse consórtes. Per Dóminum.*

Which I translate as:

> O God, who dost manifest Thine omnipotence chiefly by sparing and showing mercy: increase Thy mercy upon us, that Thou mayst make us, who are running towards Thy promises, partakers of Thy heavenly goods. Through Our Lord.

The puzzle is not the appeal to mercy or its connection to humility, which the Publican demonstrates clearly when he strikes his breast and says, "O God, be merciful to me a sinner." I remember hearing that Church officials a century ago, perhaps affected by a Jansenist spirit, were startled by St. Faustina's claim that God's greatest attribute was His mercy. Apparently, these officials didn't pay much attention to what they were praying every year on this Sunday.

No, the puzzle is the use of *currentes*, which is from the verb to run or hurry up. The image in the Gospel is of a humble man practically hiding in the shadows and not even daring to raise his eyes. The Publican is not exactly a picture of alacrity. But the Collect gives us an image of God's faithful racing, *hustling* to His promises, eager to partake of His heavenly treasures. Are these two images incompatible?

Rubbing these two sticks together, it seems to me, triggers an important spark of insight into the nature of humility. Christian humility is not masochism or self-defeat. On the contrary, as St. Thomas Aquinas so marvelously explains, whereas pride is the disordered and excessive pursuit of excellence and despair the disordered and defective pursuit of excellence, humility is the well-ordered and smoothly running pursuit of excellence, including even one's own excellence.[1] Let that sink in for a moment. *Humility is the habit for the pursuit of excellence.* It is not the state of thinking and acting like a doormat but, "so to speak, a certain disposition to man's free access to spiritual and divine goods."[2] And when that access is free, we run to it freely, unencumbered by vice or a delusional self-regard. Notice the similarity between Aquinas's wording ("spiritual and divine goods") and the Collect's ("heavenly goods"). Was the Angelic Doctor inspired by this prayer when he wrote his treatment of humility?

The point is that humility is a paradox. The virtue of lowliness gains the heights; the virtue of trusting in God and not in oneself imparts a confidence that all the pep talks in the world about high self-esteem cannot muster; and the virtue of looking down contritely and staying put looks up gleefully and runs to the prize. So run as to obtain it.

---

1 *Summa theologiae* II-II, Q. 160, art. 2; II-II, Q. 161, art. 6.
2 *Summa theologiae* II-II, Q. 161, art. 5, ad 4.

50

God Has Piety? The Collect of the Eleventh Sunday after Pentecost

N THE EPISTLE FOR THE ELEVENTH SUN-
day after Pentecost (1 Cor. 15:1–10), St. Paul goes to
great lengths to establish the historical facticity of the
Resurrection, for without it Christianity is an illusion. The Gospel
(Mark 7:31–37), on the other hand, recalls the cure of the deaf and
dumb man from Decapolis whom Our Lord healed by moistening
his finger and touching him. The Church Fathers saw in this
miracle an allegory for Baptism, and indeed the "Ephphetha"
ritual remains part of the traditional Roman Rite of Baptism.
Today's Mass therefore reminds us of the application of Christ's
victorious resurrection to the people of God through Baptism.

Extending Christ's grace is also a priority of the Collect:

> *Omnípotens sempiterne Deus, qui abundántia pietátis tuæ et
> mérita súpplicum excédis et vota: effúnde super nos misericór-
> diam tuam; ut dimíttas quæ consciéntia métuit, et adjícias
> quod orátio non præsúmit. Per Dóminum nostrum.*

Which I translate as:

> Almighty and eternal God, who in the abundance of Thy
> loving kindness goest beyond the merits and desires of
> the suppliant, pour out Thy mercy upon us, that Thou
> mayst forgive what our conscience fears and add onto
> what our prayer does not dare [ask]. Through Our Lord.

"Pour out" (*effunde*) is a liquid metaphor, a possible tie-in to the
waters of Baptism and the very earthy way that Jesus cured the deaf
and dumb man. It also has a Eucharistic overtone, since it is the
verb used for "shed" when the priest consecrates the wine. Mercy
is what led Jesus to cure the man, mercy is what led Jesus to pour
out His blood for us, and mercy is what we ask for in the Collect.

The word *pietas* appears in this prayer, which I have translated
as "loving kindness." In classical Latin, *pietas* is a human virtue
betokening loyalty to the gods, one's country, one's family, etc.

If we trust Vergil's *Aeneid*, it is the signature virtue of the hero Aeneas, and by extension of the Roman people, the one thing that makes them superior to those impressive but sneaky Greeks. In Christian Latin, *pietas* is a proper respect or attitude that the believer has towards God; it is both a moral virtue and one of the seven gifts of the Holy Spirit.

But Christianity also added a new and revolutionary meaning to the word by turning the tables and applying it to *God's* attitude to man. And what is that attitude? Thankfully, one of loving kindness. When ascribed to the divine, *pietas* is essentially a synonym for mercy or clemency. And thankfully, according to this Collect, God has plenty of it.

There is one more twist. Whereas most Christian literature favors the "human" meaning over the "divine," the Orations of the Roman Missal are the opposite. In the sermons of Pope St. Leo the Great, for example, *pietas* is used 53 times as a human attitude or habit and only 7 times as a divine quality. In the Orations, by contrast, *pietas* is used 27 times in reference to God and only 3 times in reference to man.[1] The Collect for this Sunday is one of those 27 times.

The purpose clause is especially beautiful: forgive what our conscience is afraid of, and add on(to) what our prayer does not dare ask for. The use of "increase" or "add onto" (*adjicias*) rather than "give" or "bestow" is interesting, for it implies that God is *already* giving us blessings that exceed our prayers' wildest dreams; we just want *more*. On and off for the past several weeks the Collects have been conditioning us to desire big and pray big; here we are told that God will outdo even the greatest of our yearnings and petitions.

Finally, to speak of what we dare not wish for acknowledges the possibility of a lingering despondency or despair about our spiritual condition. Like the Publican in the Gospel from last Sunday, when our conscience is working properly, it gives us enough self-knowledge to see the enormity of our sins; as a result, we do not even feel like looking up to heaven (see Luke 8:13). Be of good heart, the Collect is telling us: although your conscience is right about your sins, God's *pietas* will nonetheless deliver handsomely. For as St. Paul writes in this Sunday's Epistle, "His grace in me hath not been void."

---

1 Ellebracht, *Vocabulary of the Ancient Orations*, 53.

51

Heavenly Liturgy and Earthly Compassion: The Twelfth Sunday after Pentecost

HE COLLECT FOR THE TWELFTH SUNDAY after Pentecost paints an amazing scene, but only after one overcomes a number of linguistic challenges:

> *Omnípotens et miséricors Deus, de cujus múnere venit, ut tibi a fidélibus tuis digne et laudabíliter serviátur; tríbue, quǽsumus, nobis: ut ad promissiónes tuas sine offensióne currámus. Per Dóminum nostrum.*

Which I translate as:

> Almighty and merciful God, from whose liturgy comes the fact that Thou art worthily and laudably served by Thy faithful ones: grant, we beseech, that we may run without stumbling to Thy promises. Through Our Lord.

The Collect contains a grammatical rarity. In the Orations of the Roman Missal, a clause with *ut* and a verb in the subjunctive mood is almost always a purpose clause: "O God, give us X, Y, or Z so that we can have A, B, or C," where *ut* would be translated as "so that" or "in order to." Here, however, we have a "noun clause," where the entire clause functions as a noun (specifically, as the object of the verb "to come"), and thus we have translated *ut* as "the fact that."[1]

The Collect also contains a verbal rarity. Of the 111 times that the rich and nuanced word *munus* appears in the Orations of the Roman Missal, over 75% are in a Secret.[2] *Munus* appears less frequently in the Postcommunion Prayers and the Lenten Prayers over the People and least of all in the Collects. This is one of those outliers.

---

1 My thanks to Dr. David White for help with this clause and his insight into the use of the passive voice.
2 Ellebracht, *Vocabulary of the Ancient Orations*, 163.

Most hand missals translate *munus* in this Collect as "gift," and that indeed is how the word is used most of the time in the Roman Rite. In the Secrets, for example, *munera* are usually the "material gifts destined for the sacrifice." Every now and then, however, *munus* can mean "the rite itself which is performed with and over the gifts," and I believe this to be the meaning that is operative here.[3] For the ancient Roman, a *munus* was a public, religious service (similar to "the rite itself performed over the gifts"), and that meaning, which ties into the serving mentioned in the noun clause, better fits the context here.

The Collect is essentially stating that God has a service, and from it flows our serving Him "worthily and laudably." Or to use another word for a public, religious service (this time from Greek), God has a "liturgy" (*leitourgia*), and it is by virtue of His liturgy, the divine liturgy, that humans are able to worship Him properly. Paradoxically, even our ability to praise God and give Him gifts is a gift from God. The author of the Collect could have put the noun clause in the active voice ("the fact that Thy faithful serve Thee…"), but he instead chose the more unwieldy passive voice, which puts the focus on the action done rather than the faithful who are doing it. Even grammatically, the author of the Collect is emphasizing God and His agency in the liturgy rather than us.

The same truth is expressed in this Sunday's Epistle, 2 Corinthians 3:4-9, where St. Paul reminds the Corinthians that the Holy Spirit has made us, through no merits of our own, ministers of the New Covenant. Even though human hands have obviously played a part in its historical development, sacred liturgy, which participates in and anticipates the cosmic liturgy described in the Epistle to the Hebrews and the Book of Revelation, is ultimately not the "work of human hands," but the product of the Holy Spirit and the ongoing action of Jesus Christ the High Priest. Divorcing the human from the divine in sacred liturgy is a fool's errand, as foolish as trying to separate the humanly composed from the divinely inspired in the Sacred Scriptures.

The Collect, then, is offering an astonishing metaphysical map. It is not the case that liturgy is a primarily human phenomenon, the concept of which we then apply to what is happening in

---

3   Ellebracht, 163, 164.

Heaven, albeit weakly and metaphorically. On the contrary, the realest of real liturgies is what is happening in Heaven at the altar of the Lamb who was slain and is now at His Wedding Feast; what we do on earth in our churches is the derivative act. But since it is derivative, our earthly liturgies are truly partaking of the Heavenly Liturgy right now. So many of the liturgical controversies of the last century could have been avoided if liturgists actually understood and believed the theology brilliantly encapsulated in these thirteen words of the Collect.

The same Collect asks God to enable us to run to His promises. Only two weeks ago we made essentially the same prayer: "Increase Thy mercy upon us, that Thou mayst make us, who are running towards Thy promises, partakers of Thy heavenly goods."[4] Both Collects link participation in the heavenly with running towards divine promises. Here, however, we add an additional request: to run without stumbling (*sine offensione*). In the Vulgate, *offensio* is the word for the famous biblical "stumbling block," that which causes one to sin or offend (see Ezech. 20:7; 2 Cor. 6:3; 1 Pet. 2:8), but it can also be our very selves. As St. Anselm laments in the *Proslogion*: *Tendebam in Deum, et offendi in meum* — "I was heading for God, and I stumbled over myself."[5] May sin or our own egos not trip us up, we pray, as we race to the prize promised us.

The rather frenetic quality of this Collect also matches the tone of this Sunday's Gospel (Luke 10:23–37). When one loves the Lord God will all of one's heart, soul, strength, and mind, one is indeed sprinting flawlessly to God. The Good Samaritan in the Parable is not literally described as running, but it is difficult not to picture him hustling, rushing to the man's aid, binding up his wounds, and finding him shelter. And there is an additional dimension as well. The Church Fathers saw in the Good Samaritan a figure for Christ: the oil and wine which he poured into the wounds of the injured man symbolize the sacraments poured into our souls wounded by sin, and the sacraments are, of course, what we receive in the divine liturgy. May the heavenly goods in which we partake endow us with the same compassion for our neighbor as that of the Good Samaritan.

---

4 See chapter 49, "Running Humble: The Tenth Sunday after Pentecost."
5 St. Anselm, *Proslogion* 1, translation mine.

52
The Theological Virtues and the Thirteenth Sunday after Pentecost

HE READINGS FOR THE THIRTEENTH
Sunday after Pentecost have as their focal point the
power and importance of supernatural faith. It is faith,
the Gospel tells us (Luke 17:11–19), that makes us whole; and it
is faith, the Epistle tells us (Gal. 3:16-22), that helps us inherit
God's promises. But lest we slip into the heresy of *sola fides*, the
Collect provides a succinct and yet packed framework in which
to understand this precious gift:

> *Omnípotens sempitérne Deus, da nobis fídei, spei et caritátis
> augméntum: et, ut mereámur ássequi quod prómittis, fac nos
> amáre quod prǽcipis. Per Dóminum.*

Which I translate as:

> Almighty and everlasting God, grant unto us an increase
> of faith, hope, and charity: and so that we may merit to
> obtain what Thou dost promise, make us love what Thou
> dost command. Through Our Lord.

There is much in this brief Collect. Like clever children who know
how to get their Mom and Dad to say Yes, the Orations of the
Roman Missal usually flatter God by praising His attributes in a
"who" clause before asking Him for a favor. This prayer, however,
cuts right to the chase: there isn't even the standard deferential
"we beseech Thee."

Moreover, by requesting the theological virtues of faith, hope,
and charity, the Collect reminds us that faith alone does not
save, but must be accompanied by hope and charity, especially
the latter. St. Thomas Aquinas goes so far as to call charity
the "form" or animating principle of faith, that without which
faith is a lifeless corpse (for even the demons believe in God,
but it does them little good [see James 2:19]). Stephen Beale
rightly argues that the key difference between Protestants and
Catholics is a soteriology not of "faith alone" versus "faith

and works" but of "faith alone" versus "faith and charity."[1]

But the Collect aims even higher, praying not simply for faith, hope, and charity, but their increase. These virtues were infused into our souls by the sheer generosity of God when we received the sacrament of Baptism, but they can increase or decrease after that signature event, and we obviously want them to increase. God may have infused these virtues "in us, without us" as Aquinas puts it, but they cannot be maintained without us. The Council of Trent cites this Sunday's Collect in its articulation of the Catholic doctrine of sanctification, which involves progressing in the state of justice until death.[2]

Indeed, the amount of charity a person has at the moment of his death is the amount that he will have for all eternity (with faith giving way to vision, and hope to possession). Purgatory does not increase one's virtues but pays off the debt of temporal punishment that is owed to God. This decontamination shower (or refiner's fire, to speak more biblically) at Heaven's doorstep simply burnishes what is there; it does not bestow what is not there. There is no growth in Heaven either, only perfection of various kinds that creates a holy ranking of heavenly souls and spirits, or to use the Greek term, a "hierarchy." Therefore, if you wish your soul to have in Heaven a maximum of the goods corresponding to faith, hope, and charity, now is the time to go for it. The theme of increasing the theological virtues also pairs nicely with the Postcommunion for this Sunday, which prays that, through the working of the sacraments we have just received, "we may advance in the *increase* of eternal redemption" (*ad redemptionis æternæ, quæsumus, proficiamus augmentum*), that is, an increase in the effects of the Redemption on our souls.

The second half of the Collect teaches us how to increase the theological virtues, although the answer seems contradictory. Does the Catholic Church teach that we are saved by God's grace or by human merit? Yes, the Collect replies. We need merit to obtain God's promises, and merit is obtained by good works and the exercise of virtue. But it is still God who gives the increase

---

1 Stephen Beale, "How Protestants Still Get Justification Wrong," *Crisis Magazine*, October 30, 2017, www.crisismagazine.com/2017/protestants-still-get-justification-wrong.
2 See session vi, chapter 10.

(1 Cor. 3:6). As the well-trained Thomist Blessed Columba Marmion explains, God is the efficient cause of the increase of virtue in our souls while our acts are "the meritorious cause," which simply means that "by our acts, we merit that God should augment these vital virtues in our souls."[3]

And what makes these acts meritorious? The Collect has an answer to that question as well: we must love what God commands. As Aristotle pointed out long ago, simply doing good deeds does not make one a just man, for if one acts only out of fear of punishment or a desire for reward, one is not truly just. What makes a good man good is that he loves the good as well as does it. But to love the good—that is, to love what God commands—takes nothing less than a root-and-branch conversion that only God can give us, for our hearts are desperately wicked from their youth (see Jer. 17:9). We again return to the theme of reordered desire that emerges during this portion of the Time after Pentecost and to the paramount importance of undergoing an internal transformation.

Put differently, there is no "works righteousness" doctrine undergirding this Collect, and still less is there Luther's belief in an "imputed righteousness" according to which even souls in Heaven remain piles of dung covered by gracious blankets of snow. The Catholic dogma concerning salvation does not teach that we earn our way into Heaven by sole dint of our own efforts but rather that any merit we have earned and must earn is, paradoxically, a gift from God. For, as we never tire of citing, when God rewards the merits of His saints, He is rewarding His own gifts (see Gallican Preface for All Saints Day).

In the case of this Collect, the Church asks for an increase of faith, hope, and charity through a two-step process. First, she begs God to make us true lovers of His will, which we have absolutely no hope of accomplishing on our own but which, when accomplished by God's grace, internally transforms our dark hearts into shiny, bright Temples. Next, the Church asks God to give us, based on the merits that flow from being God's true lovers, what He has promised to such blessed folk (see Jas. 1:12, 2:5). Not a bad plan, that.

---

3 Marmion, *Christ the Life of the Soul*, 222.

53

Perpetual Propitiation in the Fourteenth Sunday after Pentecost

ORTIFICATION OF THE FLESH IS NOT exactly running rampant in the Church these days, and yet St. Paul tells us in this Sunday's Epistle (Gal. 5:16–24) that those who belong to Christ "have crucified their flesh with its vices and concupiscences." The vices that Paul lists (fornication, uncleanness, immodesty, etc.) do not spring from our bodies *per se*, but from the disordered passions of our soul that lead to bad bodily habits and even addictions. The antidotes to them are the virtues mentioned by the Apostle (charity, joy, peace, etc.), which spring from the Spirit of God.

Living according to the flesh does not lead to pleasure but to endless dissatisfaction and anxiety; hence the Gospel (Matt. 6:24–33) reminds us to serve the only Master who truly takes care of us, and not be worried about the things of this world. The Gospel, which contains the familiar verse, "Consider the lilies of the field," ends with the even more famous command, "Seek ye first the Kingdom of God and His justice, and all these things shall be added unto you." As a fervent seeker of God's Kingdom, we become like the author of the Introit, who can sing out with sincerity, "How lovely are Thy tabernacles, O Lord of hosts! My soul longeth and fainteth for the courts of the Lord" (Ps. 83:2–3).

The Collect of this Sunday contributes to these sound teachings by offering a clue into how to transition from a carnal-minded soul to someone who longs and faints for the courts of the Lord, and seeks Him and His justice above all else:

> *Custódi, Dómine, quǽsumus, Ecclésiam tuam propitiatióne perpétua: et quia sine te lábitur humána mortálitas; tuis semper auxíliis et abstrahátur a noxiis, et ad salutária dirigátur. Per Dóminum nostrum.*

Which I translate as:

> Keep, we beseech Thee, O Lord, Thy Church in perpetual propitiation; and because without Thee human mortality perishes, by Thy aids may she always be drawn away from things hurtful and led to things salutary. Through Our Lord.

Several phrases make this a difficult Collect to translate. *Propitiatione perpetua* is a rhetorical gem: it has nice alliteration with a prominent "t" sound.[1] But what does it mean? *Propitiatio* is sometimes used in the Vulgate as a synonym for *misericordia*, and hence most lay missals understandably translate it as "mercy"[2] or "kindness."[3]

There may, however, be a secondary meaning at play. As 1 John 2:2 makes clear, *propitiatio* also means atonement or appeasement. In ecclesiastical Latin, Jesus Christ is both our propitiation and our propitiator—that is, He is both the means of our reconciliation with God and the agent of that reconciliation.[4] To be kept in perpetual propitiation, then, can also mean to be kept in a state of constant reconciliation with the Father through His Son, the High Priest of an eternal sacrifice of which we partake through this Mass. The connotation is reinforced in the Sunday's Secret, which prays that this salutary sacrifice may become a purgation of our sins and a propitiation [appeasement] of God's power.

Another tricky phrase is *labitur humana mortalitas*, which I have translated as "human mortality perishes." *Labor/lapsus* is the verb for gliding on a smooth surface or beginning to fall, but it also came to mean perishing or making a mistake or falling away (as in "lapsed Catholics"). Given the context, perishing seems to be what the author had in mind: *with* God, not even human mortality is mortal, but without God it certainly is. Of course, "fall" could work here, too.

The final petition is almost comical, for instead of asking for protection from harmful things it asks that we be drawn away from them. The image is one of foolish children playing with

---

1 Haessly, *Rhetoric in the Sunday Collects*, 102.
2 *Saint Andrew Daily Missal* (1952), 801, and *The Saint Joseph Daily Missal*, 477.
3 *The New Roman Missal*, ed. Rev. F. X. Lasance and Rev. Francis Augustine Walsh, OSB (Palmdale, CA: Christian Book Club of America, 1993), 686.
4 Jerome, *Ep.* 21.2; Ambrose, *Commentary on Luke*, prol. 7.

matches next to a gas station who must be dragged home kicking and screaming for their own good. Or perhaps the image is of soldiers wounded on the battlefield who must be carried off on stretchers. The word for "aids" here is *auxilia*, which, since it is in the plural, can mean auxiliary troops or reinforcements. Perhaps personified graces or even angels are acting as medics and doing the hauling.

And actually, it is not the faithful, strewn on the battlefield or not, for which the Collect prays (although they are certainly implied): it is the Church. The Church as a unit must also be constantly dragged away from harmful things, either because she has sinful or foolish pilots at the helm or because the whirlpools of this world are trying to suck her down to the bottom of the sea. Or both. Similarly, keeping the *Church* in perpetual propitiation has a sacramental overtone. Make sure, we pray to God, that the Church is able to offer always and everywhere the sacrifice of the Holy Mass worthily.

The image of dragging is contrasted neatly with being led to salutary things. Initially, we must be pulled away from what is hurting us, voluntarily or not; then, after we come to our senses, we can be led (freely) to what may heal us. *Salutaria* is an interesting choice. One other place we see this word is the first sentence of every Preface in the Mass: "It is truly meet and just, right and profitable (*salutare*) for us everywhere and always to give Thee thanks, O Lord." The thanksgiving of the Eucharist is salutary, and it is that act of giving thanks in which we are beginning to participate when we pray this Collect. Further, by making the salutary act of thanksgiving everywhere and always, our desires are healed in such a way that they seek first the Kingdom of God and His justice.

54

The Sensational Postcommunion Prayer of the Fifteenth Sunday after Pentecost

HE SUNDAY THAT IN FORMER AGES WAS called, on account of its Gospel, the Sunday of the Widow of Naim, contains the following Postcommunion Prayer:

> *Mentes nostras et córpora possídeat, quǽsumus, Dómine, doni cæléstis operátio: ut non noster sensus in nobis, sed júgiter ejus prævéniat efféctus. Per Dóminum.*

Which I translate as:

> May the working of [Thy] heavenly gift, O Lord, take possession of our minds and bodies so that not our *sensus* but its effect may ever take precedence in us. Through Our Lord.

I leave *sensus* temporarily untranslated to highlight its peculiarity. Most missals translate *noster sensus* as either "inclinations"[1] or "impulses"[2] or even "natural impulses."[3] But these choices are problematic from a grammatical point of view. As a fourth declension noun, *sensus* can be either singular or plural. In the Collect for the Monday of the Third Week of Lent, we find it in the plural, when the Church prays that by abstaining from carnal meats we may be able to "steer our senses (*sensus*) away from harmful excesses." In that context *sensus* can indeed mean "impulses" or "inclinations." In the Postcommunion Prayer of the Fifteenth Sunday after Pentecost, however, the noun is singular, a fact we know from the adjective *noster* modifying it. Thus, *sensus* refers to a single faculty like "sensation" rather than a number of activities or conditions.

---

1 *St. Joseph Daily Missal*, 482, and *My Sunday Missal*, ed. Msgr. Joseph F. Stedman (New York: Confraternity of the Precious Blood, 1942), 272.
2 *Fr. Lasance Missal*, 692, and *The Daily Missal and Liturgical Manual* (London: Baronius Press, 2007), 819.
3 *Saint Andrew Daily Missal* (1952), 809.

With the notion of sensation in mind, I argue that *noster sensus* means "our perception," or better, "our sense of things," which I take to include not only our initial perception but our entire judgment and opinion. If my hypothesis is correct, the prayer asks that a "Eucharistic worldview," or at least a worldview nourished by the Eucharist, take precedence over our own warped perception of reality. One of the goals of the Christian believer is to see the world through the eyes of God. As one of the seven gifts of the Holy Spirit, knowledge is that which "makes us see created things in a supernatural way as only a child of God can see them."[4] There is nothing wrong with human perception or judgment per se; indeed, it is a rather impressive faculty for an animal. Nevertheless, it cannot see all there is to see. A scientific understanding of the world, for example, is a splendid thing, but if a scientist knows nothing more, he misses out on the great sacramental mystery of creation. As St. Augustine points out, it would be better for him to know nothing more than "only God can make a tree" than for him to know everything about trees except the fact that God made them (see *Confessions* 5.4.7).

And seeing through the eyes of God is far more than seeing that nature is a divine gift. It is seeing everything *sub specie æternitatis*; it is seeing through the eyes of Love and service; it is seeing through the eyes of the Spirit. The Postcommunion, accordingly, ties in nicely with the Epistle reading for this Sunday. In Galatians 5:25–26, 6:1–10, St. Paul exhorts us to live and walk in the Spirit, to bear one another's burdens, and not to deceive ourselves with an inflated self-knowledge. How can we do any of these things if we do not see through the eyes of God?

The Postcommunion also indicates the means by which we can replace our eyes with God's, so to speak: the grace of the Eucharist. In powerful language, the prayer asks that the Holy Communion we have just received may take possession of our minds and our bodies and that its effect may forever take precedence over our own sense of things. Or rather, it asks that the working (*operatio*) of Holy Communion may take possession of us. It is a vigorous prayer, conjuring up the image of Eucharistic grace working its way through our minds and our bodies, kneading, loosening,

---

4 Marmion, *Christ the Life of the Soul*, 122.

strengthening, healing, transforming. It is also worth noting that the prayer asks for our bodies to be taken possession of as well as our minds in order to have our perception of things changed. There is a profound union between body and soul, and perhaps in order to see through the eyes of love we need to change certain bodily habits. The word *sensus*, after all, straddles the line between the mental and the physical.

55

The Overcoming Orations of the Sixteenth Sunday after Pentecost

AITH, CHARITY, AND HUMILITY ARE among the themes found in today's Sunday. It is not the person who is proud or self-sufficient but rather the one "who humbles himself" (Gospel) and is "needy and poor" in spirit (Introit) that is able to comprehend the "breadth and length and height and depth" of things (Epistle). According to St. Thomas Aquinas, the reason for this is that pride is the attempt to exalt oneself in an excessive and hence irrational way, and thus it sabotages man's quest for the true, the beautiful, and the good.[1] Nothing makes us happy and wise like a love or charity born of faith and humility, especially when we have been cleansed (Secret) and purified (Postcommunion) by the saving action of Jesus Christ in the Eucharist.

Each in its own way, the Orations of the Sunday illustrate or support these points. The Collect is:

> *Tua nos, quæsumus, Dómine, grátia semper et prævéniat et sequátur: ac bonis opéribus júgiter præstet esse inténtos. Per Dóminum.*

Which I translate as:

> May Thy grace, we beseech Thee, O Lord, forever come before us and follow after us: and may it make us ever intent on good works. Through Our Lord.

We are intent upon good works as good Christians, but we cannot start them or finish them without God's grace, which must therefore precede us and follow us. If we do a good work without God, we are proud of our accomplishments and thus ungrateful and haughty; if we do a good work with God's grace and then pride ourselves that we did it, we have spoiled the broth. We need God's grace always: beginning, middle, and end. In his *Moralia*, St. Gregory the Great describes how the great sin of pride can ensnare

---

1 *Summa theologiae* II-II, Q. 161, art. 1, ad 2.

the soul before we do something, as we are doing something, or after we do something. I can become proud as I am about to do an action, I can become proud as I do the action, or I can become proud afterwards as I think about what a great action I did. We therefore need grace to flank us every step of the way to keep pride from ambushing and spoiling all our good works. In doing so, we become not less of ourselves but authentically more. "Overcome us," C. S. Lewis prays, "that, so overcome, we may be ourselves."[2]

And good works is the prayer's final petition, or rather that we remain ever intent on them. How great indeed it would be to have a purely good intention, not one subtly mixed with a proud self-love or self-promotion. How great it would be to be intent on doing good—nothing more, nothing less. Then we would be truly ourselves.

Good works and good intentions also occupy our attention in the Gospel of the day (Luke 14:1–11), in which Our Lord cures a man on the Sabbath while the Pharisees look on. After the Pharisees refuse to answer Jesus's question about whether it is lawful to heal on the Sabbath day, He asks them a second question: "Which of you shall have an ass or an ox fall into a pit, and will not immediately draw him out on the Sabbath day?" They won't touch that question, either. Rescuing an animal from danger is a compassionate and selfless act, but since it is also one's livestock (and therefore a possession of value), it is also a self-interested act. That, of course, does not mean that one should let one's ox languish in the pit, but it does point to the complexity of human intentions. Jesus's curing of the man with the dropsy, on the other hand, is purely selfless. Our Lord is ever intent on good works, as we wish to be.

The Secret is:

> *Munda nos, quǽsumus, Dómine, sacrifícii præséntis efféctu: et pérfice miserátus nobis: ut ejus mereámur esse partícipes. Per Dóminum.*

Which I translate as:

> Cleanse us, we beseech Thee, O Lord, through the effect of this present sacrifice: and in Thy mercy make us worthy to partake thereof. Through Our Lord.

---

2   C. S. Lewis, *The Great Divorce* (New York: Harper One, 1946), 113.

"Present sacrifice" is an interesting phrase, since the "Sacrifice of the Mass" (understood as the Consecration of the bread and wine) has not yet occurred. But the Offertory is also a sacrifice in its own right, insofar as it is a sacrifice of prayer, the people's offering of themselves to God in a spirit of true worship. We are essentially praying for a union of sacrifices, the sacrifice of ourselves and the sacrifice of Jesus Christ on the Cross, made present during the Sacrifice on the altar. When the priest places the host on the corporal, it is meet to place ourselves symbolically on the corporal as a living oblation to God. And we do so with the hope of being not only cleansed (which is important) but participants or partakers of the Divinity of Jesus Christ Himself, as the beautiful prayer over the mixing of water and wine attests.[3]

The Postcommunion Prayer is:

> *Purífica, quǽsumus, Dómine, mentes nostras benígnus, et rénova cæléstibus sacraméntis: ut consequénter et córporum prǽsens páriter, et futúrum capiámus auxílium. Per Dóminum.*

Which I translate as:

> Kindly, O Lord, purify our souls, we beseech Thee, and renew them by the heavenly sacraments: that equally in both the present and the future, even our bodies therein may take hold of a relief. Through Our Lord.

The Postcommunion continues the Secret's theme of cleansing or purifying. We cannot be intent on good works if our souls are not thoroughly reordered or purified. Despite all his criticisms of the Platonists, St. Augustine liked them because, in his opinion, they recognized that a mind cannot ascend to God unless it has been made clean of disordered desires.[4] But Augustine, and all Christendom with him, further asserts that we Christians hope for something more: a purification of our bodies now, during this earthly sojourn, and for all eternity once our bodies are glorified.[5] Not even Socrates in his wildest dreams could have hoped for such, but we participate in such a transformation at every Mass.

---

3 See chapter 57, "An Exchange to Remember: The Secret of the Eighteenth Sunday after Pentecost," and chapter 62, "Divine Participation and Human Dangers in the Postcommunion Prayer for the Twenty-Third Sunday after Pentecost."

4 Augustine, *City of God* 8.6–8.

5 Augustine, *City of God* 12.26.

56

Unity versus the Devil: The Collect of the Seventeenth Sunday after Pentecost

N FORMER AGES THIS SUNDAY WAS called the Sunday of the Love of God because in the Gospel reading (Matt. 22:34–46) Our Lord proclaims that the two greatest commandments are to love God with one's whole heart and to love one's neighbor as oneself. It could, however, just as easily be called Unity Sunday or Oneness Sunday, since it is this theme that unites so many of its propers. The love of God and the love of neighbor may be listed as two separate commandments, but they are not two separate and disconnected loves. Rather, the love of God grounds the love of neighbor and makes it possible, for true charity (*agape* or *caritas*) is a single, supernaturally infused love that, proceeding from God and aiming at God, bubbles over into a love of our fellow man. The Christian love of neighbor is clearly a superhuman achievement impossible to achieve without grace. Think of martyrs forgiving their torturers, saints kissing the sores of lepers, and the old religious orders whose members offered themselves up as slaves in order to free Christian captives from Muslim slavers. In his commentary on this Sunday, Ildefonso Schuster contrasts the goods works of the Church with the efforts of secular powers and concludes, "The so-called philanthropy which aims at being Christian charity dechristianized never rises to this supernatural level."[1]

In the Epistle reading (Eph. 4:1–6), St. Paul is all about oneness. "Keep the unity of the Spirit in the bond of peace," he exhorts the Church at Ephesus. "One body and one spirit, as you are called in one hope of your calling. One Lord, one faith, one Baptism. One God and Father of all."

The theme of a single God uniting us *may* explain the inclusion of this Sunday's Collect, which makes a similar reference to "the only God":

---

1 Schuster, *The Sacramentary*, 3:148.

*Da, quǽsumus, Dómine, pópulo tuo diabólica vitáre contágia:
et te solum Deum pura mente sectári. Per Dóminum.*

Which I translate as:

Grant, O Lord, to Thy people for us to avoid all diabolical
contagion, and with pure minds to follow Thee, the only
God. Through Our Lord.

Whether or not *solum Deum* is meant to introduce the theme of
unity for this Mass, it is surprising to see mention of the devil in
a Sunday Collect; in fact, it is the only mention of the devil in a
Sunday Collect. Dom Guéranger does not address this peculiarity
but ties the Collect to the theme of love: "The most hateful of all
the obstacles which divine love has to encounter upon earth is
the jealousy of Satan, who endeavours, by an impious usurpation,
to rob God of the possession of our souls—souls, that is, which
were created by and for Him alone."[2]

The noun that "diabolical" modifies is also interesting. *Conta-
gium* is in the plural as *contagia*, and so it contrasts nicely with
the one true God (*solus Deus*). We cannot follow the one God,
enjoy the unity of the Spirit, or be infused with the unifying
virtue of charity when we are distended by a myriad of spiritual
pollutions. But since the word *contagia* only appears in Latin
literature in the plural, we can also translate it as "contagion"
in the singular. *Contagia* is like the English word "news," which
is used in the plural even when it is meant in the singular, as
when we say: "The evening news *is* on."

"Contagion" in modern English has a clinical or medical ring
to it, but in Latin *contagia* was used only by poets in the post-
Augustan age. I wonder how that colored the Christian reception
of the word during the late Patristic and early medieval periods.

What is diabolical contagion? For those first generations
of Christians, it was quite straightforward. The early Church
took seriously Psalm 95 (96):5—"All the gods of the gentiles are
devils"—and viewed the Greco-Roman deities accordingly. Pagan
shrines and temples were obviously diabolically contaminated, but
so were groves and other natural locales. John Henry Newman
sums up this attitude well in his novel *Callista* when a Christian
character from the third century is out in the woods and declares:

---

2 Guéranger, *The Liturgical Year*, 11:373.

> O that I did not find the taint of the city in these works
> of God! Alas! Sweet nature, the child of the Almighty, is
> made to do the fiend's work, and does it better than the
> town. O ye beautiful trees and fair flowers, O bright sun
> and balmy air, what a bondage ye are in, and how do ye
> groan till you are redeemed from it![3]

Reading this Sunday Collect almost a century ago, liturgical
commentators identified "spiritualism" and "theosophy" as the
diabolical threats of their day. Our own age, of course, can boast
of so much more: New Age spirituality, the occult, neopaganism,
witchcraft (Wicca), and even explicit Satanism, the "temples" of
which enjoy the same legal status under U. S. law as Catholic
churches. And, of course, if we take "diabolical" in its broader
sense we can include *all* sin, starting with those acts committed
under the influence of the "spirit of fornication," a spirit from
whom we pray for deliverance in the Litany of the Saints and
who seems particularly busy these days. The fact that the Collect
also contrasts diabolical contagion with "pure minds" suggests
perhaps this broader, moralized view.

René Girard's theory of mimetic contagion also comes to mind.
The idea of Satan whipping up mobs into a violent frenzy often
seems strange when you read in the Bible the shouts of "Crucify
Him!" or when you think of people coming to watch Christians
being eaten by lions in the Coliseum, but as the 2020 summer of
rioting demonstrated, diabolical contagion and mob frenzy are
still alive and well.

But whether we speculate narrowly or broadly, it is good to
speculate. The Time after Pentecost corresponds to the age in
which we live, the age in between the first Pentecost and the last
Judgment, and already by the Seventeenth Sunday after Pentecost
the season is beginning to become more eschatological in tone
and content as it anticipates the Last Sunday of the Year and
its foreshadowing of the end of the world. It is as if the Church
were inviting us, in light of impending Doomsday, to recognize
the reality of our invisible enemies and identify them right now
in preparation for the final struggle, a struggle that relies on the
armor of one Lord, one faith, one Baptism, and on one double-
edged sword of the love of God and neighbor.

---

3   St. John Henry Newman, *Callista* (New York: Cosimo Classics, 2007), 8.

57

An Exchange to Remember: The Secret of the Eighteenth Sunday after Pentecost

OU COULD SAY THAT THE EIGHTEENTH Sunday after Pentecost marks the beginning of the ending. According to Blessed Ildefonso Schuster, "The Introit, instead of being taken from the Psalms, is from Ecclesiasticus 36:18 and begins a series of Antiphons for the Introit, altogether peculiar to these last Sundays after Pentecost."[1] Schuster does not elaborate, but he seems to be pointing to how the remaining Sundays form a kind of mini-season characterized (with the help of other features) by a heightened awareness of the Parousia and Last Judgment.

The Secret for the Eighteenth Sunday after Pentecost is also distinctive:[2]

> *Deus, qui nos, per hujus sacrificii veneránda commércia, uníus summæ divinitátis partícipes éfficis: præsta, quæsumus: ut, sicut tuam cognóscimus veritátem, sic eam dignis móribus assequámur. Per Dóminum.*

Which I translate as:

> O God who, through the venerable *commercia* of this sacrifice dost cause us to be partakers of the one supreme Godhead: grant, we beseech Thee, that as we come to know Thy Truth, so too may we attain it by worthy lives. Through Our Lord.

In Latin, *commercium* (from which we derive the words "commerce, commercial," etc.) can refer to a trade or transaction, the location of trading (e.g., a marketplace), or even the articles of trade themselves. *Commercium* came to have a technical, legal meaning for a merchant's right to trade, but it could also signify

---

1 Schuster, *The Sacramentary*, 3:167.
2 It is also the Secret for the Fourth Sunday after Easter.

a non-mercantile exchange of goods, such as the *strenæ* or gifts that the Romans would offer each other on New Year's Day.[3]

Commercium does not appear in the Vulgate Bible, but the word is no stranger to Patristic literature. St. Augustine uses it to describe the Atonement, the salvation of sinners in exchange for the Precious Blood of Jesus Christ. In Rome's sacred liturgy, *commercium* can refer to the Incarnation, the exchange of humanity and divinity in which, to paraphrase Saint Athanasius, God became man so that men could become gods. The first Antiphon during Vespers for the Feast of the Circumcision/Octave Day of Christmas on January 1[4] (channeling and surpassing the old Roman *strenæ*?) proclaims:

> *O admirábile commércium! Creátor géneris humáni, animá-tum corpus sumens, de Vírgine nasci dignátus est: et procédens homo sine sémine, largítus est nobis suam Deitátem.*

Which I translate as:

> O admirable interchange! The Creator of the human race, assuming a living body, hath deigned to be born of a Virgin: and becoming man, from no human seed, hath bestowed upon us His divinity.

Commercium appears five times in the 1962 Roman Missal (four times in a Secret and once in a Postcommunion Prayer) and always in the plural. During the Offertory rite, there are several exchanges: in exchange for God's Body and Blood and a participation in His divinity, there is an offering of bread, an offering of wine, and an offering of self. Not a bad deal, that. These ritual exchanges, of course, have their efficacy because they are grounded in the exchange that took place in the Incarnation and the exchange that took place during the Atonement. Indeed, the offering of the wine includes a beautiful description of the former in ways that evokes a sense of exchange:

> O God, who in creating human nature didst wonderfully dignify it, and still more wonderfully restore it, grant that, by the Mystery of this water and wine, we may be

---

3   See Suetonius, *Tiberius* 34.
4   See Gregory DiPippo, "The Ancient Character of the Feast of the Circumcision," *New Liturgical Movement*, January 1, 2019, www.newliturgicalmovement.org/2019/01/the-ancient-character-of-feast-of.html.

made partakers of His divinity who deigned to be made partaker of our humanity, Jesus Christ Our Lord, Thy Son, Who liveth and reigneth with Thee in the unity of the Holy Spirit, God, forever and ever. Amen.

Because *commercium* is an important notion, one that unites the mysteries of Jesus Christ with the mystery of the Eucharist, it was something of a surprise to see how preconciliar lay missals translated the term. The 1959 *St. Andrew Daily Missal* has "the communion of this adorable sacrifice"[5] while the *Father Lasance Missal* has "august communication."[6] The *St. Joseph Daily Missal* simply skips the word altogether: "O God, Who by means of this adorable sacrifice ..."[7]

In the new Missal, this oration is used six times during Paschaltide. In the 2011 U. S. edition, *veneranda commercia* is translated as "wonderful exchange."[8] They got the *commercia* right (albeit in the singular: see below), but *veneranda* connotes respect or veneration rather than wonder.

Unfortunately, perhaps the best English word for *commercium* is one that can be used only with a certain risk. "Intercourse" implies any kind of exchange that brings about a union or intimacy between two parties and would be ideal were it not for the fact that the term was applied so often in the mid-twentieth century to copulation that the sexual meaning is now foremost. A century ago, it was not uncommon to see the Christmastide *O admirabile commercium* translated as "O wonderful intercourse!" but today that phrasing might elicit shock or perhaps some snickering. For the Secret's *veneranda commercia*, the Baronius Missal has "by Thy venerable intercourse with us in this Sacrifice."[9] The addition of "Thy" makes the use of "intercourse" less jarring, but the use of the singular for *commercia* overshadows the fact that several exchanges are taking place in the Eucharistic sacrifice.

Finally, an appreciation of the ritual, sacrificial exchanges of the Mass helps us understand the Secret's petition: "Grant, we

---

5 *Saint Andrew Daily Missal* (1959), 744.
6 *Fr. Lasance Missal*, 719.
7 *Saint Joseph Daily Missal*, 502.
8 *The Roman Missal*, 3rd ed. (Washington, DC: USCCB Publishing, 2011), 399, 408, 414, 418, 422, 428.
9 *The Daily Missal* (Baronius), 846, and *Saint Andrew Daily Missal* (1952), 840.

beseech Thee, that as we come to know Thy Truth, so too may we attain it by worthy lives." It can be said of well-catechized and practicing Catholics that they have come to know God's truth, but knowing a truth (even *the* Truth that is Jesus Christ) and instantiating the truth in a life worthy of the name Christian are two different things. To move from a noetic assent to a saintly way of life, we need the "venerable exchanges" that bring about, as Eastern Christians would put it, our divinization. And surely, getting divinized as much as possible is an excellent way to prepare for the Parousia.

58

The Liberating Collect of the Nineteenth Sunday after Pentecost

HE COLLECT FOR THE NINETEENTH SUN-
day after Pentecost is:

Omnípotens et miséricors Deus, univérsa nobis adversántia propitiátus exclúde: ut mente et córpore páriter expedíti, quæ tua sunt, líberis méntibus exsequámur. Per Dóminum.

Which I translate as:

Almighty and merciful God, kindly keep out everything opposing us; that, being equally unencumbered both in mind and body, we may arrive with free minds at those things which are yours. Through Our Lord.

The participle that we have translated as "being unencumbered" is an interesting one. *Expeditus*, which is from *ex* and *pes/pedis*, literally means to free the foot from a snare. But it also has a military connotation: an *expeditus* was a light-armed Roman infantryman who is unencumbered by a heavy rucksack and able to march quickly. Yet again during this Time after Pentecost, the Church is praying in kinetic terms, using images of running or moving swiftly. And the logic is fairly straightforward. Keep us from the bad so that, freed up, we may attain the good with free minds.

There are three other details in this Collect that I like. First, I appreciate the particular bad/good juxtaposition. The Collect contrasts "all things opposing us" (*universa nobis adversantia*) with "those things which are yours" (*quæ tua sunt*). *Adversantia* literally means things that are turned against us, and *universa* implies all these things taken together as a whole. Its opposite in this Collect is "those things which are God's." None of God's things, in other words, are against us. God is on our side, and so are all His things.

Second, I am intrigued by the relationship between an equally unencumbered mind and body and a free mind. Why do we pray that the mind and body be equally unencumbered, and why do we pray only for a free mind and not a free body as well (i.e., a body free from illness)? To this last question we may answer that it is an unrealistic expectation. Our hope as Christians is not to be free of the burden of our bodily mortality (until the creation of the new Heaven and new earth, that is); rather, it is to be free in spirit as we await the Parousia or bodily death, whichever comes first.

As for the former question, the Church frequently prays for the welfare of both soul and body, but why in this Collect does she pray for an equal (*pariter*) deliverance from encumbrance for both? Perhaps the intention is simply that we want nothing about us, spiritual or physical, to interfere with our race towards the prize.

Third, the Collect jeopardizes rhetorical excellence by its quick repetition of the word "mind" (*mens*). Would not a synonym such as heart or soul lend greater verbal panache? Indeed, not a single lay missal I consulted translated *mens* with the same word twice. They supplied their own variety to spice up the Collect.

They did not err in doing so, for *mens* in liturgical Latin can indeed refer to the soul or the heart, but perhaps the Epistle provides a clue as to why we should nonetheless leave well enough alone. Barely have the words *liberis mentibus* left our ears than we hear the opening words of Ephesians 4:23–28: "Brethren: Be ye renewed in the spirit of your mind (*mens*)." A renewed mind is a free mind, and a free mind is one that puts "on the new man, who according to God is created in justice and holiness of truth." A free mind, because it is free and not cowardly or servile, puts "away lying" and is courageous enough to speak "the truth . . . with his neighbor." A free mind is not enslaved to its own lust for honor or respect, and so it is not moved to disordered or sinful anger: when it has anger, it has righteous anger, and thus it sins not. And of course, a free mind does "not give place to the devil."

Combining the Collect and the Epistle, we may say that protection from the snares of the devil liberates our minds to possess the goods of God, a "possession" which renews us and transforms our behavior. Finally, this possession must above all include the virtue of charity, which is implied in this Sunday's Gospel, the Parable of the Wedding Feast. For charity is the "wedding garment" that we must "put on" in order to feast at the nuptials of the God who frees our feet from the snares and our minds from their bondage.

59

A Worthy Location? The Postcommunion Prayer of the Twentieth Sunday after Pentecost

HE POSTCOMMUNION PRAYER FOR THE Twentieth Sunday after Pentecost presents something of a puzzle:

> Ut sacris, Dómine, reddámur digni munéribus: fac nos, quǽ-sumus, tuis semper obedíre mandátis. Per Dóminum nostrum.

Which the *St. Andrew Daily Missal* translates as:

> That we may become worthy, O Lord, to receive Thy holy gifts, make us ever, we beseech Thee, obedient to Thy commandments. Through Our Lord.[1]

The puzzle lies in the fact that this is a *Postcommunion* prayer, and yet it would seem to function better as a prayer for the proper reception of Holy Communion. *Munera* in liturgical Latin almost always refers either to the Eucharistic offerings or to the ritual action of the Mass, so the prayer is not referring to generic gifts from God. And reinforcing the preparatory dimension is the petition for obedience to God's commandments. Commenting on this facet of the oration, Bl. Ildefonso Schuster writes:

> The Sacraments work indeed by divine institution, but their effect is proportionate to the capacity and the dispo-sition of him who receives them. What better disposition can a soul possess in order to receive the sacramental body of Christ than that of communicating constantly with the Spirit of Christ himself and of faithfully obeying his holy will?[2]

As this explanation reveals, Schuster interprets this *Postcommu-nion* prayer "as a most helpful preparation for Holy Communion" but does not explain why we should be preparing for something

---

1 *St. Andrew Daily Missal* (1952), 851.
2 Schuster, *The Sacramentary*, 3:178.

after it has happened.[3] The authors of the 1970 *Missale Romanum* likewise seem to think that this is more of a preparatory prayer than anything else: assuming that the Prayer over the Offerings for the 34th Sunday in Ordinary Time is a modified version of this oration, they eliminated the confusion by relocating it to the Offertory rite.[4]

But the authors of the 1570/1962 Missal do not seem to have made a mistake, or if they did, it is a mistake they made twice, since the same prayer also appears as the Postcommunion for the Tuesday after the Second Sunday of Lent. And the same "mistake" (in both locations) is at least as old as the Gregorian Sacramentary in the late eighth century.[5]

There are two ways to resolve the dilemma. First, we need a more literal translation. The *St. Andrew Missal* took the considerable liberty of adding "to receive," as if we had not just received the Body and Blood of Christ in Holy Communion. The *Father Lasance Missal*, along with other editions, has a better version:

> That we may be rendered worthy of Thy sacred gifts, O Lord, grant us, we beseech Thee, ever to obey Thy commandments. Through Our Lord.[6]

There is nothing unreasonable about asking to be worthy of a gift after one has received it. If I can pray to be made worthy of the gift of eternal life that I was given decades ago through the sacrament of Baptism, I can pray to be made worthy of the gift of the Eucharist that I was given moments ago. Nor is there anything unreasonable about praying that the effect of Holy Communion

---

3 Ibid.

4 *Suscipe, Domine, sacra munera, quæ tuo nomini iussisti dicanda, et, ut per ea tuæ pietati reddamur accepti, fac nos tuis semper oboedire mandatis. Per Christum.* Which ICEL translates as: "Accept, O Lord, the sacred offerings which at your bidding we dedicate to your name, and, in order that through these gifts we may become worthy of your love, grant us unfailing obedience to your commands. Through Christ Our Lord."

5 In the *Gregorianum*, the prayers for what is currently the Twentieth Sunday after Pentecost appear as the prayers for the Twenty-First Sunday after Pentecost (*The Gregorian Sacramentary*, ed. H. A. Wilson [London: Harrison and Sons, 1915], 176). The same oration, incidentally, appears as the Postcommunion for the Twenty-Fourth Sunday after Pentecost in the so-called Gelasian Sacramentary (*The Gelasian Sacramentary*, ed. H. A. Wilson [Oxford: Clarendon Press, 1894], 360).

6 *Father Lasance Missal*, 726.

be a greater adherence to the law of God. True, to be properly disposed to receive the graces of the sacrament one must have a certain amount of moral rectitude, but it is also true that the graces of the sacrament help with the increase of moral rectitude.

And for the Twentieth Sunday after Pentecost, there is a further consideration. The Introit of the day is taken from Daniel 3:31, 29, and 35:

> All that Thou hast done to us, O Lord, Thou hast done in true judgment; because we have sinned against Thee, and we have not obeyed Thy commandments: but give glory to Thy name, and deal with us according to the multitude of Thy mercy. *Ps* 118:1. Blessed are the undefiled in the way; who walk in the law of the Lord.

Daniel the prophet is referring to the Babylonian Exile which, he asserts, was a just punishment on the Hebrews because of their consistent failure to keep God's law. Divine chastisement was real then and, as these Mass propers imply, it is real now.[7] And so it is fitting that just as we began Mass acknowledging the justice of being punished for not obeying God's commandments, so too do we end Mass by praying for the Eucharistic grace, paid for by the death of our Savior, to obey God's commandments unfailingly. Rather tidily, the Postcommunion Prayer brings us full circle.

Finally, the Introit's allusion to the Babylonian Exile is not random, for it is also the explicit theme of the Offertory verse: "Upon the rivers of Babylon there we sat and wept; when we remembered Thee, O Sion" (Ps. 136:1). We are in the final phase of the Time after Pentecost, a mini-season that anticipates the final days of human history. The Epistle of the day contributes nicely to this theme. "Walk with care," the Apostle warns, for "the days are evil" (Eph. 5:15–21). During the End Times, faithful Catholics will feel very much out of place, perhaps more than they have ever felt before. Or to put it in today's jargon, the Church will then have "a heightened awareness" of the fact that she is in exile, far from her true home. All the more reason to "walk in the law of the Lord" (Introit) and to "walk with care" (Epistle) by ever obeying God's commandments.

---

7   Michael P. Foley, "Divine Chastisement in the Traditional Roman Missal," *New Liturgical Movement*, October 14, 2020, www.newliturgicalmovement.org/2020/10/divine-chastisement-in-traditional.html.

60

The Final Conflict and the Orations of the Twenty-First Sunday after Pentecost

HE SUNDAYS NEAR THE END OF THE traditional liturgical year are increasingly concerned with the Last Judgment and the end of time, and increasingly alarmed. Whereas the previous Sunday had a somewhat joyful tone, the Twenty-First Sunday after Pentecost is more somber. In the background, from the Divine Office during the month of October, is "the astonishing annals of the heroic warriors, the Machabees," writes Fr. Pius Parsch. "Their deeds, as it were, illustrate the Epistle of the 21st Sunday, which describes the armor needed in the spiritual conflict."[1] In the foreground of the Mass is an array of different biblical texts involving some kind of conflict between two parties:

• The Introit is from the Book of Esther, when Mordecai and Esther plead with God to save the Jews from a new Babylonian law decreeing their extermination;

• The Alleluia, from Psalm 113, pits the Jews against the "barbarous" Egyptians—apparently, there is more to being civilized than impressive architecture, political stability, and mummification;

• The Epistle, from Ephesians 6, describes the Christian spiritual warrior and the armor that he needs to defeat the demons, who are especially active during the final days;

• The Gospel, the Parable of the Unforgiving Servant (Matt. 18:23–35), presents Christ the King as the Judge who will not forgive those who do not forgive others;

• The Offertory verse presents the miserable figure of Job who is beset with misfortune at the hands of Satan;

• The Communion verse, from Psalm 118, turns the fear of judgment, which is evident in the Gospel, into an appeal for judgment against our enemies. A sharp distinction is drawn between wicked persecutors and innocent victims.

---

1 Parsch, *The Church's Year of Grace*, 5:65.

THE TIME AFTER PENTECOST

The orations for this Sunday shed further light on the conflict that we must win in order to be judged well. The Collect is:

> *Famíliam tuam, quǽsumus, Dómine, contínua pietáte custódi: ut a cunctis adversitátibus, te protegénte, sit líbera; et in bonis áctibus tuo nómini sit devóta. Per Dóminum nostrum.*

Which I translate as:

> Keep, we beseech Thee, O Lord, Thy household in continual piety; that, with You protecting it, it may be free from all adversities and devoted to the glory of Thy name through good works. Through our Lord.

Pietas, as we have seen elsewhere,[2] can be a difficult word to translate, since it means two different things depending on whether it is used to describe God or man, and it is not entirely clear in this Collect which one it is. I have translated *continua pietate* as "in [man's] continual piety" (one of the seven gifts of the Holy Spirit), but the phrase can also be an ablative of means and thus refer to God's continual mercy. If it is the latter, the meaning of the petition is, "Guard Thy household with Thy continual lovingkindness."

The second half of the Collect includes a double petition: to be free from all adversities and to be devoted to good works. The former asks for the bad to be removed, the latter for the good to be added. And the good is devotion to the glory of God's Holy Name. Among other things, glory is what is bestowed on those who have emerged victorious in a conflict. It is God who wins the battle for us; we only ask to participate in the spoils of victory and to have the grace to do our share in the fighting.

The Secret presents a peculiar challenge:

> *Súscipe, Dómine, propítius hóstias: quibus et te placári voluísti, et nobis salútem poténti pietáte restítui. Per Dóminum nostrum.*

Which I translate as:

> Graciously receive, O Lord, these offerings, by which Thou hast also willed to be appeased: and restore salvation to us through Thy powerful lovingkindness. Through our Lord.

---

2   See chapter 50, "God Has Piety? The Collect of the Eleventh Sunday after Pentecost."

Hostias ("offerings") refers to sacrificial victims in the plural. But is there not one Victim, offered on the Cross? The reference is, no doubt, to the double offering of Christ's Body and Blood, which is about to happen. It is through the Sacrifice of the Cross, offered through the different species of bread and wine, that God's will is appeased. And the petition is bold: to have salvation restored through God's powerful lovingkindness (*pietas*). Piety shifts from the loyalty of man to the mercy of God. And the sacrifice of the Eucharist restores our salvation, marred and compromised by sins committed after our cleansing in Baptism.

Finally, the Postcommunion prayer is:

> *Immortalitátis alimóniam consecúti, quǽsumus, Dómine: ut, quod ore percépimus, pura mente sectémur. Per Dóminum.*

Which I translate as:

> Having obtained the food of immortality, O Lord: we beseech Thee, that what we have received with our mouth, we may continually follow with a pure mind. Through our Lord.

"Food of immortality" is a common reference to the Eucharist in the Postcommunion prayers, but in context here (with Doomsday looming nigh), it has the sense of the viaticum, the provisions necessary for a journey and the eternal food that is given to a dying Catholic (his last Holy Communion) before he passes to the next world. There is also a kind of parallel between the past participle "having obtained" (*consecuti*) and the main verb of the petition, "may we continually follow" (*sectemur*), since the former can also mean to follow after or pursue. As we enter into the final struggle, we pray that we may follow Jesus Christ with a pure mind, the same Jesus Christ whom we have just received in our mouths.

61

Thinking Out Loud? The Collect of the Twenty-Second Sunday after Pentecost

HE TWENTY-SECOND SUNDAY AFTER Pentecost continues the apocalyptic theme of this final phase of the liturgical year. For the last two Sundays, the Epistle has referred to a special day, e.g., the days that are evil or the day of the Second Coming of Jesus Christ. This Sunday's reading continues along the same lines. Philippians 1:6–11 mentions "the day of Christ" twice, along with our need to be to be ready for it. The Introit and the Secret, however, mention our iniquities and our guilt before the Lord, and if He observes them, who shall endure it (Ps. 129:3)?

The Gospel, the famous passage from Matthew 22 that includes the command to render unto God what is God's, reminds us of the obligation to make a sacrifice of our entire selves to God, for just as Caesar can have his silly lucre because it is made in his image, so too must we make a complete self-donation to God, for we are made in His image. And that's a tall order. Perhaps it is this undercurrent of heightened alert that explains the Offertory verse, which prays for the ability to pray:

> Remember me, O Lord, Thou who rulest above all power; and give a well-ordered speech in my mouth, that my words may be pleasing in the sight of the prince. (Esther 14:12-13)

We are so nervous, the Church seems to be saying, we need Your help to avoid getting tongue-tied.

With these considerations in mind we turn to the day's Collect:

> *Deus, refúgium nostrum et virtus: adésto piis Ecclésiæ tuæ précibus, auctor ipse pietátis, et præsta: ut, quod fidéliter pétimus, efficáciter consequámur. Per Dóminum nostrum.*

Which I translate as:

> O God, our refuge and our strength: be present to the pious prayers of Thy Church, O very author of piety! And grant that what we ask in faith we may obtain in effect. Through our Lord.

The Collect is distinctive for having two appositions, one in the prelude or protasis ("our refuge and our strength") and one in the petition or apodosis ("O very author of piety"). The second apposition comes as a surprise, almost interrupting the prayer's train of thought. It is as if the author were working it out as he was going along, thinking (or rather, praying) out loud. First he addresses God, who is our refuge and strength. And because He is, He can answer our prayers. But of course, God will not answer all prayers but only those that are pious or just. Thus, the author asks God to be present to the pious prayers of the Church. I like the use of the imperative "be present" (*adesse*) when another expression could have been used like "incline Thine ear to" or "hearken to." From the verb "to be" (*sum*) and the preposition "towards" (*ad*), the verb *adsum* can almost mean "Be yourself towards us" or perhaps, "bring your Being here."

Then comes the surprising second apposition, the vocative exclamation, "O very author of piety." In terms of the structure of a Roman Collect, this outburst is unique and disrupts the normal order of the prelude, and yet it follows the logic of the author who, we continue to surmise, is acting as if he is working it out as he goes along. As Sr. Mary Gonzaga Haessly observes: "The Church prays God to be attentive to her *piis precibus*; the word *piis* reminds her that prayers cannot be *piae* unless God Himself, the Author of *pietas*, inspires them."[1] And so the Church exclaims as if she just remembered something fundamental or just discovered something new: "O very author of piety"! Our prayers cannot be pious unless God infuses them with piety.

The final petition, "grant that what we ask in faith we may obtain in effect," works within the same paradigm. Just as the prelude limits the prayers in question to those that are pious, the petition is limited to what is asked for in faith (*fideliter*). And just as God is the grounding and source of our piety, so too is He the grounding and source of our petitions' efficacy. Thus, despite the appearance of being extemporaneous and haphazard, the Collect amply qualifies as an example of a "well-ordered speech" as mentioned in the Offertory verse. There is hope after all that we will be ready for the day of Christ.

---

1   Haessly, *Rhetoric in the Sunday Collects*, 117.

62

Divine Participation and Human Dangers in the Postcommunion Prayer for the Twenty-Third Sunday after Pentecost

HE TWENTY-THIRD SUNDAY AFTER PEN-
tecost inaugurates, if you will, a season within a season
within a season. The main season is the Time after
Pentecost, which corresponds to that period of human history
stretching from the first Pentecost to the Last Day. Within that
season, beginning around the Eighteenth Sunday, things take on
a more eschatological or apocalyptic note. And within *that* season,
beginning on the Twenty-Third Sunday, the antiphonary of the
Mass (Introit, Gradual/Alleluia, Offertory, and Communion) is frozen: however many Sundays of the Time after Pentecost remain, the
Antiphonary stays the same while the rest of the propers change.

The effect of this freezing is both reassuring and unsettling:
reassuring because, as the Introit states, these selections from
the Antiphonary emphasize that the Lord thinks thoughts of
peace and not of affliction (Jer. 29:11); unsettling because their
repetition implicitly confirms the threat of a real danger. One
does not feel the need to remind oneself of the Lord's peaceful
intentions when the birds are chirping and a warm sun is rising
over the serene surface of a lake, but one may feel that need in
the midst of a violent storm. And the Offertory, "From the depths
I have cried out to Thee, O Lord" (Ps. 129:1), would suggest that
we are not to imagine ourselves in an ideal situation right now.

Danger is the subject of the Postcommunion Prayer of the
Twenty-Third Sunday after Pentecost:

> *Quæsumus, omnípotens Deus: ut, quos divína tríbuis par-*
> *ticipatióne gaudére, humánis non sinas subjacére perículis.*
> *Per Dóminum.*

Which I translate as:

> We beseech Thee, almighty God, that Thou wouldst not permit us, whom Thou givest to rejoice in divine participation, to be subject to human dangers. Through Our Lord.

Before the Church pleads for freedom from human dangers, she rejoices in divine participation. Since this is a Postcommunion prayer, "divine participation" first and foremost refers to the reception of Holy Communion, for the faithful have just received the Body, Blood, Soul, and Divinity of Jesus Christ—or to put it more simply, human persons have just received within the marrow of their being a Divine Person. That is quite a participation. And yet, divine participation begins not with the Eucharist but with the Incarnation. When the priest mixes water and wine during the Offertory rite, he prays:

> O God, who in creating human nature didst wonderfully dignify it and still more wonderfully restore it, grant that, by the mystery of this water and wine, we may be made partakers of His divinity who deigned to be made partaker of our humanity, Jesus Christ Our Lord, Thy Son, Who liveth and reigneth with Thee in the unity of the Holy Spirit, God, forever and ever. Amen.

And it continues to the end of time. "Even at this moment He is, as man, making representation for my salvation, until He makes me divine by the power of His incarnate manhood," writes St. Gregory of Nazianzus of Jesus Christ sitting at the right hand of God and ever making appeal for us.[1]

It is therefore appropriate, especially during this apocalyptic leg of the liturgical year, to think of "divine participation" in terms of both the Eucharist and the Resurrection of the dead (which is also the theme of the Gospel reading, Matt. 9:18–26), when God will be all in all. But in between our current condition and our fully actualized participation in the Godhead lies a host of "human dangers." In some respects, the expression is a pleonasm: any danger to a human is a human danger, and we are obviously more concerned in this prayer with dangers to us than dangers to, say, armadillos. Still, the addition of the adjective "human" forms a contrast to the "divine" in "divine participation." It is an effective rhetorical antithesis.

---

1 *Oration* 30.14.

What is dangerous to humans? We can start with ourselves. In the Collect for the First Sunday of Advent we pray for deliverance from the "imminent dangers of our sins." Perhaps the old adage exaggerates when it states that we are our own worst enemy, but it is admittedly on to something. And, of course, the snares of the devil (which often exploit our sinful proclivities) would also qualify as dangers to us humans.

Finally, the verb that we have translated as to be "subject to" is *subjacere*, which literally means "to lie under." It is a colorful image. Were we not mindful of liturgical propriety, we might be tempted to translate the petition as "Do not, O Lord, allow us to be thrown under the bus of human dangers." The verb choice is another antithesis; there is an implicit contrast between divine participation, which is a participation in the good that is *above*, and the perils of being *under* the thumb of what is bad. May our mingling with the high keep us from succumbing to the low, now and to the very end.

63

New Meanings and the "Leftover" Sundays

HE FIRST TWENTY-TWO SUNDAYS after Pentecost are the same every year—unless, of course, a higher-ranking feast like that of the Assumption of the Blessed Virgin Mary falls on a Sunday. What happens after that depends on the date of Easter. If Easter comes late in the season, the Mass for the Twenty-Third Sunday after Pentecost is replaced by the Mass for the Last Sunday after Pentecost, the Mass for the Sunday before Advent. If there are twenty-four Sundays after Pentecost, Mass for the Last Sunday after Pentecost is used then. If there are twenty-five Sundays, the sixth Sunday after Epiphany (which had not been celebrated earlier that year) becomes the Twenty-Fourth Sunday after Pentecost; if there are twenty-six Sundays, the Fifth Sunday after Epiphany holds that honor; if twenty-seven, the Fourth Sunday after Epiphany; and if twenty-eight (the maximum number of Sundays there can be after Pentecost), the Third Sunday after Epiphany.

Lay missals refer to these Sundays as the "Additional Sundays after Pentecost"; they also call them the "Movable Sundays after Epiphany" or the "Resumed Sundays after Epiphany." The latter two headings are less accurate because not all the propers of a Sunday after Epiphany are "moved" when it becomes a Sunday after Pentecost. The Orations (Collect, Secret, and Postcommunion), the Epistle, and the Gospel are moved, but the Introit, Gradual/Alleluia, Offertory verse, and Communion verse (the so-called Antiphonary) are repeated from the Twenty-Third Sunday after Pentecost. The official Latin sobriquet for these Sundays is *Dominicæ quæ superfluit post Epiphaniam* — the "Sundays that are left over after Epiphany." But like some leftovers in the culinary world, these Sundays are not simply reheated; they are altered and enhanced before being served to the faithful. Hence we consider them not so much resumed but reconfigured.

The Leftover Sundays afford a clear example of the power of context in shaping the meaning of what is read, heard, or prayed. As we saw in part III, the Time after Epiphany meditates on the earthly ministry of Jesus Christ and the manifestation of His divinity during that ministry; and as we have seen in this part, the Eighteenth to the Last Sundays after Pentecost focus on the end of the world and the Last Judgment. Thus, the Orations and biblical readings from these Sundays will be colored either by an epiphanic ambiance or an apocalyptic overtone. For example, the chants that are repeated from the Twenty-Third to the Last Sunday after Pentecost present "every mood in harmony with the Church's Harvest Time" — fear, heavenly homesickness, confidence in God's deliverance, reassurance, etc.,[1] and hence they frame the reception of the Orations and Lessons in terms of that Harvest.

---

1   Parsch, *The Church's Year of Grace*, 5:125.

64

Jew, Gentile, and the Orations of the Reconfigured Third Sunday after Epiphany

N THE WORLD OF SUNGLASSES, POLAR-ized lenses remove glare and some colors from the surface of the water, but they also reveal more clearly what is below the surface. In the world of sacred liturgy, the apocalyptic subtext of the last Sundays after Pentecost reveals additional currents in the propers of the Third Sunday after Epiphany, specifically, the mass conversion of the Jews at the end of time.

Regarding the lessons: The Epistle reading (Rom. 12:16–21) commands us not to be wise in our conceits and to overcome evil with good. The latter admonition makes sense at all times, of course, but it has added meaning during the last times, when the "days are evil" (Eph. 5:16; see the lesson for the Twentieth Sunday after Pentecost). But the phrase "be not wise in your own conceits" also reminds us of Romans 11:25–26, where Paul writes:

> For I would not have you ignorant, brethren, of this mystery (lest you should be wise in your own conceits), that blindness in part has happened in Israel, until the fulness of the Gentiles should come in. And so, *all* Israel [shall] be saved [emphasis added].

In the Gospel (Matt. 8:1–13), Jesus cures a leper in order to induce the (Jewish) priests to convert. As far as we know, the priests to whom the cured leper appeared did not convert, and thus we are sad when we hear Jesus say: "the children of the kingdom shall be cast out into the exterior darkness." But then again, when we recall Romans 11:25–26, we are reminded that Israel is in God's hands and that all is not lost.

As for the Orations, the Collect is:

> *Omnípotens sempitérne Deus, infirmitátem nostram propítius réspice: atque ad protegéndum nos, déxteram tuæ majestátis exténde. Per Dóminum.*

Which I translate as:

> Almighty, eternal God, kindly look upon our infirmity and,
> in order to protect us, stretch forth the right hand of Thy
> majesty. Through Our Lord.

Emphasis is placed on the image of God stretching forth His
hand to us by its placement at the end of the prayer, and it is
precisely by Jesus stretching forth His hand that the leper was
cured. The leper, of course, was cleansed, but in the Collect we
ask to be protected, lest we be overcome by evil (see the Epistle).
Cleansing, however, comes in the Secret:

> *Hæc hóstia, Dómine, quǽsumus, emúndet nostra delícta: et ad*
> *sacrifícium celebrándum, subditórum tibi córpora mentésque*
> *sanctíficet. Per Dóminum.*

Which I translate as:

> May this offering, O Lord, we pray Thee, cleanse away our
> offenses, and sanctify the bodies and minds of Thy sub-
> jects for the celebration of this sacrifice. Through Our Lord.

Both Jew and Gentile are subject to God, and both need cleansing.
The petition to sanctify both body and mind in order to be able
to celebrate this Eucharistic sacrifice again brings to mind Paul's
Letter to the Romans: "I beseech you therefore, brethren, by the
mercy of God, that you present your bodies a living sacrifice,
holy, pleasing unto God, your reasonable service" (Rom. 12:1).

As we have seen elsewhere, "reasonable service" (*logiké latreia*)
is the *obsequium rationabile* that is the holy sacrifice of the Mass.[1]
But as Pope Benedict XVI observes, "the celebration is not only
a ritual, it is not only a liturgical game, but it is intended to be
'*logiké latreia*', a transformation of my existence in the direction
of the Logos."[2] And this transformation takes on added urgency
as time runs out.

Finally, the Postcommunion in the original Latin is a bit of
a brain-twister:

> *Quos tantis, Dómine, largíris uti mystériis: quǽsumus; ut*
> *efféctibus nos eórum veráciter aptáre dignéris. Per Dóminum*
> *nostrum.*

---

1 See chapter 16, "Reasonable Meditation and the Collect of the Sixth
Sunday after Epiphany."
2 Magister, "Homilies."

Which I translate as:

> We beseech Thee, O Lord: deign to make those whom
> Thou generously allowest to benefit from such great mys-
> teries to truly conform to their effects. Through Our Lord.

Veraciter ("in reality") implicitly juxtaposes the actions of the
sacred mysteries which we have just performed with their spiritual effect, but it also shows a link between the external sign
and the internal reality. *Aptare* ("conform") is more difficult to
translate. The verb literally means to adapt or fit, but in liturgical Latin it has the sense of "make our lives be in harmony
with what we are doing ritually."[3] The priests who received the
cured leper were performing rites that were sacred, but insofar
as they refused to believe in the Messiah to whom those rites
pointed, they were not living in harmony with what they were
performing. We pray, especially at this time of year, to have a
better fate than that.

---

3   Ellebracht, *Vocabulary of the Ancient Orations*, 147, n. 5.

65

The Extra Stormy Orations of the Reconfigured Fourth Sunday after Epiphany

HEN COMMENTING ON THE FOURTH
Sunday after Epiphany, we noted that the Gospel image
of a ship in a storm held allegorical meaning for the
Church Fathers.[1] The raging wind is a type for the devils whose
pride stirs up waves of persecutions against God's people, and the
sea becomes troubled by the passions and malice of men which,
as Dom Gaspar Lefebvre, OSB, puts it, is "the great source of
disobedience to authority and of fraternal strife."[2]

We also noted the prevailing theme of human frailty and the
need for strength in the Orations of this Sunday. Both themes
take on a new urgency in light of the Apocalypse. When Jesus
chides the Apostles for screaming out "Lord, save us, we perish!"
he asks them, "Why are you fearful, O ye of little faith?" The
phrasing is redolent of another question that Our Lord asks about
the end of days: "But yet the Son of man, when He cometh, shall
He find, think you, faith on earth?" (Luke 18:8).

A lack of faith characterizes the End Times; once-great Christian civilizations will likely go awash in apostasy and infidelity.
The storm that the Gospel reading describes is the storm that
characterizes the final conflict; it is the storm described in the
Fourth Sunday after Epiphany but now ratcheted up to a new
level of terror. And it is tempting, with such mighty winds and
waves about us, to wonder about the sleeping Christ. Why is
He not waking up and helping us while the devil roams about,
seeking whom he may devour, more, it seems, than he has ever
done before? Yet just as we despair, we hear the voice of the
Christ: "Why are you fearful, O ye of little faith?" It is time to

---

1   See chapter 14, "The Stormy Orations of the Fourth Sunday after
Epiphany."
2   *Saint Andrew Daily Missal* (1952), 156.

buck up, and like good and faithful sailors weather the storm.

And the Orations give us the naval manuals for good seamanship. The Collect reminds us that God's help is the only sure antidote to human frailty, the Secret reminds us that we must sacrifice ourselves body and soul in order to profit from the Eucharist, and the Postcommunion reminds us that profiting from the Eucharist helps free us from earthly snares and helps give us our sea legs. May it be so as we confront either the end of the world or the end of our lives.

66

The Orations of the Reconfigured Fifth Sunday after Epiphany

HE GOSPEL READING FOR THIS SUNDAY is Matthew 13:31–35, the Parable of the Wheat and the Tares. The parable consists of three main parts: the sowing of grain and weeds, the owner's decision to let them grow up side-by-side, and the harvest. When this Gospel is read during the Fifth Sunday after Epiphany, our attention turns to the second part, Christ's announcement that the members of His Church will be a mixed bag, a fact that we will need to learn to accept. But when the Gospel is read as one of the last Sundays of the year, our attention naturally turns to the third part and its warning of the Final Judgment, with the rewards of Heaven and the punishments of Hell.[1]

And whereas the Gospel describes the actual Church, the Epistle (Col. 3:12–17) describes the ideal Church, a brotherhood of believers united in charity, thankful to God, and abounding in virtues. During the Fifth Sunday after Epiphany, this description offers us a goal towards which to strive. But when read near the end of the Church calendar, that goal is made more urgent, for if we have not lived this way so far, we may be counted among the tares rather than the wheat.

And what is true of the readings is true of the Orations. The Collect for this Sunday is:

> *Famíliam tuam, quǽsumus, Dómine, contínua pietáte custódi: ut quæ in sola spe grátiæ cæléstis innítitur tua semper protectióne muniátur. Per Dóminum.*

Which I, following Sr. Mary Gonzaga Haessly, translate as:

> Guard Thy family, we beseech Thee, O Lord, with continual lovingkindness: that, as it leans upon the hope of heavenly grace alone, it may ever be walled about with Thy protection. Through Our Lord.[2]

---

1   Parsch, *The Church's Year of Grace*, 5:124–25.
2   Haessly, *Rhetoric in the Sunday Collects*, 40.

Munio is usually translated as "defend," but it literally means to "build a wall," and that siege mentality, if you will, is justifiable during the final conflict between good and evil. There is also a nice pairing of a solid wall of defense and the people leaning on something secure. And when prayed after the Introit of the day (Jer. 29:11, 12, 14), an image emerges. Thinking thoughts of peace, the Lord God gathers His people from a diaspora of captivity into one place, where he then builds a wall of safety around them, much like how the master in the parable gathers the wheat and puts it into his barn.

Context shapes our praying of the Secret as well. The End Times on their minds, the faithful hear today's Gospel with its image of tares burning eternally, and they are unsettled. In the Offertory verse they cry from the depths of their being and beg for mercy and help (the *De profundis*, Ps. 129). And in the Secret they continue in this vein, asking not only for a forgiveness of their sins through the offering of this sacrifice but that God guide their wobbly hearts:

> *Hóstias tibi, Dómine, placatiónis offérimus: ut et delícta nostra miserátus absólvas, et nutántia corda tu dírigas. Per Dóminum.*

Which I translate as:

> We offer unto Thee, O Lord, the sacrifices of appeasement, that Thou mayest mercifully absolve our sins, and do Thou Thyself direct our wavering hearts. Through Our Lord.

Our hearts are wavering, shaking in their boots, because of how the readings and the meaning of this season have affected them; they are afraid of the opening verses of the *Dies Irae*, which they hear around this time of year on All Souls' Day (November 2): "That day of wrath, that day [which] will melt the world into glowing embers." And they ask for guidance from God Himself. The verb *dirigo*, which I have translated as "direct," forms a good contrast to wavering (*nutans*), for it literally means to set in a straight line (*dis+rego*). Because our hearts are apt to zigzag and not stay within the lines, we need God to steady us and keep us on course. And there is an emphasis on God's agency with the pronoun *tu* (you yourself). We don't want a representative of God to guide us; we want God Himself, we insist, to take the tiller.

Finally, in the Postcommunion we pray:

Quǽsumus, omnípotens Deus: ut illíus salutáris capiámus efféctum, cujus per hæc mystéria pignus accépimus. Per Dóminum.

Which I translate as:

We beseech Thee, almighty God, that we may take hold of the effect of that salvation, the pledge of which we have received through these mysteries. Through Our Lord.

Despite proceeding in reverse chronological order, the petition is relatively straightforward. We have a received a pledge of salvation by virtue of the mysteries we have just received in Holy Communion; now we ask to take possession of the effect of that salvation. *Capio* (which I have translated as "take hold") is an aggressive verb that means to seize or grab. There is *almost* a hint of the legend of Proteus, the god whom you must continue to grab despite the various appearances he assumes before he will relent and tell you the truth. In the case of the Eucharist, the appearance of bread and wine "hides" the Truth (who is a Divine Person) and a pledge of salvation. We ask to take hold of that salvation, even though our senses cannot detect it.

And that pledge's eschatological meaning becomes clearer around this time of year. The pledge of our salvation includes the pledge of our bodies rising from the dead after the Last Judgment and taking on the miraculous qualities of Christ's risen and glorified body, for, as the Postcommunion Prayer of Corpus Christi says, the Eucharist is the "pledge of our future glory."

And so our closing prayer for this Mass is that we be counted among the grains of wheat that, safely gathered into God's barn, will be transformed into the glorious, risen, eternal bread that is Christ's Mystical Body.

67

Yearning for the Reasonable during the Reconfigured Sixth Sunday after Epiphany

HE RECONFIGURED SIXTH SUNDAY after Epiphany is a liturgical mutt: the Orations and biblical readings are from the Sixth Sunday after Epiphany, while the antiphonary (Introit, Gradual, Alleluia, Offertory, and Communion) is repeated from the Twenty-Third Sunday after Pentecost.

The result is another fascinating lesson in how context can shape the interpretation of a text. When hearing this Sunday's Epistle (1 Thess. 1:2–10) during the Time after Epiphany, the verse about having just "turned to God from idols" assumes greater prominence, since the Time after Epiphany indirectly continues to celebrate the conversion of the Gentiles that began with the visit of the Magi. But during the apocalyptic leg of the Time after Pentecost, other verses from the same reading, such as Jesus delivering us "from the wrath to come," will naturally exert a stronger gravitational pull.

One prayer that is fascinating both on its own and in different contexts is the Collect for this Sunday:

> *Præsta, quǽsumus, omnípotens Deus: ut semper rationábilia meditántes, quæ tibi sunt plácita, et dictis exsequámur et factis. Per Dóminum nostrum.*

Which I translate as:

> Grant, we beseech Thee, almighty God, that ever meditating upon reasonable things, we may thoroughly carry out the things that are pleasing to Thee both in words and in deeds. Through Our Lord.

In our essay on the Sixth Sunday after Epiphany, we explained the rich meaning of the word *rationabilia* in the Collect of this Mass, and we concluded that meditating on "the reasonable things" is a meditation on spiritual things but also a sacrificial self-offering that transforms our existence in the direction of the Logos.[1] To meditate on God's reasonable things and to make ourselves a rational, spiritual offering are the gladsome duties of all Christians at all times and in all places, but they take on new meaning and urgency in the shadow of the world's end. It is reasonable to expect that the final chapter of human history, awash with false prophets and Antichrists, will not be a Golden Age of Reason, let alone of Faith. It is reasonable to expect that tyrannical passions, a dictatorship of noise, and Orwellian new-speak will take the place of dispassionate discourse, quiet contemplation, and clear, honest communication. It is reasonable to expect (since it will be an age of persecution) that the few who keep their heads will be blamed by the many who have lost theirs. In short, it is reasonable to expect that during the End Times, it will be more difficult to meditate on the reasonable. And that is all the more reason to pray that we may ever meditate upon reasonable things and thoroughly carry out the things that are pleasing to God both in words and in deeds.

Finally, whether or not the world will end tomorrow, we should remain solidly enrolled in the school of love.[2] The Postcommunion for this Mass is:

> *Cæléstibus, Dómine, pasti delíciis: quǽsumus: ut semper éadem, per quæ veráciter vívimus, appetámus. Per Dóminum nostrum.*

Which I translate as:

> Having been fed, O Lord, on heavenly delights, we beseech Thee: that we may ever hunger after those same things by which we truly live. Through Our Lord.

The use of the passive voice (*pasti*) in the opening clause is noteworthy: we did not feed on heavenly delights; we were fed on heavenly delights: the emphasis is on our receptivity in the act of Holy Communion, a receptivity that is reflected well in the practice of receiving Holy Communion on the tongue.

---

1 See chapter 16, "Reasonable Meditation and the Collect of the Sixth Sunday after Epiphany."
2 Pope Benedict XVI, "Message of the Holy Father Benedict XVI to the Youth of the World on the Occasion of the 22nd World Youth Day, 2007."

The prayer itself is a delightful contrast of good satiation and good hunger. Normally the goal of eating is to end hunger, but our goal in receiving the Eucharist is to increase it, to give us an appetite for the right things. The Eucharist brings peace but it also brings passion, a desire for the reasonable things, characterized here "as the things by which we *truly* live." We are most alive when we are most intent on Him who is Life itself.

68

The Stirring Collect of the Last Sunday after Pentecost

S WE HAVE NOTED OVER THE PAST SEVeral weeks, the Last Sunday after Pentecost corresponds to the Last Days of history. According to the Church Fathers, the Gospel reading (Matt. 24:15–25) combines a prophecy of the destruction of the Holy Temple (which took place in AD 70) with a prophecy of Doomsday, when the world will be dissolved in a globe of fire and replaced with a new Heaven and a new earth. The Last Sunday after Pentecost thus anticipates the Second Coming of Our Lord.

But as we saw in the first part of this book, so too does Advent (the season immediately following this apocalyptic crescendo of the liturgical year), for *Adventus* or "coming" remembers the first coming of Our Lord to Bethlehem, implores His coming into our hearts now, and prepares for His coming in glory at the end of time. The last and first parts of the 1962 Roman calendar overlap, functioning as two interlocking clasps that connect the dazzling necklace of the year's feasts and seasons.[1]

One of the more interesting components of this clasp are the Collects. During Advent, the Church betrays impatience in her opening prayers: three out of four of the Sunday Collects of this season beg the Lord to rouse Himself up (*excitare*) and come. But that impatience is so impatient that it cannot even wait for the season of Advent. The Last Sunday after Pentecost has an *excita* Collect as well:

> *Excita, quǽsumus, Dómine, tuórum fidélium voluntátes: ut divíni óperis fructum propénsius exsequéntes; pietátis tuæ remédia majóra percípiant. Per Dóminum nostrum.*

Which I translate as:

---

1   See chapter 1, "The Tempestuous Collect of the First Sunday of Advent," and chapter 5, "The Key to the Season: The Collect of the Vigil Mass of Christmas Eve."

> Stir up the wills of Thy faithful people, we beseech Thee,
> O Lord: that as they more eagerly strive after the fruit
> of divine work, they may receive greater remedies of Thy
> loving kindness. Through Our Lord.

We examined the extended use of *excita* in part I. Here, it is sufficient to note the word order. By placing this imperative at the head of the statement, without fanfare or introduction, the Church emphasizes her impatience. O Lord, make haste to help us—now!

The Collect introduces us to a theme found in the Epistle, namely, "being fruitful in every good work" (Col. 1:10). Here, however, the Church speaks of the fruit of a *divine* work, perhaps to emphasize the agency of God in making our works righteous and fruitful, for it is God who gives the increase (1 Cor. 3:7). Reinforcing the fruit imagery is *propensius* ("more eagerly"), which is derived from the verb *propendeo*, to hang down. Although the adverb is applied to the faithful and not to the fruit of divine work, the mind is nonetheless inclined to think of low-hanging fruit, ready for the taking. It is almost the Garden of Eden in reverse: with a will properly roused and weighted towards the Good, we will be eager for the right fruit, and from it we will receive diving healing rather than punishment.

But in order to receive "greater remedies," do we need to obtain the fruit or merely seek after it? *Exsequi* is a robust verb by virtue of the perfective force of *ex*. Usually in the Roman Orations, it implies an action that has been completed. But *exsequi* can also mean to seek after, and I agree with Sr. Mary Pierre Ellebracht that that is its meaning here.[2]

Either way, whether we are taking fruit or about to take it, we are engaged in an activity of harvesting. As St. Mary Gonzaga Haessly notes: "On this last Sunday of the Ecclesiastical year, the Church prays God to rouse the wills of the faithful, in order that they may reap the harvest, as it were, of all the good things that He has worked in them during the year."[3]

---

2   Ellebracht, *Vocabulary of the Ancient Orations*, 101. The English edition of the new Missal likewise interprets *exsequentes* in this prayer as "striving." Unlike my interpretation, however, it then goes on to translate *divini operis fructum* in terms of human agency: "that striving more eagerly to bring your divine work to fruitful completion" (see the Collect for the Thirty-Fourth Sunday in Ordinary Time).

3   Haessly, *Rhetoric in the Sunday Collects*, 170.

And, we may add, it is a good idea to petition for a roused-up will near the end of a harvest or a long journey, when our spirits are prone to flag or grow weary. Although such a reaction is understandable, it must (at least in the spiritual life) be resisted. Whether it is the end of the world or the end of one's life, the devil will make a last-ditch effort to entrap souls and drag them to Hell. With the finish line in sight and the Enemy on our tail, now is the time not to relax the reins but to apply the spurs. For only he that shall persevere to the end shall be saved.

VIIII

THE
SANCTORAL
CYCLE

69

The Purifying Orations of Candlemas, February 2

N THE POST-VATICAN II CALENDAR, FEB-
ruary 2 is the Feast of the Presentation of the Lord; in
the Byzantine Rite it is the "Meeting of the Lord"; and
in the traditional Roman or Tridentine calendar it is the Feast of
the Purification of the Blessed Virgin Mary. All three highlight
one of the things that took place when Mary and Joseph brought
Jesus to the Holy Temple forty days after His birth (Luke 2:21–40).
The Novus Ordo feast recalls that Jesus, a firstborn male, was
"redeemed" or consecrated to the Lord in conformity with the
Mosaic Law.[1] The Byzantine feast focuses on the meeting of Simeon and Anna with the long-awaited Messiah. And the Tridentine
feast emphasizes that Mary presented herself at the Temple to be
ritually purified from childbirth according to the Law of Moses.

Or was it according to the Law? Mary was free of every moral
impurity, but she was also free of ritual impurity, which was contracted when a woman, "having received seed," gave birth to a man
child (Lev. 12:2). The Mother of God gave birth to a man child,
but she did not receive seed from a man, having instead conceived
of the Holy Spirit.[2] Mary therefore obliged the Law out of her
great humility and condescension rather than out of necessity.

The Feast of the Purification is nicknamed "Candlemas" because
the day is marked in the historic Roman Rite with a blessing of
candles and a great procession. Having a light ceremony is an
appropriate way to end the Christmas season, and it ties in well
with Simeon's epithet of Jesus as a Light to the Revelation of
the Gentiles (Luke 2:32).

Further, according to figures such as St. Anselm of Canterbury,
candles are an excellent symbol for Christ. The wax, made from

---

1 Exodus 13:2, 12–13; Numbers 18:15–16.
2 See St. Thomas Aquinas, *Summa theologiae* III, Q. 37, art. 4, ad 2.
Aquinas even states that it appears as if Moses chose his words precisely
in order to exclude the Mother of God from the requirement.

the "virginal bee," signifies the pure flesh of Our Lord taken from His mother; the wick symbolizes His human soul; and the flame represents His divinity. Candles blessed on Candlemas Day can be taken home and used as sacramentals throughout the year.

Simeon's prophecy and the focus on light also led to a peculiar folk belief that the weather on February 2 had a particularly keen prognostic value. If the sun shone for the greater part of Candlemas, there would be, it was claimed, forty more days of winter, but if the skies were cloudy and gray, there would be an early spring. In Germany this lore was amended by bringing into the equation the badger or the hedgehog, but when German immigrants arrived in Pennsylvania, they could find none of these creatures around. Instead they saw plenty of what the local Native Americans called a *wojak* or woodchuck. Since the Indians considered the groundhog to be a wise animal, it seemed only natural to appoint the furry fellow, as they say every year in Punxsutawney, "Seer of Seers, Sage of Sages, Prognosticator of Prognosticators, and Weather Prophet Extraordinary." The Feast of the Purification thus gave rise not only to a beautiful tradition of candle-blessing but to Groundhog Day.

The Collect for the Mass is:

> *Omnípotens sempitérne Deus, majestátem tuam súpplices exorámus: ut, sicut unigénitus Fílius tuus hodiérna die cum nostræ carnis substántia in templo est præsentátus; ita nos fácias purificátis tibi méntibus præsentári. Per eúndem Dóminum.*

Which I translate as:

> Almighty, everlasting God, we humbly beseech Thy Majesty: that as Thine only-begotten Son was on this day presented in the Temple with the substance of our flesh, so too wouldst Thou grant us to be presented unto Thee with purified minds. Through the same Our Lord.

The Collect hearkens to the laws of purification concerning a child-bearing woman but also focuses on the marvelous fact that the Son of God was presented "with" the substance of human flesh on this day. Most translators opt for "in" the substance of our flesh, but I believe that "with" emphasizes the fact that the Incarnate Divine Person brought His human nature with Him, so to speak, to the Holy Temple, and that in itself is a wondrous mystery. How long Israel longed for God to visit her in the Temple! And when He does, it is not just with His Divinity but with His humanity as well.

And if the Word humbled Himself by taking on our lowly human flesh, we can ask in return for a purification of our minds. Our bodies need purifying too, but our bodies are not the problem: it is our disordered thoughts and desires, which spring from our sinful minds, that are the chief cause of our woes. The Collect aims high: neither the flesh nor the soul of Jesus Christ, neither the flesh nor the soul of His mother, needed purifying, but we do. On this day that commemorates a Purification, we ask for a purifying of the seat of our identity, and our problems.

The Secret is:

> *Exáudi, Dómine, preces nostras: et, ut digna sint múnera, quæ óculis tuæ majestátis offérimus, subsídium nobis tuæ pietátis impénde. Per Dóminum.*

Which I translate as:

> Graciously hear our prayers, O Lord; and so that the gifts which we offer in the sight of Thy Majesty may be found worthy, spend on us the help of Thy mercy. Through Our Lord.

The Secret subtly recalls that an exchange happened on the Feast of the Purification: Joseph and Mary spent two turtle doves, in return for which Mary was purified. During the Offertory rite we "spend" the gifts of bread, wine, money, and ourselves (not least of all), and we humbly ask that God spend something on us: His mercy.

The Postcommunion is:

> *Quǽsumus, Dómine Deus noster: ut sacrosáncta mystéria, quæ pro reparatiónis nostræ munímine contulísti, intercedénte beáta María semper Vírgine, et præsens nobis remédium esse fácias et futúrum. Per Dóminum.*

Which I translate as:

> We beseech Thee, O Lord our God: that by the intercession of blessed Mary ever Virgin, Thou wouldst make the sacrosanct mysteries, which Thou hast bestowed upon us as a fortification of our reparation, both a present and future remedy. Through Our Lord.

The Eucharist is sacrosanct, namely, both sacred and holy, and it bestows upon us a remedy, or rather, a fortification, against our sins. The same subordinate clause (*ut sacrosancta ... contulisti*) appears in the Postcommunion for the Sunday after Easter, where it is regarded "as a protection of our new life."[3] Here, however, we pray for the Pure One who is the Mother of God to apply the remedy both now and in the future. Although we have not been pure, we hope that God's grace through Our Mother will render us clean both ritually and morally.

---

3   Ellebracht, *Vocabulary of the Ancient Orations*, 175.

70

The Expectant Orations of the Feast of the Annunciation, March 25

HE ANNUNCIATION, ONE OF THE OLD-est and greatest Marian feasts that we have, is filled with meaning and expectation. First, it marks the beginning of the end of Satan's rule over mankind. Just as the first Eve's no to God led to our slavery under sin, the New Eve's yes or *fiat* to God opens the way to our salvation. Pope Benedict XVI beautifully describes this fiat as saying Yes to a marriage proposal: "As Mary stood before the Lord, she represented the whole of humanity. In the angel's message, it was as if God made a marriage proposal to the human race. And in our name, Mary said yes."[1]

And just as the Annunciation is a kind of wedding between God and man, it is also a kind of wedding between Mary and the Third Person of the Blessed Trinity. The Mother of God is hailed as the Spouse of the Holy Spirit because on this day the Holy Spirit overshadowed her (see Luke 1:35). As if that weren't enough, the Annunciation is, along with Christmas, a great feast of the Incarnation. This is the day that that the Second Person of the Holy Trinity united Himself to our humanity by humbly becoming a zygote, a single eukaryotic cell, in Our Lady's womb. Or to put it more plainly, this is the day that the Word first became flesh and dwelt among us (John 1:14), and the place where He first chose to dwell—or to translate the original Greek more literally, to pitch His tent—was within this maiden of Nazareth, making her a holy tabernacle and a new and truer Ark of the Covenant. This is the day, as the Maronite liturgy proclaims, that "the peace of God is planted, and the heights and depths cry out: 'O come, Lord Jesus!'"[2]

---

1 Pope Benedict XVI, "On God's Marriage Proposal," Angelus address at the 2008 World Youth Day Closing Mass, Zenit News, July 19, 2008, http://zenit.org/article-23282?l=english. St. Bernard of Clairvaux also has a beautiful commentary on this theme in his Homily 4.8–9.
2 *The Book of Offering According to the Rite of the Antiochene Syriac Maronite Church* (Beirut, Lebanon: Patriarcat Maronite, 2012), 28.

Some of these themes are present in the traditional Roman Orations for the feast. The Collect is:

> *Deus, qui de beátæ Maríæ Virginis útero Verbum tuum,*
> *Angelo nuntiánte, carnem suscípere voluisti: præsta supplícibus*
> *tuis; ut, qui vere eam Genitrícem Dei crédimus, ejus apud te*
> *intercessiónibus adjuvémur. Per eúndem Dóminum nostrum.*

Which I translate as:

> O God, who hast willed that Thy Word should take flesh
> from the womb of the Blessed Virgin Mary during the
> Angel's announcement: grant to Thy suppliants, that we,
> who believe her to be truly the Mother of God, may be
> helped by her intercessions in Thy presence. Through
> the same Our Lord.

For the first part or protasis, most translations have "in the womb" of Mary instead of "from the womb," but the preposition in question is not *in* but *de*, the latter of which means "from" or "out of." We can forgive the ancient author for the biological inaccuracy: babies are not formed from the tissue of their mother's womb but from an ovum that is in the womb, a fact which was not discovered until the nineteenth century. But the main point is worth contemplating: when the Word became flesh, Its flesh came entirely from Mary's flesh rather than from a commingling of a mother's flesh with a father's. To put it in modern terms, 100% of Jesus Christ's DNA came from Mary of Nazareth. So as it turns out, the ancient author was right.

In the second half or apodosis of the prayer, we ask for help from God through Mary's intercession in almost a plea-bargain manner: we are going out on a limb and believing that this maiden bore God; in return, can't we have some special favors from her? The expression *ejus apud te intercessionibus* can be translated as "through her intercessions with Thee," but I choose "by her intercessions in Thy presence" to highlight the distinctive character of the preposition *apud*, which is the Latin equivalent of the French *chez* ("in the house of"). There seems to be an implicit contrast between the Incarnate Word being in the womb of Mary and Mary now being in the eternal abode of God. She who "enclosed" God is now enclosed in His Paradise.

The Secret is:

> *In méntibus nostris, quǽsumus, Dómine, veræ fídei sacraménta confirma: ut, qui concéptum de Vírgine Deum verum et hóminem confitémur; per ejus salutíferæ resurrectiónis poténtiam, ad ætérnam mereámur perveníre lætítiam. Per eúndem Dóminum.*

Which I translate as:

> Strengthen in our minds, we beseech Thee, O Lord, the mysteries of the true Faith: that we who confess the Virgin's Son to be truly God and man, may deserve, by the power of His saving resurrection, to reach eternal joy. Through the same Our Lord.

Sacramenta, which I have translated as "mysteries," also means "sacraments." Given that the sacrament of the Eucharist is about to be confected, it is a fitting ambivalence. *Salutiferus*, which I have translated as "saving," literally means "salvation-making." The prayer pivots from the beginning of Christ's earthly life (the Incarnation) to the end (the Resurrection) and its salvation-making power.

The Postcommunion is:

> *Grátiam tuam, quǽsumus, Dómine, méntibus nostris infúnde: ut qui, Angelo nuntiánte, Christi Fílii tui incarnatiónem cognóvimus; per passiónem ejus et crucem, ad resurrectiónis glóriam perducámur. Per eúndem Dóminum.*

Which I translate as:

> Pour forth, we beseech Thee, O Lord, Thy grace into our hearts: that we, to whom the Incarnation of Christ Thy Son was made known by an angel announcing it, may, by His passion and cross, be brought to the glory of His resurrection. Through the same Lord.

The prayer is well-known to Catholics as the conclusion to the Angelus, which in itself is an interesting choice, insofar as a Marian devotion ends with a prayer that makes no explicit mention of Mary. As the Postcommunion to the Feast of the Annunciation, the prayer contributes to an interesting pattern of mysteries that are or are not mentioned. The pattern is:

- The Collect mentions Mary, the Angel, and the Incarnation;
- The Secret mentions Mary and the Incarnation;
- The Postcommunion mentions the Angel and the Incarnation.

Again our thoughts proceed from the Incarnation to the Passion to the glory of the Resurrection. Why did God become man? To die for us and to rise again to give us glory. It is a message from an angel almost too good to be true. But it is so good that it has to be true.

71

The Votive Mass of St. Thomas More

N THE 1969 GENERAL CALENDAR, THE celebration of Saints John Fisher and Thomas More is an optional memorial on June 22, whereas in England and Wales it has the rank of a feast. Neither appeared on the universal calendar prior to that date, but in England and Wales their combined feast was celebrated on July 9 after they were both canonized in 1935. (Yes, it took four hundred years for these heroic men to be raised to the altar.) I suspect that the reason for the choice of July 9 was practical. St. John Fisher was martyred on June 22, 1535, but in the 1935 General Calendar late June was rather full: June 22 was the feast of St. Paulinus of Nola, and the first available feria day was not until June 27. St. Thomas More, on other hand, was martyred on July 6, 1535, the Octave of Saints Peter and Paul. (More himself considered it an honor to die on the octave day of St. Peter, to whose See he had remained loyal at all costs.) Because July 7 is the feast of Saints Cyril and Methodius and July 8 that of St. Elizabeth of Portugal, the first free day after July 6 was July 9.

In addition to a July 9 Mass for Saints John Fisher and Thomas More, which can be celebrated in the dioceses of England and Wales, there is a Votive Mass of St. Thomas More (which is not to be confused with the Mass for his feast day). Although it does not appear in the 1962 Roman Missal, it has been celebrated before outside of England without raising too many eyebrows. Moreover, its propers are an excellent example of how the traditional liturgy tailors its petitions and lessons to the "genius" of a particular saint.[1]

---

1 The new Missal takes all the propers of the feast from the Common of Martyrs, with the sole exception of the Collect. And the Collect, aside from mentioning Fisher and More by name, could easily be used for any martyr since it has nothing distinctive about their lives. The new Collect is: "O God, who in martyrdom have brought true faith to its highest expression, graciously grant that, strengthened through the intercession of Saints John Fisher and Thomas More, we may confirm by the witness of our life the faith we profess with our lips. Through our Lord."

The Introit is:

> In Thy strength, O Lord, the just man shall joy: and in
> Thy salvation he shall rejoice exceedingly: Thou hast given
> him his heart's desire. Ps. 20:4. For Thou hast prevented
> him with blessings of sweetness: Thou hast set on his
> head a crown of precious stones.

These verses (Ps. 20:1–4) are used as the generic Introit for a martyr
who is not a pontiff, but the verse about coming before the martyr
(the meaning of "preventing him") with the blessings of sweetness
holds special meaning in reference to the gentle St. Thomas More,
and it anticipates a key theme of the Collect, which is:

> *Deus, qui beáto Thomæ Mártyri inter sǽculi illécebras et
> cárceris mortísque dolóres hílari fortíque ánimo crucem tuam
> amplécti tribuísti: concéde, quǽsumus, ejus intercessióne et
> exémplo, ut pro fide et justitia alácriter decertántes, ad ætérna
> gáudia læti perveníre mereámur. Per Dóminum.*

Which I translate as:

> O God, who didst empower blessed Thomas Thy martyr,
> amidst the allurements of the world and the pains of prison
> and death, to embrace Thy cross with a merry and coura-
> geous spirit: grant, we beseech, that by his intercession
> and example we may be quick to fight for faith and justice,
> and so, filled with cheer, deserve to attain eternal joys.

It is an excellent description of the witty and playful Saint.
Erasmus famously called Thomas More a "man for all seasons"
because he was the kind of man you wanted and could depend
on in any circumstance or situation. He was a joy to be around.
And his generous heart was quick to forgive, as he did when
his judges condemned him to be hanged, drawn, and quartered.
(Henry VIII had the sentence reduced to a beheading the night
before his execution.) Rather than express outrage at the unjust
verdict and recoil at the gruesome way he thought he was to die,
More prayed that they would all meet "merrily together" one
day in heaven. The adjective *hilaris*, which I have translated as
"merry," is the perfect word to describe More. It is the only time
that it appears in the traditional Mass.[2]

---

2 It appears once in the 2002 *Missale Romanum*, in the *Oratio super
Oblata* for St. Philip Neri on May 26. The 2011 English edition translates
the word as "cheerfully."

The choice of 2 Maccabees 6:18–28 for the Epistle is also distinctive: the only other time it appears in the traditional liturgy is the combined feast of Fisher and More. The passage tells the story of an old and pious scribe named Eleazar who was told by the Hellenistic occupiers of Israel to eat swine's flesh or be executed. Eleazar chose a "most glorious death" over a "hateful life," but his friends, moved by a "wicked pity," suggested a clever way out: he could eat something that only looked like pork and thereby not violate the Law of Moses. Without delay Eleazar replied that it was not becoming for a man his age to dissemble, and that he would be giving bad example to the youth. "And having spoken thus, he was forthwith carried to execution."

The reading is perfect for the two martyrs but especially for More. His most famous work, *Utopia*, is proof that he could be a master of dissembling when he wanted to. The ironic fantasy fiction is written in such a way that the bitter truth about political life is cleverly hidden by "honeyed" absurdities (see his Letter to Peter Giles). And after his resignation from the Chancellorship of England, More could have remained quiet, but he continued to write veiled critiques of Henry VIII's decision to marry Anne Boleyn and declare himself Head of the Church of England. It is possible that a shrewd lawyer like More could have found a loophole in the Oath of Supremacy, but instead of using a casuistic approach, he followed the path of Eleazar, even though he was not an old man but at the height of his skills.

The Gospel reading (Matt. 10:34–42) is equally appropriate, for among other things it contains the verses: "And a man's enemies shall be they of his own household. He that loveth father or mother more than Me is not worthy of Me." Thomas More truly and sincerely loved his country's father, the King, but he did not love Henry more than God.

The Secret is:

> *Hoc sacrificium redemptiónis nostræ, quæsumus, omnípotens Deus, cleménter réspice: et intercedénte beáto Thoma Mártyre tuo, pro hac família tua placátus assúme. Per Dóminum.*

Which I translate as:

> Look mercifully, we beseech Thee, Almighty God, on this sacrifice of our redemption: and by the intercession of

blessed Thomas, Thy martyr, graciously accept it on behalf of this Thy household. Through our Lord.

The prayer uses language that is common in Secrets: "Graciously accept," for example, appears thirty-one times in the Secrets of the 1962 Roman Missal either as *benignus assume* or, as here, *placatus assume*. Nor is it unusual to refer to the Church as God's household or family (*familia*), but in the over hundred times that the word appears in the Roman orations, it is in the Collect or the Postcommunion rather than the Secret.

The Postcommunion is:

Sint tibi, omnípotens Deus, grata nostræ servitútis obséquia: ut hæc sancta quæ súmpsimus, intercedénte beáto Thoma Mártyre tuo, nobis ad capessénda pérpetis vitæ præmia profícere sentiámus. Per Dóminum.

Which I translate as:

O Almighty God, may the homage of our service be pleasing unto Thee, with the result that, by the intercession of blessed Thomas, Thy martyr, we may feel these holy things which we have received bring about a snatching up of the rewards of perpetual life. Through our Lord.

Again, the language is and is not familiar. Petitions to feel the effects of the Eucharist (*sentiamus*) are common in Postcommunion Prayers, but the construction of this prayer is unusually elaborate, as is the use of the verb *capesso* (to snatch up, seize eagerly), which is nowhere to be found in the traditional Missal. I wonder—and this would take a much more extensive study to confirm—if the diction is an implicit homage to the Renaissance humanist Latin in which More excelled.

In 1929, G. K. Chesterton wrote that "Thomas More is more important at this moment than at any moment since his death, even perhaps the great moment of his dying; but he is not quite so important as he will be in about a hundred years' time." As we approach the centenary of G. K.'s prophecy, let us pray that an increased use of the well-crafted Votive Mass of Thomas More will duly reflect the Saint's ever-growing importance in the world today.

72

The Orations of the Feast of the Transfiguration, August 6

IKE ALL MYSTERIES OF THE FAITH, THE Transfiguration of Jesus Christ (Matt. 7:1-9) contains an inexhaustible treasury of meaning. Its immediate purpose was to fortify the Apostles (Peter, James, and John) who were to witness the demoralizing Agony in the Garden, which is why the Gospel is assigned to the Second Sunday of Lent as well. But the Transfiguration is much more than a morale booster, which is why it is meet that we celebrate it as a feast unto its own on August 6.

The Collect for today's feast refers to other meanings in the mystery:

> *Deus, qui fídei sacraménta in Unigéniti tui gloriósa Transfig-uratióne patrum testimónio roborásti, et adoptiónem filiórum perféctam voce delápsa in nube lúcida mirabíliter præsignásti: concéde propítius; ut ipsíus Regis glóriæ nos coherédes effícias, et ejúsdem glóriæ tríbuas esse consórtes. Per eúndem Dóminum.*

Which I translate as:

> O God, who in the glorious Transfiguration of Thine only-begotten Son didst confirm the divine signs of the Faith by the testimony of the Fathers, and who by Thy voice flowing down from the shining cloud didst wonderfully foreshadow the perfect adoption of sons: kindly concede that Thou wouldst make us coheirs with Him who is the King of glory, and grant that we may become partakers of that same glory. Through the same our Lord.

There are at least two things about the Transfiguration that are causes for rejoicing.

First, "the Fathers"—that is, Moses and Elijah—confirmed the authenticity of Jesus's Transfiguration and indeed of His entire mission. The word I have translated as "divine signs" is *sacramenta*, which is, it seems to me, its primary meaning in this context: when Jesus was transfigured, it was a divine indication of His hidden identity as the Son of God. But *sacramenta* can also be translated as "mysteries" or "sacraments," and these meanings should be kept in mind as well. The "divine signs" of the Faith also pair nicely with the use of "foreshadowing" later on, for the word there is *praesignasti*: "pre-signified."

As for the Fathers, Moses represents the Law and Elijah the Prophets, the two most important parts of the Old Testament. Representatives of the Old Covenant are appearing in order to confirm the validity of the New Covenant in the person of Jesus Christ.

Second, when a voice from the cloud declares, "This is My beloved Son: Hear ye Him," it is not only a confirmation that Jesus Christ is consubstantial with the Father, but also an anticipation of our divine adoptions as sons of God. As we have discussed elsewhere,[1] the doctrine of divine adoption is key to understanding our salvation; it is, so to speak, the Latin way of speaking about the Greek concept of *theosis* or the divinization of the believer. And if the adoption is "perfect," it will grant the main petition of the prayer: it will make us coheirs with Jesus Christ, and we will participate in His glory—which, among other things, means that we too will have transfigured bodies after the Resurrection of the Dead, bodies with impassibility, agility, subtlety, and clarity.[2]

The Secret is:

> *Obláta, quǽsumus, Dómine, múnera, gloriósa Unigéniti tui*
> *Transfiguratióne sanctífica: nosque a peccatórum máculis,*
> *splendóribus ipsíus illustratiónis emúnda. Per eúndem nostrum.*

Which I translate as:

> Sanctify, we beseech Thee, O Lord, the gifts we have offered in [memory of] the glorious Transfiguration of Thine only-begotten Son; and by the splendors of His shining, cleanse us from the stains of sin. Through the same our Lord.

---

1   See chapter 7, "The Orations of the Sunday after Christmas."
2   A final note on the language of the Collect. *Voce delapsa in nube lucida*, which I have translated as "by Thy voice flowing down from the shining cloud," gives the impression of rain gently falling down to the earth. The verb, for example, can be used for flowing downstream.

Splendoribus ipsius illustrationis, which I have translated as "By the splendors of His shining," is difficult to capture. *Illustratio* is an illumination or shining, which certainly characterizes the Transfiguration, and it was obviously splendid. But it is curious that *splendor* is in the plural. The prayer presupposes that there were many splendid things about Christ's illumination, not just one.

There is also a neat contrast between the dark spots on our souls ("the stains of sin") and the shining of our transfigured Lord. We are essentially asking for a spiritual version of sun bleaching in order to participate worthily in the Sacrifice of the Lamb moments away.

The Postcommunion is:

> *Præsta, quæsumus, omnípotens Deus: ut sacrosáncta Fílii tui Transfiguratiónis mystéria, quæ solémni celebrámus offício, purificátæ mentis intelligéntia consequámur. Per eúndem Dóminum nostrum.*

Which I translate as:

> Grant, we beseech Thee, almighty God, that with the intelligence of a purified mind, we may reach the sacrosanct mysteries of the Transfiguration of Thy Son, which we celebrate with solemn liturgy. Through the same our Lord.

We hope that the petition of the Secret was answered and that our sinful stains were bleached away; and we certainly hope that our participation in Holy Communion has had a similar effect. And so, with this "purified mind," we now ask that it be put to good use, namely, to understand the many "sacrosanct mysteries" of the Transfiguration. We thus return full circle to the petition of the Collect and its reference to the "divine signs" or mysteries of the Faith. And in seeking to understand the mysteries of the Transfiguration, we are essentially asking for what we are doing now: studying the Orations of our liturgical patrimony in order to be enlightened.[3]

---

3 Speaking of our liturgical patrimony, I have translated *officium* as "liturgy," whereas most translate it as "worship" (which is also valid). *Officium* is the Latin equivalent of the Greek *leitourgia*, a public service done on behalf of the community by a duly appointed official (the "Divine Office," for instance, is the Church's equivalent of the Greek polis's solemn festivities).

73

The Newer Old Propers for the Feast of the Assumption of the Blessed Virgin Mary, August 15

ROM WHAT WE CAN TELL, THE GREAT feast of the Assumption of the Blessed Virgin Mary began in Palestine around the fifth or sixth century, spread throughout the East, and was celebrated in Rome by the seventh century. Aside from a couple of outliers, the feast has always been kept in the West and Byzantine East on August 15. Initially, the apostolic Churches called the feast the Dormition or "Falling Asleep" of the Virgin, in reference to the belief that Mary's body suffered death but did not decay; later, the West changed the title to her Assumption to stress her glorious bodily transition to Heaven.

Whereas Protestants tend to reject this doctrine on the grounds that it is not explicitly found in the Scriptures, the only real question among Catholic and Orthodox Christians has been not whether the Blessed Virgin was assumed, but how. Was she was taken up to Heaven without tasting death, like Enoch and Elijah?[1] After all, since she was conceived without original sin, she would not be required to suffer its penalties. And why should Enoch and Elijah be accorded an exit superior to that of the Queen of Angels and Mother of God? Thus, St. Epiphanius (315–403) writes:

> Like the bodies of the saints, however, [Mary] has been held in honor for her character and understanding. And if I should say anything more in her praise, she is like Elijah, who was virgin from his mother's womb, always remained so, and was taken up, but has not seen death.[2]

And yet, Epiphanius seems to be in the minority. Both East and

---

1 See Genesis 5:21–24 and 2 Kings 2:11.
2 *Panarion/Refutation of All Heresies* 79.5,1, quoted in Tim Staples, *Behold Your Mother* (San Diego: Catholic Answers Press, 2014), 224.

West have versions of a story that all of the Apostles except Saint Thomas were miraculously transported from all over the world to be present at Mary's death and that they remained at her tomb for three days. On the third day, Saint Thomas arrived and asked "to worship the Tabernacle of God," that is, the body of the Blessed Virgin.[3] When they opened the coffin, they were greeted by only her burial wrappings and an incredible fragrance (some versions of the story describe lilies in the tomb). The Byzantine icon of the Dormition captures most of these details, including a beautiful image of Christ holding in His arms the soul of His mother prior to the reunion of her body and soul and heavenly assumption, the way that she held Him when He was a baby. St. Gregory of Tours, on the other hand, states that Our Lord appeared with His angels at the moment of His mother's death and gave her soul to St. Michael. The Apostles buried her remains and then witnessed Our Lord taking her body up to Heaven, where it was reunited with her soul.[4]

Private revelation (which holds no doctrinal weight but is interesting nonetheless) has an intriguing solution to this dilemma. According to the visions of Blessed Anne Catherine Emmerich, Our Lord appeared to His Mother at the end of her life and gave her the option of transitioning to Heaven without experiencing death or experiencing death and then being assumed into Heaven. Our Lady humbly chose death on the grounds that she was not superior to her Lord and Son.

Another option is to remain agnostic on the question. When on November 1, 1950, Pope Pius XII infallibly defined the dogma of Mary's bodily assumption into Heaven in his Apostolic Constitution *Munificentissimus Deus*, he alluded several times to the ancient belief that the Mother of God suffered temporal death, but in his solemn definition, he merely states that the Blessed Virgin, "having completed the course of her earthly life, was assumed body and soul into heavenly glory."[5] The key point, it would seem, is that her body did not suffer corruption but joined that of her Son in Heaven. The pontiff also laid stress on the heavenly glory bestowed on Mary by this privilege, and

---

3   St. John Damascene, *Second Homily on the Dormition of Mary* 10.18.
4   St. Gregory of Tours, *Eight Books of Miracles* 1.4.
5   Pope Pius XII, *Munificentissimus Deus* 44.

indeed one of the purposes of defining this dogma, he states, is to increase her glory.[6]

The Holy Father's proclamation also had a liturgical effect. The day before the promulgation of *Munificentissimus Deus,* the Sacred Congregation of Rites approved a new Mass for the feast "so that in the sacred liturgy there may also be a memory of this most auspicious event."[7] Although the new Orations do not explicitly commemorate the solemn definition, they do echo its language. Whereas the Collect from the 1570 Roman Missal makes no mention of the Assumption at all, but merely prays for forgiveness through Our Lady's intercession, the 1950 Collect states:

> *Omnípotens sempitérne Deus, qui Immaculátam Vírginem Maríam, Fílii tui Genitrícem, córpore et ánima ad cæléstem glóriam assumpsísti: concéde, quǽsumus; ut ad supérna semper inténti, ipsíus glóriæ mereámur esse consórtes. Per eúndem Dóminum nostrum.*

Which I translate as:

> Almighty and everlasting God, who hast assumed the Immaculate Virgin Mary, Mother of Thy Son, body and soul into heavenly glory: grant, we beseech, that ever intent on the things above, we may deserve to be partakers of her glory. Through the same Our Lord.

The new Collect is the first liturgical prayer that explicitly references the assumption of Mary's "body and soul," and its use of "immaculate" hearkens to a point made by Pius XII, namely, that the definition of the Immaculate Conception of the Blessed Virgin by his predecessor Blessed Pius IX helped lay the groundwork and increase desire for doctrinal clarity regarding the Assumption.[8]

The Collect follows a similar line of thinking to that of the Ascension of Our Lord. When we think of a body rising up to heaven, our imagination naturally starts to think vertically. This verticality, however, should transcend concern with physical altitude and move to an even higher plane, the spiritual realities that are "above" the material. The Mother of God, "who pondered

---

6 Ibid.

7 *Ut etiam in sacra liturgia memoria huius faustissimi eventus haberetur* (*AAS* 42 [1950], 795). The following year the Congregation approved a new Office (*AAS* 43 [1951], 399).

8 *Munificentissimus Deus* 4.

these things in her heart" (Luke 2:19), certainly qualifies as someone intent on the high in the best possible way. Similarly, the 1950 Secret eloquently pairs the assumption of Mary with the rising flames of our love and a continual longing for God.

Unlike the 1570 Orations, the 1950 prayers also strike an eschatological note. Our goal, the 1950 Collect states, is to be partakers of Mary's heavenly glory, which entails enjoying (at the end of time) a similar reunion of our bodies and souls. This eschatological theme is reinforced by the 1950 Postcommunion Prayer, which prays that the intercession of "Mary, assumed into Heaven," may lead us to the "glory of resurrection," that is, the general resurrection of the dead made possible by Our Lord's Resurrection and presaged by Our Lady's Assumption.

The one conspicuous change, which returns us to the debate about Mary's temporal death, is the omission of the 1570 Secret, variations of which can be traced back to the fifteenth and possibly twelfth century:[9]

> *Subvéniat, Dómine, plebi tuæ Dei Genitrícis orátio: quam etsi pro conditióne carnis migrásse cognóscimus, in cælésti glória apud te pro nobis intercédere sentiámus. Per Dóminum.*

Which I translate as:

> May the prayer of the Mother of God assist Thy people, O Lord: although we know that she passed according to the condition of the flesh, may we nevertheless feel her interceding for us in heavenly glory. Through Our Lord.

And for those who think that "passing according to the condition of the flesh" is not explicit enough, we turn to another ancient prayer that appears in the eighth-century Gregorian Sacramentary and is still used as the Collect for the feast in the Dominican use:

> *Veneránda nobis, Dómine, hujus diei festívitas opem cónferat salutárem; in qua sancta Dei Génitrix, mortem súbiit temporálem, nec tamen mortis néxibus deprími pótuit, quæ Fílium tuum Dóminum nostrum de se génuit incarnátum. Qui tecum vivit et regnat.*

Which I translate as:

---

9 See *Corpus Orationum 4: Orationes 2390–3028*, E. Moeller, J.-M. Clément, and B. Coppieters 't Wallant, eds. (Turnholt, Belgium: Brepols, 1993), n. 2723.

> May the venerable feast on this day, on which the holy
> Mother of God underwent temporal death (although she,
> who brought forth Thy incarnate Son Our Lord, could not
> be shackled by death's bonds), bring us salvific assistance.
> Who liveth and reigneth with Thee.

This prayer, incidentally, was used at the beginning of a great
litany and procession through the streets of Rome that began on
the night of the feast (when it was believed that the Assumption
took place) and stretched into the morning. The all-night vigil,
which was practiced from the seventh until the mid-sixteenth
century, was held to be of great importance and was the occasion
of numerous miracles. Peter the Venerable and other witnesses
testify that torches used for the procession burned all night but
in the morning contained the same amount of oil as the night
before. In 847, when the procession passed the church Santa Lucia
in Selci, a monstrous serpent that lived in a nearby cavern and
liked to terrorize the locals fled and was never seen again. To
commemorate this happy event, Pope St. Leo IV added an octave
to the feast, which remained in effect until 1955.[10]

Aside from the Collect in the Dominican use, one wonders why
these prayers are no longer in use. Are these explicit mentions
of Our Lady's temporal death out of step with the new caution
apparent in the solemn definition? Was the use of "we know"
(*cognóscimus*) too presumptuous? Could the phrase "according
to the condition of the flesh" be misinterpreted to mean that
Mary was not free of the effects of original sin and thus lead to
a denial of the rather newly defined doctrine of the Immaculate
Conception? On the other hand, is the suppression of these
prayers a violation of the principle *lex orandi lex credendi*, or rather,
an attempt to change the Church's *lex credendi* by changing her
lex orandi? At the very least, the Church's liturgical tradition
both old and new affords us an opportunity to marvel at the
ever-mysterious end of Our Lady's singular life on earth.

---

10 Guéranger, *The Liturgical Year*, 13:367.

74

The Orations of Michaelmas, September 29

HE FEAST OF ST. MICHAEL HAS A LONG and storied history in the Roman Rite. In the 1962 Missal it is known as the feast [of the anniversary] of the Dedication of St. Michael, a basilica that was dedicated to the Archangel on the Salarian Way about seven miles from Rome in AD 530 by Pope Boniface II. In the traditional rite, the feast maintains this title, even though the basilica it commemorates disappeared over a thousand years ago.

In the new Missal, the feast is that of "Saints Michael, Gabriel and Raphael, Archangels," although it is indirectly extended to all Angels. The old rite has separate feasts for Gabriel and Raphael (March 24 and October 24, respectively), but the September 29 feast also shares a broader sensibility for all of God's faithful heavenly spirts. Thus the Collect:

> *Deus, qui, miro órdine, Angelórum ministéria hominúmque dispénsas: concéde propítius; ut, a quibus tibi ministrántibus in cælo semper assístitur, ab his in terra vita nostra muniátur. Per Dóminum.*

Which I translate as:

> O God, who through a wonderful order dost manage the ministries of Angels and men: graciously grant that as our life is forever assisted by those ministering to Thee in Heaven, it may also be defended by them on earth. Through our Lord.

The 2011 English translation of the new Missal (which retains this Collect) gets the gist of the prayer's grammar where the 1952 *St. Andrew's Missal* does not, for the latter less clearly connects the ministry of the Angels in Heaven to our life on earth:

> O God, who in a wonderful order hast established the ministry of angels and of men, mercifully grant that even as Thy holy angels ever do Thee service in heaven so at

all times they may defend our lives on earth. Through our Lord.[1]

The key is that when the Angels are ministering to God in Heaven, they are ministering to us, preparing us for heavenly rewards. We know this, for this is what these marvelous spirits do: they serve God, who wants them to serve us. Our only petition is that they do the same on earth as well. There is a nice contrast between *assistitur* ("assisted"—literally, to sit or stand by) and *muniatur* ("defended"—building a wall). Just as the Angels stand at the court of Heaven to help us, like soldiers on guard, so too do we hope that they will build a wall on earth to protect us against evils.

The subordinate clause for God, "He who dispenses ministries of Angels and men through a wonderful order," is also noteworthy. God has delegated roles for His two intellectual creatures, the pure spirits known as Angels as well as human beings, a unique combination of reason/intellect and animality. He allocates these roles through a *mirus ordo* ("wonderful order"), that is, an order that is not fully grasped by the human mind but elicits wonder and awe. We will never know, this side of the grave, all that the Angels do for us.

The Secret is:

Hóstias tibi, Dómine, laudis offérimus, supplíciter deprecántes: ut eásdem, angélico pro nobis interveniénte suffrágio, et placátus accípias, et ad salútem nostram proveníre concédas. Per Dóminum.

Which I translate as:

O Lord, we offer up to Thee the sacrifice of praise, humbly praying that by the angelic suffrage interceding for us, Thou wouldst graciously receive it and grant to attain our salvation. Through our Lord.

Unlike the fallen angels, who resent our inclusion in the economy of salvation, the good Angels, though superior beings, want us measly creatures to be saved. We offer up our Mass that God will accept their intercession and make it so. *Suffragio*, which I have translated as "suffrage," can also mean "applause." The Angels,

---

1   *The Saint Andrew Daily Missal* (1952), 1584.

these great spirits, are cheering for us in Heaven! Commenting on the Epistle to the Hebrews, Monsignor Ronald Knox writes: "If you are ever feeling rather down-hearted about your second-rate efforts to live a good Christian life, think of the Saints in heaven bending over the balconies in front of them and shouting out 'Stick it!' as people do when they are watching a race."[2] And thanks be to God, the nine choirs of Angels are doing the same.

The Postcommunion is:

> *Beáti Archángeli tui Michaélis intercessióne suffúlti: súpplices te Dómine, deprecámur; ut, quod ore proséquimur, contingámus et mente. Per Dóminum nostrum.*

Which I translate as:

> Propped up by the intercession of Thy blessed Archangel Michael, we humbly beseech Thee, O Lord, that what we have pursued through our lips may also touch our souls. Through our Lord.

Ah, finally a reference to St. Michael on Michaelmas! *Suffulti* ("propped up") is rare in the Roman Orations: it appears only one other time, in a Secret in a Votive Mass to Saint Joseph. If we are propped up by Saint Michael, the implication is that we need propping up, that we are constantly tottering without him in a world full of demons and other dangers.

But here we make a more specific request: that St. Michael may help us have a more efficacious Holy Communion (which we have just received). Unlike the great Archangel who needs no physical goods, our heavenly aid is mediated through sacraments like the Eucharist, which we take through our carnal lips. But such a reception means nothing if it does not touch our souls, and so we ask God that through His faithful servant, Michael, our physical reception of the Eucharist may lead to a spiritual union with Him. Perhaps Michael is even guiding our souls to the divine target as he yells, "Stick it!"

---

2 Ronald Knox, *The Creed in Slow Motion* (New York: Sheed & Ward, 1949), 122.

75

The Feisty Orations of the Feast of Christ the King, Last Sunday of October

ONTRARY TO A POPULAR MISCONCEPTION, the Feast of Christ the King was not transferred or modified in the new Missal; it was, according to Pope Paul VI's own language, replaced, the chief difference being the stress placed on the social reign of Jesus Christ in the here and now.[1] Today, we examine all three Orations of that feast in the hopes of gaining a better understanding of what this social reign entails.

But first, a stylistic curiosity. Most Orations in the Roman Missal are addressed to God the Father, and most do not mention the Son until the conclusion. When the Son is mentioned at the beginning of the prayer, the ending is changed from "Through Our Lord Jesus Christ" to "Through the same Our Lord Jesus Christ." And when the Son is mentioned near the end of the prayer, the ending is changed to "Who with Thee liveth and reigneth..." It is rare to have all three Orations in the same Mass (the Collect, Secret, and Postcommunion) end like this. In fact, the only two times in the 1962 Missal that they do are at the Christmas Midnight Mass and on the Feast of Christ the King.

The Collect for the traditional feast is:

> *Omnípotens sempitérne Deus, qui in dilécto Fílio tuo, universórum Rege, ómnia instauráre voluísti: concéde propítius; ut cunctæ famíliæ géntium, peccáti vúlnere disgregátæ, ejus suavíssimo subdántur imperio: Qui tecum vivit.*

Which I translate as:

> Almighty everlasting God, who in Thy beloved Son, King of all men, hast willed to restore all things; mercifully grant that all the families of nations, rent asunder by the wound of sin, may be placed under His most pleasant rule. Who liveth.

---

1   See Michael P. Foley, "A Reflection on the Feast of Christ the King," *New Liturgical Movement*, October 21, 2020, www.newliturgicalmovement. org/2020/10/a-reflection-on-fate-of-feast-of-christ.html.

A few observations about diction. Used in the plural as it is here, *universus* can mean either "the whole word" or "all men," and thus has more of a social or political connotation than a cosmic one. *Disgregatæ*, the past participle translated as "rent asunder," is a nice choice. *Grego* means to gather, and *grex* can be a flock of sheep. *Disgrego* means to break up, but with the ovine association, one cannot help but think of what Jesus told the disciples before His agony in the Garden: "All you shall be scandalized in me this night. For it is written: 'I will strike the shepherd, and the sheep of the flock shall be dispersed'" (Matt. 26:31). Finally, "to restore all things in Christ" is from Ephesians 1:10. It was the motto of Pope St. Pius X, Pius XI's predecessor, who likewise wished to see a renewed Christian society replace a rudderless or pernicious secularism.

The Collect diagnoses an international disease and prescribes a spiritual cure. The cause of division and rancor among nations is not nationalism *per se* but sin, and the solution is not a one-world government or a stronger United Nations or any other international agency, but global subjection to the most sweet rule of Christ (*imperium suavissimum*). "Subjection" is, of course, a dirty word these days, an affront to our egalitarian sensibilities. But Jesus Christ Himself deigned to be subject to Mary and Joseph (Luke 2:51); indeed, as St. Gregory of Nazianzus points out, He made Himself "subject to all that He saved," becoming a slave to flesh, to birth, and to all our human experiences.[2] To be subject to such a King, who lovingly subjected Himself to death for our sake, is to accept a yoke that is easy and a burden that is light. To be subject to such a Lord is at last to breathe the air of freedom.

Such subjection, incidentally, need not involve changes to existing political structures since it is an internal conversion, but it will obviously have beneficent social effects.

The Secret for the feast is:

> *Hóstiam tibi, Dómine, humánæ reconciliatiónis offérimus: præsta, quǽsumus; ut quem sacrifíciis præséntibus immolámus, ipse cunctis géntibus unitátis et pacis dona concédat, Jesus Christus, Fílius tuus, Dóminus noster: Qui tecum vivit.*

Which I *temporarily* translate as:

> We offer Thee, O Lord, the victim of human reconciliation; grant, we beseech Thee, that He whom we immolate in

---

2 *Oration* 30.3.

the present sacrifices, may Himself concede to all nations
the gifts of unity and peace, Our Lord Jesus Christ Thy
Son, who with Thee liveth and reigneth.

The arresting phrase "human reconciliation" is found in the
Collect of Easter Friday, "O God, who didst institute the Paschal
Sacrament as a covenant of human reconciliation," where it is
unclear whether *paschale sacramentum* means the actual events
of the Paschal Mystery or the Blessed Sacrament. The adjective
keeps the focus on the Atonement; through Christ *all things* have
been reconciled to the Father (Col. 1:20), but we are particularly
interested in His reconciliation of us (2 Cor. 5:18). And, of course,
He reconciles us by "making peace through the Blood of His
Cross" (Col. 1:20), the same peace we pray that God will give to
all the nations and the same Blood that, even if we receive only
the Host, we will be receiving shortly.

The clause *ut quem sacrificiis præsentibus immolamus* indirectly
reminds us of the importance of a good translation. The word
immolare here is potentially dangerous, which may explain why
the 1970 Missal omits this phrase entirely in its Prayer over the
Offerings for the Solemnity of Our Lord Jesus Christ, King of
the Universe. The *St. Andrew Daily Missal* translates the clause
as: "He whom we immolate in the present sacrifices."[3] Usually
in the 1962 Missal, the Church immolates the "victim of praise"
(*hostia laudis*) or the offertory gifts (*munera*) or the "sacrifice"
(*sacrificium*), which in this case means the ritual action itself. But
to say that we are immolating Jesus Himself makes it sound like
we are sacrificing Him on the altar repeatedly (which was Martin
Luther's fear) and that the sacrifice of the Mass and the sacrifice
of Calvary are not one. The solution is to recall that *immolare* can
also mean to "present as an offering" and does not require the
shedding of blood. "Offer up" is therefore a safer translation than
the English "immolate," which maintains a link to ritual violence.
If you have a *St. Andrew Daily Missal*, pencil out "immolate."

The Postcommunion Prayer of the feast is:

> *Immortalitátis alimóniam consecúti, quǽsumus, Dómine: ut,*
> *qui sub Christi Regis vexíllis militáre gloriámur, cum Ipso in*
> *cælésti sede júgiter regnáre possímus: Qui tecum vivit.*

---

3   *Saint Andrew Daily Missal* (1952), 1639.

Which I translate as:

> Having received the food of immortality, we beseech Thee,
> O Lord, that we who glory in our service under the stan-
> dards of Christ the King, may be able to reign with Him
> forever on His heavenly throne. Who with Thee.

Immortalitatis alimonia is not a common phrase in the Roman
Orations, but when it does occur, it is in a Postcommunion Prayer.
(Coincidentally, one such occurrence in the Time after Pentecost
besides the Feast of Christ the King is the Twenty-First Sunday
after Pentecost, which sometimes happens to fall on this Sunday
as well.) *Alimonia* means food, but it also means provisions or
support (hence the word "alimony"), and thus fits in well with
the military imagery of this prayer. And biblically, *alimonia* has
a liturgical meaning: in the Vulgate's Leviticus 3:16 and 1 Maccabees 14:10, it is the food used in a burnt offering.

Christi Regis vexillis. The phrase is adapted from Fortunatus's
magnificent hymn *Vexilla Regis*, which was composed for a grand
procession of a relic of the True Cross from Tours, France, to
St. Radegunda's monastery in Poitiers on November 19, 659.[4]
A *vexillum* (in the singular) is a military ensign or standard or
banner. As Orations on the Feasts of the Holy Cross and the
Finding of the Holy Cross make clear, the supreme *vexillum* of
Jesus Christ is the Cross on which He was crucified. Fortunatus
and the Postcommunion Prayer for Christ the King, however,
speak of the standards (plural) of Christ. According to one theory,
the various instruments of the Passion, such as the lance and
the scourge, are Our Lord's other *vexilla*.

"We glory in our service under the standards of Christ the
King." This stirring image is worthy of a scene from *The Lord
of the Rings*, *The Chronicles of Narnia* or Henry V's St. Crispin's
Day speech. Clad in the armor of God (see Eph. 6:10), we hear
the call of the trumpet and join our lion-hearted Lord on the field
of battle, where we enter into spiritual combat to advance the
Kingdom of God in ourselves and in others, all the while suffering the slings and arrows of a world that increasingly holds us
in contempt. The word translated as "in our service" is *militare*,
which literally means to serve in the army as a solider; it is the

---

4   The hymn is used during Passiontide in the traditional Breviary.

source of our term "the Church Militant."

Apparently, this muscular martial metaphor was deemed too militaristic for the cosmological focus of the new rite's Solemnity of Our Lord Jesus Christ, King of the Universe, which replaces this clause with "we glory in obedience to the commands of Christ." I can't quite see Good King Harry winning the Battle of Agincourt with that one. The new wording is also out of tune with the biblical and liturgical use of "glory" and "obedience" and omits all reference to spiritual combat or struggle in the public square. But "if the trumpet give an uncertain sound, who shall prepare himself for the battle?" (1 Cor 14:8).

The new rite also replaces the petition that we may *reign with Him* with the less ambitious "live with Him." I can understand why. Although the idea of co-reigning with Christ is taken from 2 Timothy 2:12, it sounds too good to be true. We started out as mere creatures (and sinful ones at that); then we were promoted to servants of God and then to His friends (see John 15:14–15). Moreover, we were endowed with the incredible dignity of being adopted sons of God (see Eph. 3:20) who participate in His divinity and are coheirs of the Kingdom (see Gal. 4:1–7). And now we dare to look forward to sharing in Christ's rule—and on His very own throne no less. In a transferred sense, *in cælesti sede* means "in His heavenly abode" (the *St. Andrew* rendering), but it literally designates Christ's "heavenly seat" and thus hearkens to Matthew 19:28: "Amen, I say to you, that you who have followed me, in the regeneration, when the Son of man shall sit on the seat (*sedes*) of His majesty, you also shall sit on twelve seats judging the twelve tribes of Israel."[5] In one Oration, we move from being lowly privates in the trenches to Joint Chiefs of Staff working with the Commander-in-Chief in the Situation Room, where together we shall rule the earth (Rev. 5:10) and judge angels (1 Cor. 6:3).[6] Christ's rule is indeed most sweet and rewarding.

---

5 That said, the only other time that *in cælesti sede* is used in the Roman Missal (an alternative Collect for a deceased priest), it means "heavenly abode": *Præsta, quæsumus, Domine: ut anima famuli tui N. Sacerdotis, quem, in hoc sæculo commorantem, sacris muneribus decorasti; in cælesti sede gloriosa semper exsultet. Per Dominum.* For Christ the King, context supports a more literal translation.

6 For other instances of co-reigning or co-judging with Christ, see Revelation 20:4, 6; Daniel 7:27; 1 Corinthians 6:1–3.

76

The Orations of All Saints' Day, November 1

HE COLLECT OF THE FEAST OF ALL Saints' Day in the traditional Roman Rite is:

Omnípotens sempitérne Deus, qui nos ómnium Sanctórum tuórum mérita sub una tribuísti celebritáte venerári: quǽsumus: ut desiderátam nobis tuæ propitiatiónis abundántiam, multiplicátis intercessóribus, largiáris. Per Dóminum.

Which I translate as:

Almighty and everlasting God, who hast given us under one celebration [the opportunity] to venerate the merits of all Thy saints; we beseech Thee, that with this increased number of intercessors, Thou mayst grant to us the abundance of Thy mercy for which we long. Through Our Lord.

The prayer attributes the Feast of All Saints not, as a historian might, to Pope Gregory III (d. 741), who in the eighth century replaced a May 13 celebration of the feast of Holy Mary and the Martyrs with an expanded Feast of All Saints on November 1, or to Pope Sixtus IV (d. 1484), who made All Saints' Day a holy day of obligation for the entire Latin Church, and gave it an octave that was observed until 1955. Rather, the prayer claims that *God* gave us this feast. It is not unusual for the Christian imagination to prescind from intermediary causes and to focus our gratitude on God as the ultimate and highest cause. The traditional blessing for beer in the *Rituale Romanum* does as much when it credits the production of beer to God's "kindness and power" and fails to mention the wheat and hops farmers and the brewer, and so does Jesus Christ when He credits God the Father rather than a host of natural processes with feeding the birds of the air (Matt. 6:26). In the case of the Collect, the exclusive focus on God's role in instituting the feast reminds us of the agency of the Holy Spirit in guiding the organic development of the sacred liturgy.

Our liturgical traditions are more than the work of human hands; they are a divine gift for which we should be grateful.

Both parts of the Collect (the subordinate clause and the petition) are wonderfully crowded. The word *celebratio* technically refers to a festival celebrated *in great numbers*. Perhaps this is an allusion to the vast numbers that came to Rome for the feast day, so many that the pope, it has been speculated, transferred the feast from May 13 to November 1 in order to better feed the pilgrims with the bounty from the autumn harvest.[1] But it could also be a reference to the great Cloud of Witnesses themselves, the Saints rejoicing in Heaven (Heb. 12:1). Either way, the Collect aspires to take advantage of the great number of heavenly intercessors now gathered for the occasion, so to speak, in order to increase God's mercy upon us.

The Secret for the feast is:

> *Múnera tibi, Dómine, nostræ devotiónis offérimus: quæ et pro cunctórum tibi grata sicut honóre justórum, et nobis salutária, te miseránte, reddántur. Per Dóminum.*

Which I translate as:

> We offer to Thee, O Lord, the gifts of our devotion, that they may be pleasing to Thee in honor of all the Saints and that, by Thy mercy, they may be salutary for us. Through Our Lord.

The interesting word here is *justi*, which I have translated as "saints." According to Sr. Mary Ellebracht, the word migrated from meaning a Christian or someone who lived according to the divine law to "a technical term for the saints in heaven, those fixed in justice."[2] (This migration in some respects parallels that of *sanctus* or "holy.") In any event, the wording, which is also found in the Secret for several martyrs, nicely complements the feast's Offertory verse from Wisdom 3:1-3 —

> The souls of the just are in the hand of God, and the torment of malice shall not touch them: in the sight of the unwise they seemed to die, but they are in peace. Alleluia.

---

1   Weiser, *Handbook of Christian Feasts and Customs*, 307-8. See Gregory DiPippo for other thoughts on "The Origins of All Saints' Day," *New Liturgical Movement*, November 2, 2017, www.newliturgicalmovement.org/2017/11/the-origin-of-all-saints-day.html.
2   Ellebracht, *Vocabulary of the Ancient Orations*, 39.

The Postcommunion Prayer is:

Da, quǽsumus, Dómine, fidélibus pópulis ómnium Sanctórum semper veneratióne lætari: et eórum perpétua supplicatióne muníri. Per Dóminum.

Which I translate as:

Grant, we beseech Thee, O Lord, that Thy faithful people may ever rejoice in the veneration of all Thy Saints and may be defended by their unceasing supplication. Through.

In the Collect at the beginning of Mass, the Church prays that this celebration may bring an abundance of mercy. In the Postcommunion, the Church prays that the effects of this celebration will last far beyond the close of day. The word used here for being defended is *munire*, originally a military verb for building a wall (*munus*) in order to protect. In Postcommunion Prayers, *munire* is often used to signify the effects of the Eucharistic action on our souls. It is also often paired with verbs of purification, an arrangement that echoes the idea articulated by Our Lord in Luke 11:21–16, namely, that once you purge a space from a demon, you need to fortify it to keep him and seven of his more wicked friends from reconquering it.[3] Contemporary political rhetoric likes to praise bridges and condemn walls, but in the spiritual life at least, walls are essential as a bulwark against evil. The contribution of this Postcommunion Prayer is that it identifies the intercession of the Saints as a part of the wall keeping our spiritual enemies at bay.

---

3   See chapter 23, "The Succinct Collect of the Third Sunday of Lent."

77

The Illuminating Orations of the Feast of the Immaculate Conception, December 8

ECEMBER 8 IS THE CHURCH'S ONLY UNI-versal Marian feast in December, that of the Immacu-late Conception. The feast has its origins in the eighth century, when it was celebrated in the East under the title "The Conception of Saint Anne." Soon after it spread to the West, usu-ally under the title of the Immaculate Conception of the Blessed Virgin Mary. Saint Norbert (1075–1134) and his Premonstratensian Order were among the first Western-rite Christians to celebrate the feast and had their own proper Office for it. They were fol-lowed by the Franciscans, also supporters of the doctrine of the Immaculate Conception, who celebrated the feast with a Mass and Office adapted from that of the Papal Chapel.

The feast was on the universal calendar of the first liturgical books of the Tridentine reform, but without a proper Office or Mass; the texts were those of the Nativity of the Blessed Virgin Mary, as Gregory DiPippo points out in his article on the subject, with the word "Nativity" changed to "Conception."[1] In 1708, Pope Clement XI made the feast a holy day of obligation, but the Mass and Office remained unchanged. In 1847, Pope Blessed Pius IX approved a proper Office for the feast and extended it to the entire Church. Seven years later, Pius solemnly defined the doctrine of the Immaculate Conception, and nine years after that, he issued a new Office and Mass for the feast. Some of the 1863 propers were borrowed from the Franciscan feast of the Immaculate Conception (e.g., the Collect) while others (like the Secret and Postcommunion) were new compositions.

In his Apostolic Constitution *Ineffabilis Deus*, in which he defines the dogma of Mary's Immaculate Conception, the Supreme Pontiff speaks of the law of prayer establishing the law of belief

---

1   Gregory DiPippo, "Liturgical Notes on the Immaculate Conception," *New Liturgical Movement*, December 8, 2019, www.newliturgicalmovement. org/2019/12/liturgical-notes-on-immaculate.html.

(*lex credendi ipsa supplicandi lege statueretur*). The Orations chosen for the feast are a good illustration of this principle, as each prayer brings to light a different facet of this glorious mystery concerning the Mother of God. The Collect is:

> *Deus, qui per Immaculátam Vírginis Conceptiónem dignum Fílio tuo habitáculum præparásti: quǽsumus; ut, qui ex morte ejúsdem Fílii tui prævísa, eam ab omni labe præservásti, nos quoque mundos ejus intercessióne ad te perveníre concédas. Per eúndem Dóminum.*

Which I translate as:

> O God, who through the Immaculate Conception of the Virgin didst make a worthy dwelling place for Thy Son, grant, we beseech Thee: that Thou who, having foreseen the death of Thy same Son, didst preserve her from all stain, may grant that we also, by her intercession, may reach Thee cleansed. Through the same Our Lord.

The key concept in this prayer, which is owed to the Franciscan friar Blessed John Duns Scotus, is "foreseen." Scotus was able to solve a riddle that stumped even the great St. Thomas Aquinas: if Mary was conceived without original sin, how could she call Jesus Christ her Redeemer or Savior? Scotus's insight was that just as someone who rescues you from a ditch after you have fallen into it is your savior, so too is someone who keeps you from falling into it in the first place.

According to Pius IX in *Ineffabilis Deus*, almighty God foresaw several things. For all eternity and before the Heavens and the earth were created, God foresaw that Adam would fall and that the best remedy for the tragedy of sin would be to have His own Son become incarnate and atone for our sins through His suffering and death. God also foresaw that the best mother for His Son would be Mary of Nazareth, and God knew for all eternity that He would preserve her from all sin and endow her with a holiness nothing greater than which can be imagined. Most of all, because God foresaw the death of His Son, He preapplied the graces won on the Cross to His Son's Mother at the moment of Her conception to prevent the stain of original sin from contaminating her soul. This preapplication means that Jesus Christ is the Savior of His Mother just as much as He is ours, even though Mary is without sin. He saved her from falling into the ditch in order to have, among other things, a "worthy dwelling place."[2]

The Secret further describes this process of preapplication:

> *Salutárem hóstiam, quam in solemnitáte Immaculátæ Concep-*
> *tiónis beátæ Vírginis Maríæ tibi, Dómine, offérimus, súscipe*
> *et præsta: ut, sicut illam tua grátia præveniénte ab omni labe*
> *immúnem profitémur: ita ejus intercessióne a culpis ómnibus*
> *liberémur. Per Dóminum.*

Which I translate as:

> Accept, O Lord, the saving victim which we offer Thee
> on the Solemnity of the Immaculate Conception of the
> Blessed Virgin Mary, and grant that as we confess her to
> have been made immune by Thy prevenient grace to every
> stain, so through her intercession we may be delivered
> from all our faults. Through Our Lord.

The key phrase in the Secret is "prevenient grace." Usually this term, which literally means "grace that comes before," refers to the grace that enables a soul to undergo conversion and thus receive sanctifying grace. Here, it means that and more: the graces of the Crucifixion, still decades away from happening, preceded Mary every moment of her life.

The idea of applying the grace of Christ prior to the Passion of Christ should not come as a surprise, for *all* grace comes from the Cross. "Every supernatural good given to us," writes Blessed Columba Marmion,

> all the lights God lavishes on us, all the helps with which
> he surrounds our spiritual life, are bestowed on us in
> virtue of the life, passion, and death of Christ; all the
> graces of pardon, justification, perseverance God gives and
> ever will give to souls *in all ages* have their own source
> in the Cross.[3]

All of which is to say that if Abraham, Moses, and Job had sanctifying grace (and they did), then that grace came to them from

---

2 The foresight of God's eternal plan for Mary is reinforced in the Lesson of the feast's Mass and Lauds: "The Lord possessed me in the beginning of His ways, before He made anything, from the beginning. I was set up from eternity, and of old, before the earth was made. The depths were not as yet, and I was already conceived" (Prov. 8:22–24).

3 Marmion, *Christ the Life of the Soul*, 68, emphasis added.

an event that had not yet happened. The Blessed Virgin Mary was not alone in receiving prevenient grace. What distinguishes her from all other holy figures before the Paschal Mystery (and all since) is that this prevenient grace was applied at the moment of her conception. Such is the lesson of the Postcommunion:

> *Sacraménta quæ súmpsimus, Dómine Deus noster, illíus in nobis culpæ vúlnera réparent, a qua Immaculátam beátæ Maríæ Conceptiónem singuláriter præservásti. Per Dóminum.*

Which I translate as:

> May the sacraments which we have received, O Lord our God, repair in us the wounds of that fault from which Thou didst singularly preserve the Immaculate Conception of Blessed Mary. Through Our Lord.

The key word here is "singularly." According to Catholic tradition, several Saints have been preserved from committing a mortal sin, and some have even been preserved from committing a venial sin, for they were sanctified by the Holy Spirit in the womb: Jeremiah the prophet is believed to be one such Saint, and John the Baptist another (and, depending on which theologian you consult, some claim that Saint Joseph also received an *in utero* sanctification that enabled him to not commit any personal sins). But as blessed as these men were, they still contracted the stain of original sin and were then washed clean of it. Mary alone among lowly mortals was preserved from original sin as well as all actual sin. She is unique, and on this feast day we thank God for that.

IX

THE ADJURATION OR ENDING

S WE MENTIONED IN THE INTRODUC-
tion, every *oratio* in the Roman Missal has three parts:
a protasis, an apodosis, and an adjuration to the Holy
Trinity. The adjuration is usually *Per Dominum nostrum Jesum
Christum Filium tuum qui tecum vivit and regnat in unitate Spiritus
Sancti Deus per omnia sæcula sæculorum. Amen*—"Through Our
Lord Jesus Christ Thy Son who liveth and reigneth with Thee
in the unity of the Holy Spirit, God, forever and ever." When
the Son of God is mentioned in the body of the prayer near the
beginning, the word "same" is added in front of "Our Lord" in
the adjuration, and when the Holy Spirit is mentioned in the
body of the prayer, "same" is added in front of "Holy Spirit" in
the adjuration. But when the Son of God is mentioned in the
body of the prayer near the end, the adjuration is changed to
"Who liveth and reigneth with Thee ... " Finally, when the prayer
addresses God the Son, it is changed to "Thou who livest and
reignest with God the Father in the unity... "

It is easy to take the adjuration for granted. We hear it or read
it at the end of every Collect, Secret, and Postcommunion, and at
other times in the Mass as well. But let us be on guard against
familiarity breeding contempt. Stylistically, this conclusion to our

prayer is magnificent. As Adrian Fortescue writes: "Who first wrote this no one knows. Whoever he was, he has immortalized himself by words that for centuries have closed our prayers with the splendid rhythm of their accent and the roll of their vowels."[1] It is a delight just to say the Latin words aloud; it almost feels like a game in which one recites a rollicking mystical nursery rhyme in order to open up Heaven.

Theologically, there is much we can learn from this compact conclusion to the Orations. The variations, along with the frequency of their usage, reveal much about the nature of the liturgy. By far the most common ending is the original (*Per Dominum nostrum* ...), and this tells us one thing: even though the Mass is the re-presencing of the Paschal sacrifice of Jesus Christ, these liturgical prayers are overwhelmingly addressed to God the Father. Indeed, it is most likely *because* the Mass is the re-presencing of Christ's Paschal sacrifice that the Church directs her prayers to the Father, following Our Lord in His footsteps and orienting herself in precisely the same way that He did when He offered Himself to the Father for the sake of the many.

Even though there are parts of the Mass that invoke Jesus Christ directly (such as the *Gloria in excelsis*), Orations directed to the Son in the Roman Missal are far less frequent than those directed to the Father. Most of them hail from a later era (the Middle Ages or thereafter), and almost all of them are for a special occasion such as the Feast of Corpus Christi or the Sundays of Advent. Among the latter, there are Collects beseeching the Lord Jesus to come. The petition makes sense for a season commemorating the coming of the Lord to Bethlehem and anticipating the coming of the Lord on Doomsday, but it also highlights another curiosity about the Orations of the Roman Missal: they sometimes ask the Son to come, and (as we will see in a moment) the Holy Spirit as well, but never the Father. The picture that emerges is not of a distant deity but of a loving Father who sends His Son and His Spirit out to redeem and sanctify us and bring us back to Him. One of our goals as Christians is to be caught up in this dynamism of emanation and return, so to speak, and to come back to the Father who eagerly waits for us at home, ready with a feast of fatted calf. But in order for this to happen, He needs to stay put and not leave the house.

---

1 Fortescue, *The Mass*, 250.

Further, completely absent from the Orations are addresses to the Holy Spirit. Even during Pentecost and its octave, the Church prays in her Collects, Secrets, and Postcommunions that the Father and the Son send the Holy Spirit, but in these Orations she never prays *to* the Holy Spirit; even in the *Gloria in excelsis*, both the Father and the Son are addressed, while the Holy Spirit is only mentioned. The lesson to be gleaned from this usage is not that one should never pray to the Holy Spirit, for the Church addresses the Holy Spirit directly in her sequence *Veni Sancte Spiritus* and her hymn *Veni Creator Spiritus*. Rather, the curious custom reinforces the dynamic pattern of the Eucharistic liturgy, which is an act *of* the Son (Christ the High Priest) directed *to* the Father made possible *by* the Holy Spirit.

Regardless of the variation, the concluding adjuration serves as a nice entry point for meditating on the Trinity. Jesus Christ, who is Our Lord, is the Son of God the Father. Together they live and reign (and so both are equal in their divinity and equal in their kingship) "in the unity of the Holy Spirit." Why unity? The *Gloria in excelsis* ends with a similar sentiment but instead speaks of the Son and Holy Spirit dwelling in the *glory* of the Father. The Persons of the Trinity share all divine attributes equally, but through a process called appropriation we tend to associate some attributes with one Person more than another. Unity is a fitting attribute for the Holy Spirit, for He is the bond of love that proceeds from and unites Father and Son.

And they are united "forever and ever," for the procession of the Divine Persons is an eternal act that took place (takes place) outside of time. The Latin *per omnia sæcula sæculorum* has an impressive biblical pedigree. It appears in various forms nineteen times in the Vulgate translation of the New Testament as a translation of the Greek *eis tous aiōnas tōn aiōnōn*. In most of these instances, the phrase is followed by the word "Amen," suggesting that it already had a place in the worship of the early Church even before it was committed to writing by the authors of the New Testament. It certainly occupies a certain pride of place in the liturgies of both East and West to this day.

But what does it mean? A literal translation of *per omnia sæcula sæculorum* is "throughout all ages of ages." Strictly speaking, "throughout all ages" conjures an image of God proceeding infinitely through time, but the quirky "ages of ages" is meant to evoke something different than infinity: it is meant to evoke eternity. Eternity is not infinity. It is not simply the absence of cessation or limit but all time (past, present, and future) as present, the "eternal now." Consider this: God does not exist in time and space; time and space exist in God, and they are real only insofar as they are present to the mind of God.

The Orations of the Missal use the plural "ages of ages" (*sæcula sæculorum*), but some passages in the New Testament (and other Christian prayers) instead have "age of ages" (*sæculum sæculorum*). According to St. Anselm, both point to God's eternity, which contains "the very ages of [all] times." Because "age," however, is suggestive of indivisible unity, "age of ages" refers to God's containment of all temporal things. On the other hand, because "ages" (in the plural) connotes immeasurable immensity, "ages of ages" draws our attention to eternity as containing all ages of all times themselves.[2]

If your head is starting to hurt at this point, we can at least agree on one way *not* to think about *sæcula sæculorum*, and that is the way that it is translated in one of the most popular prayers in the English language. The last line of the doxology "Glory be to the Father and to the Son and to the Holy Spirit" is *in sæcula sæculorum*, but it is rendered "world without end." The phrase incoherently shifts attention from God's glory to the alleged perdurance of His creation, and it is heretical *if* "world" is meant to designate *this* world, which will dissolve on the Last Day and therefore most certainly has an ending.

Sæculum can mean "world" in Latin (our word "secular" is derived from it), but in both the Vulgate and liturgical prayer it is usually pejorative or at best neutral. Moreover, when *sæculum* appears in the plural, as it does twice here, it means "ages" and *not* "worlds." *In sæcula sæculorum* clearly denotes God's eternity and not the world's infinity; and as Sr. Mary Gonzaga Haessly points out, construing the Christian notion of eternity as "'never ending' is far from adequate," since, among other things, eternity bespeaks a supernatural joy.[3]

---

2   St. Anselm, *Proslogion* 21.
3   Haessly, *Rhetoric in the Sunday Collects*, 21.

The authoritative culprit behind this translation is King Henry VIII, who in 1541—eight years after his break from the Catholic Church and six years after he had Saint John Fisher, Saint Thomas More, and several other faithful Catholics martyred—issued a set of standardized prayers in English, including this rendering of the "Glory be." Henry was codifying his new church and responding to a century-old movement in England to pray (at least privately) in one's mother tongue.

The "world without end" translation may have been influenced by Tyndale's translation of the Bible or it could simply be the product of ignorance, but it is difficult not to see in it the fingerprints of the new statism developing under Henry's reign, in which the City of God and City of Man were being conflated under the rule of a sovereign who was now the head of both. The novel arrangement may have demoted the City of God by subordinating it to the City of Man, but perhaps the hope was that it would immortalize the City of Man in the process, or at least one city in particular—that which Shakespeare calls *"this* little world...*this* blessed plot, *this* earth, *this* realm, *this* England."[4]

Whatever the reason, much was certainly lost in this translation.

---

4 *Richard II* 2.i.45–50, emphases added.

The Easter Sequence "Victimae Paschali Laudes"

HE ROMAN ORATIONS HAVE A SWEET and distinctive style, but they are not the only examples of artistic masterpieces in the Missal. Sequences began as mnemonic devices to help choirs remember the elaborate notes of the *jubilus*, the melismatic ending to the Gradual/Alleluia. Words were added to the notes to aid the memory, but over time they took on a life of their own and became self-standing compositions. Although they were hundreds of sequences in the Middle Ages, only four made it into the 1570 Roman Missal: *Victime Paschali Laudes*, *Veni Sancte Spiritus*, *Lauda Sion Salvatorem*, and *Dies Irae*. Later on, a fifth was added, the *Stabat Mater*. These five are in the 1962 Roman Missal and were retained in the 1970 Roman Missal, although, being optional, they do not always make it into the average Novus Ordo Mass.

The *Victimae Paschali Laudes* is a glorious composition from the eleventh century that has been attributed to Notker Balbulus, King Robert II of France, and Adam of St. Victor, but its most likely author is Wipo of Burgundy, a chaplain to the Holy Roman Emperor Conrad II. The sequence appeared in various medieval Missals, where it was assigned to different days within the Octave of Easter. The 1570/1962 Roman Missal requires its use from Easter Sunday through Easter Saturday.

I include a literal translation alongside the text, followed by my commentary.

Víctimæ Pascháli laudes	Let Christians sacrifice praise
ímmolent Christiáni.	To the Paschal Victim.
Agnus redémit oves:	The Lamb has redeemed the sheep!
Christus ínnocens Patri	Christ, who is innocent,
reconciliávit peccatóres.	Has reconciled sinners
	To the Father.

The first two stanzas abound in paradox, which is fitting for a season that celebrates Christ destroying our death by dying and restoring our life by rising (see the Preface for Easter). The first sentence is even stronger in the Latin: *immolare* also means to slay or to shed blood ritually. The verb connotes the Hebrew Passover's bloody sacrifice of a lamb, and ties into the depiction of Christ as the Paschal (i.e., Passover) Victim and Lamb, which is the dominant theme of the Easter Sunday Mass; the statement *Pascha nostrum immolatus est Christus* ("Christ our Pasch is sacrificed") appears in the Epistle, Alleluia, Preface, and Communion verse. As the verse for the Alleluia, it creates a fitting transition to the Sequence: while the Alleluia proclaims that Christ our Pasch is sacrificed, the Sequence "answers" that Christians should [therefore] offer sacrifice to the Paschal Victim.

Mors et vita duéllo	Death and Life clashed
conflixére mirándo:	In a spectacular battle:
Dux vitæ mortúus	The Commander of life, having died,
regnat vivus.	Reigns alive.

The second stanza summarizes a fortnight of violent imagery in the liturgy. Ever since Passion Sunday, the traditional Roman Rite has included readings and other propers recounting or alluding to the increasing hatred against Jesus Christ and the rising conflict between Him and His enemies. Yes, the Passion of the Christ is like that of a lamb who opened not his mouth as he was led to the slaughter, but Our Lord's pacifism is also paradoxically portrayed as a fight freely waged on our behalf. St. Luke (22:43) calls the beginning of this fight in the Garden of Gethsemane an "agony" (ἀγωνία), which in ancient Greek referred to a contest in the Games. And like many of the Greeks' violent sports, this contest in which Jesus was engaged drew blood long before the first soldier came to strike him (Luke 22:44). It is thanks to Luke's usage that "agony" eventually came to have the predominant meaning of "intense mental suffering" that it has today.

I translate *duellum* as "battle," even though it can also mean "duel," because the verse after it describes Jesus as a *dux*, which commonly refers to a military commander or head general. And I suspect that the author chose the militaristic *dux* rather than *rex* (king) because even though Jesus "reigns," and is therefore a king, not all kings fight their own battles as ours does.

Dic nobis María,	Tell us, Mary,
quid vidísti in via?	What did you see on the way?

The third stanza has the narrator, or rather the chorus of narrators, turn to Saint Mary Magdalene and ask her a question. Although her response is sung by the same choir (as opposed to a single female vocalist), I must confess that the exchange reminds me of the campy dialogic songs of the big band era, in which the female singer and the band members hold a musical conversation (think Ella Fitzgerald's "A Tisket, A Tasket" or Jo Stafford's "Whatcha Know Joe?").

The similarity is trivial and incidental, but it does recall how this humble sequence played a key role in rehabilitating the fine arts. The early Church had closed the theaters of Greece and Rome because they had grown too lewd, but the medieval Church brought them back through her liturgy. In the tenth century, a primitive liturgical drama emerged when tropes from the Introit of the Easter Sunday Mass began to be enacted by the clergy. The first medieval play consisted of only four lines comprising the conversation between the holy women and the angels at the tomb and was held after the Office of Matins in the sanctuary. Soon after, other parts of the Easter liturgy, including *Victimae Paschali Laudes*, began to inspire similar theatrical productions. From there the idea expanded to Passion plays, miracle plays, and mystery plays.

"Sepúlcrum Christi vivéntis,	"I saw the tomb of Christ
et glóriam vidi resurgéntis:	And the glory of His rising,
Angélicos testes,	Angelic witnesses,
sudárium, et vestes.	The head napkin, and the linen
Surréxit Christus spes mea:	cloths.
præcédet suos in Galilǽam."	Christ my Hope is risen!
	He will go before His own into
	Galilee."

Mary Magdalene's response is a combination of details from both Mark's and John's accounts of the Resurrection. In Saint Mark's Gospel, Mary Magdalene enters Christ's empty tomb "very early in the morning" and sees an Angel who instructs her and the other women to tell the disciples that Jesus will go before them into Galilee. Mary and the other women, however, are afraid and say nothing to anyone. Later in the morning, after

Jesus appears to Mary Magdalene (is this when she sees "the glory of His rising"?), she gains the courage to tell the Apostles what she heard from the angel.

In John's Gospel, Mary does not initially see the glory of the Rising One (another translation of *gloria resurgentis*); instead she mistakes Jesus for the gardener. Nor does she enter into the tomb but waits outside while Peter and John go in; it is they who see Christ's burial linens (see John 20:11). She also sees two angelic witnesses outside the tomb, not one within.

Scimus Christum surrexísse a mórtuis vere:	We know that Christ is truly risen From the dead:
Tu nobis, victor Rex, miserére.	Do Thou, O Christ the Victor,
Amen. Allelúja.	have mercy on us.
	Amen. Alleluia.

The sequence ends nicely with an affirmation of Christ's resurrection, which we know to be true based in large part on the testimony of St. Mary Magdalene. (The use of the Latin *scire* is quite strong, since the verb can refer to the highest grade of human knowing.) The reference to Christ as Victor brings us full circle to the beginning, where He was described as a Victim. As Saint Augustine notes, Jesus Christ was "both Victor and Victim, and Victor because Victim," and He was "both Priest and Sacrifice, and Priest because Sacrifice."[1]

One stanza of the sequence, however, you won't hear sung in Mass is the following:

Credéndum est magis soli	Truthful Mary should be believed
Maríæ veráci	All by herself rather than
quam Judæórum turbæ falláci.	The deceitful crowd of Jews.

These verses were part of the original composition and appeared after *Præcédet suos in Galilæam*, but they were removed from St. Pius V's 1570 edition of the Roman Missal. There is evidence that the editors of the Tridentine Missal did not wish the liturgy to stir up dislike of the Jews. In the last responsory of the Office of the Annunciation, they replaced a versicle that included the line *erubescat Judæus infelix, qui dicit Christum ex Joseph semine esse natum* ("Let the unhappy Jew blush, who says that Christ

---

1 *Confessions* 10.43.69, trans. Frank J. Sheed (Indianapolis, IN: Hackett, 2006).

was born from the seed of Joseph"), with *beata es, quæ credidisti: quia perfecta sunt ea quæ dicta sunt tibi a Domino* ("Blessed art thou, because the things that were said of you by the Lord have been perfected").

The old stanza can also be criticized for inaccuracy. In Matthew's Gospel, the chief priests bribe the Roman guards stationed at the tomb of Jesus to say that His disciples stole His body in the night, and the Jews believed them (Matt. 28:11–15). With the exception of the chief priests, then, the Jews are not deceitful but deceived.

The stanza can also give the impression that the Jews tried to silence or discredit Mary Magdalene's testimony (like the two lecherous elders in Daniel 13, the story of Susanna[2]), but there is no evidence for this in Scripture. While it is true that women were forbidden in Jewish society from testifying in court, the strongest attacks on the Magdalene's credibility came from pagan philosophers like Celsus, who denounced her as an "hysterical woman." (As quoted by Origen in his *Contra Celsum* 2.59–60. Celsus puts these words in the mouth of a Jew, but this is a literary conceit.)

Perhaps another reason for the deletion of this stanza is that it strikes a sour note which detracts from the joy of the sequence and of the occasion for which it is meant. Singling out death and rejoicing over its defeat leaves a good taste in one's mouth, but mulling over a mob of liars who might still be out there badmouthing our dear sincere Saint does not. Resentment (not to mention fuel for scapegoating) does not belong in a celebration of the risen Savior who forgave His murderers. Whatever the reason, it is good that this stanza was left on the cutting room floor.

---

2   Gregory DiPippo, "The Story of Susanna in the Liturgy of Lent," *New Liturgical Movement*, March 5, 2016, www.newliturgicalmovement. org/2016/03/the-story-of-susanna-in-liturgy-of-lent.html.

The Pentecost Sequence "Veni Sancte Spiritus"

OMPOSED IN THE THIRTEENTH CEN-
tury, the Mass sequence for Pentecost and its Octave,
Veni Sancte Spiritus, is not as well-known today as the
equally fine hymn *Veni Creator Spiritus*. In the Middle Ages, however, this liturgical poem was nicknamed the "Golden Sequence,"
for even amidst hundreds of sequences in use at the time, it
stood out. The sequence captures the ineluctability, so to speak,
of Him who appears in the Scriptures under mysterious guises:
flames, a dove, a cloud, etc. In thirty tight lines, the Holy Spirit
emerges as a Perfecter through contraries, and we learn to draw
closer to Him through paradox and juxtaposition. Recognizing
the value of this sacred composition, the Holy See used to grant
a plenary indulgence to anyone who devoutly recited the *Veni
Sancte Spiritus* for a month. Although this indulgence unfortunately no longer exists, the practice is still worthwhile.

An excellent companion for extended reflection on the Golden
Sequence is Fr. Nicholas Gihr's *An Explanation of the* Veni Sancte
Spiritus, an impressive fifty-four-page, line-by-line analysis.[1] I
do not aspire to surpass Gihr's achievement, but I hope to shed
some light on a few of the sequence's stanzas.

Veni, Sancte Spíritus	Come, Holy Spirit,
Et emítte cǽlitus	And send forth from Heaven
Lucis tuæ rádium.	A ray of Thy light.
Veni, Pater páuperum,	Come, O father of the poor,
Veni, dator múnerum,	Come, O giver of gifts,
Veni, lumen córdium.	Come, O light of our hearts.
Consolátor óptime,	O best of comforters,
Dulcis hospes ánimæ,	O sweet guest of the soul,
Dulce refrigérium.	O sweet refreshment.

---

1   Nicholas Gihr, *An Explanation of the* Veni Sancte Spiritus (Fitzwilliam,
NH: Loreto Publications, 2009).

In labóre réquies,	In labor, Thou are rest,
In æstu tempéries,	In sweltering heat, Thou are the cool,
In fletu solátium.	In tears, Thou art comfort.
O lux beatíssima,	O most blessed light,
Reple cordis íntima	Fill the cockles of the hearts
Tuórum fidélium.	Of Thy faithful.
Sine tuo númine	Without Thy numinosity
Nihil est in hómine,	Nothing is in man,
Nihil est innóxium.	Nothing is harmless.
Lava quod est sórdidum,	Cleanse what is dirty,
Riga quod est áridum,	Water what is parched,
Sana quod est sáucium.	Heal what is wounded.
Flecte quod est rígidum,	Bend what is rigid,
Fove quod est frígidum,	Warm up what is frozen,
Rege quod est dévium.	Guide what is astray.
Da tuis fidélibus	Grant to Thy faithful
In te confidéntibus	Who trust in Thee,
Sacrum septenárium.	The sacred sevenfold (gift).
Da virtútis méritum,	Grant the reward of virtue,
Da salútis éxitum,	Grant an exit of salvation,
Da perénne gáudium.	Grant joy unending.
Amen, Allelúja.	Amen, Alleluia.

The first general observation is the prominence of light imagery. The Holy Spirit has a light which sheds rays from Heaven (first stanza) and is a Light of hearts (second stanza), indeed, a most blessed Light that we ask to fill the cockles of our hearts (fifth stanza). The author toggles between two different Latin words for light, *lux* and *lumen*. Originally, *lux* was light (daylight in particular) and *lumen* was a source of light, like a lamp or torch. Over time, however, the two became interchangeable, so it is difficult to say whether our author has a particular meaning in mind for each. Today, by the way, lux and lumens are two different ways of measuring light: lumens (in the Anglicized plural) is how much light is emitted by a light source, while lux is how much light falls on a surface.

One thing we know: Jesus Christ is the Light of the world, but so in a way is the Holy Spirit. Saint Augustine explains it this way: If the sun is God the Father, then the sun's shining is God the Son, and the sun's illumination is God the Holy

Spirit.[2] I wonder if Augustine's distinction between shining and illuminating is similar to the aforementioned use of lumens and lux, but I hesitate to say. One thing is certain: by using this analogy, Augustine is not promoting a modalist heresy, but trying to deepen our love of the Holy Spirit as He who wakes us up (like the rosy fingers of dawn) and sheds light on the world around us and above us.

The fourth, seventh, and eighth verses (*In labore requires, Lava quod est sordidum*, and *Flecte quod est rigidum*) are a study in contrasts. According to Saint Augustine, Jesus Christ is a Divine Physician who cures our sins sometimes through contraries and sometimes through similarities. A doctor sometimes applies a cold pack to an inflamed part of the body and sometimes applies a round bandage to a round wound, and so too, in a manner of speaking, does Our Lord. Regarding contraries, Christ heals man's pride through His humility and defeats the serpent's wisdom through His folly. Regarding similarities, "He was born of a woman to deliver us who fell through a woman, came as a man to save us who are men, as a mortal to save us who are mortals, by death to save us who were dead."[3]

Contraries rather than similarities are on full display in the *Veni Sancte Spiritus*, which is appropriate for the Holy Spirit since He did not become Incarnate and hence similar to us in the way that Christ did. Indeed in sacred art, although it is permissible to portray the Father and Son in human form, it is generally forbidden to portray the Holy Spirit anthropomorphically (Andrei Rublev's famous icon *The Trinity*, it should be noted, portrays three *angels* appearing as men who are types for the Trinity).[4]

In the stanza *In labore requies*, the poet addresses the Holy Spirit as the counterpoint to his various negative experiences: "In labor, you are rest," "in the heat, you are [literally] just the

2 *Soliloquies* 1.8.15.
3 *On Christian Doctrine* 1.14.13, trans. J. F. Shaw (Mineola, NY: Dover Publications, 2009).
4 One interesting exception is the fresco on the ceiling in the sanctuary of the Mission Santa Clara de Asis in northern California, completed by Mexican artist Agustin Davila in 1825 and portraying the Trinity as three young, bearded men sitting together. I have been told that the unusual depiction was an artistic attempt to explain the Trinity to the native converts.

right mixture or temperature," and "in tears, you are comfort" (a nice allusion to the Holy Spirit as the Paraclete or Comforter). The verb "to be" is implied in all three verses (common in Latin), and the context makes clear that the action is happening in the present tense. In other words, the poet is not saying that the Holy Spirit is rest *after* labor, but that He is rest *in the midst of* labor. He is not a cold drink when the hot day is done; He is a cool breeze during hard, sweltering work. And He is not going to wait to console us after we have dried our tears; He is consoling us right now, entering into our sorrow and providing sweet relief. Happily, even amidst the entanglements of this world, we can enjoy a foretaste of the total bliss which is to come, thanks to the Holy Spirit.

The other two stanzas consist of six urgent pleas to the Paraclete, again in terms of opposites. To give one example: "Guide what is astray." *Rege* means "keep straight" while *de-vius* literally means "off-road" (etymologically, a "deviant" is someone who lives in an out-of-the-way place). Going off-road is fine when you are playing the weekend warrior on your ATV, but spiritually it means that you are the lost sheep who has gone rogue, like Dante in the opening lines of the *Comedy*:

> Midway upon the journey of our life
> I found myself within a forest dark,
> For the straightforward pathway had been lost.[5]

These two stanzas (*Lava quod est sordidum,* and *Flecte quod est rigidum*) also invite self-examination. What is in *my* life that is dirty and requires cleaning? That is dehydrated and needs watering? That is wounded and cries out for healing? That is rigid when it should be flexible? That is numb, chilly, or cool and in need of warming up? That is wandering around and can't find the way home? Fix us, O Holy Spirit: You are the Cleaner, Gardener, Healer, Chiropractor-Masseur, Warm Fire, and Park Ranger of our filthy, parched, bleeding, frozen stiff, and lost souls.

With its daily use of the *Veni Sancte Spiritus*, each of the seven days of the Pentecost Octave beckons us to answer these questions, but the vicissitudes of life being what they are, our

---

5 Dante, *Inferno* 1.1–3, trans. Henry Wadsworth Longfellow (n.p.: Royal Classics, 2021).

answers will vary over time. What is too tight one year may be too loose the next or vice versa. (With its one-year cycle, the traditional calendar acts as a measuring stick to gauge our progress as pilgrims, and this sequence is one such marker.) The spiritual life is one of constant adjustment and re-calibration, and the Holy Spirit is the Master Mechanic with whom we collaborate in the fine tuning.

The sixth stanza, *Sine tuo numine*, contains a word that is difficult to translate. *Numen* is one of the Latin terms for deity or divine majesty, but because it comes from the verb to nod or give approval, it also conveys a sense of command or will: *numen* is divine sway, divine power. Without your approval and support, our sacred poet is saying to the Holy Spirit, everything we have — our temporal goods, talents, efforts, etc. — ends up harming us. As Augustine puts it in the *Confessions*: "Without Thee [O Lord], what am I but a guide to my own destruction?"[6]

The rest of the stanza poses a mild problem. "Nothing is in man (*homine*)/ Nothing is harmless" is somewhat confusing, and so translators usually simplify it to something like "Nothing in man is harmless." But why is the Latin here somewhat clunky in an otherwise eloquent poem? The answer is that, unfortunately, somebody along the way changed the wording. The original stanza had *lumine* (light) rather than *homine* (man) and thus read:

> Without Thy numinosity,
> Nothing is in [its proper] light,
> Nothing is harmless.

The original stanza is much richer and more intelligible: it loses none of the *moral* claim that without the Holy Spirit nothing is harmless, and it adds an *intellectual* observation: without the Holy Spirit we cannot see reality properly, for to see things in their proper perspective is not simply to grasp their natural essences but to see them in light of how *God* sees them, or at the very

---

6 *Confessions* 4.1.1. Incidentally, the motto for the state of Colorado is *nil sine numine* ("Nothing without Thy Divine Will") and it comes from then-Secretary of the Territory L. L. Weld, who was descended from a long line of English recusant Catholics. When asked what the new state's motto should be, he suggested *Nil sine numine*, which was his family motto. Perhaps one of Weld's ancestors had been inspired by the sequence verse *Sine tuo numine* as he assisted at a Whitsuntide Mass.

least, to see them *sub specie æternitatis*. "In Thy light we shall see light," sings the psalmist (35:10), and rightly so, for if we only aspire to a natural knowledge of things, we will not see reality to the fullest; for instance, we will be blind to its providential meaning and its sacramental significance.

And it is the Holy Spirit who is instrumental in enabling us to see reality to the fullest. Several if not all of His seven gifts (especially wisdom, understanding, and knowledge) have as their aim a supernatural view of things. In one of his analogies of the Trinity, Saint Augustine writes that God the Father is He who is, God the Son is He who is understood (like the Word that He is), and God the Holy Spirit is He who makes all things understood.[7] The distinctions make sense, for as the Collect from the Ember Wednesday after Pentecost reminds us, the Son has promised that the Holy Spirit will lead us to all truth (see Jn. 16:13), and I take it for granted that when one understands all things, one is no stranger to the truth.

The penultimate stanza, *Da tuis fidelibus*, contains an intriguing term. *Septenarius* in Latin is an adjective for sevenfold, and *sacrum* is used here as a noun. "Give us your sevenfold sacred thing," the poet implores. It is an obvious reference to the seven gifts of the Holy Spirit, with a focus on their unity. As Augustine explains, "The Spirit is sevenfold (*septenarius*) and the Spirit is one, one by a sevenfold operation."[8] Nevertheless, the use of *sacrum* or "sacred thing" is curious, for the author could have used a word for "gift" like the expression *septiformis munere* ("by the sevenfold gift") in the hymn *Veni Creator Spiritus*.

The answer may be that our author has in mind a word play. *Septenarius* in Latin can also refer to a line in poetry that consists of seven feet, and indeed this is the definition of the English word "septenarius, n." Further, word order is not as important in Latin as it is in English. Putting these pieces together, *sacrum septenarium* can just as easily be translated "a sacred septenarius." And a sacred septenarius would be a sacred poem that consists of seven-syllable verses—a poem like *Veni Sancte Spiritus*. By asking the Holy Spirit for a poem that he has already written, the poet

---

7   *Soliloquies* 1.8.15.
8   Sermon 8.11.13, translation mine.

may be alluding to the paradoxical nature of prayer. Sometimes, our very petition to God contains the answer.

The last stanza of this remarkable sequence (*Da virtutis meritum*) encapsulates in just three verses a good Christian life, a good Christian death, and a good Christian afterlife.

A good Christian life involves moral, intellectual, and religious excellence, that is, it is resplendent with moral, intellectual, and theological virtues. Our sacred poet is asking for the *reward* of virtue, but because he knows that such a reward is a consequence of virtue, he is essentially asking for a lifetime of virtue. And he needs to ask because man cannot become virtuous without God. It is a lovely if paradoxical arrangement: God helps us grow virtuous and then gives a reward for being virtuous. As the Gallican Preface for All Saints' Day puts it, when God crowns the merits of His saints, He is crowning His own gifts.

A good Christian death is one that overcomes the final assaults of the Devil, who often makes a last-ditch effort at the dying by inducing fear or despair or defiance. And how does one exit with salvation? By persevering with the Holy Spirit who, as we learn from the Collect on the Ember Friday after Pentecost (when the *Veni Sancte Spiritus* is still being used liturgically), keeps us from being disturbed by every assault of the Enemy. "He that shall persevere to the end, he shall be saved" (Matt. 24:13).

Finally, a good Christian afterlife is one that consists of union with God the Father, Son, and Holy Spirit in the Beatific Vision. St. Augustine defines happiness as "joy in truth,"[9] but the truth only brings joy when you are in love with it. Seeing the truth causes the damned in Hell pain, for they hated the truth in life, and they hate the truth when it exposes their wicked lives. But when the saints in Heaven see the Truth, they experience pure joy, for they have at last attained what they have loved. As we learn in the Gospel reading on Pentecost Monday (likewise when the *Veni Sancte Spiritus* is being used in the Mass): "For every one that doth evil hateth the light, and cometh not to the light, that his works may not be reproved; but he that doth truth cometh to the light, that his works may be made manifest, because they are done in God" (Jn. 3:20-21).

---

9 *Confessions* 10.23.33-34.

WORKS CONSULTED

Acta Apostolicae Sedis 42 (1950) and 43 (1951).

Ambrose. *Commentary on Luke.*

Anselm. *Why God Became Man.* In *Anselm of Canterbury: The Major Works.* Edited by Brian Davies and G.R. Evans. Oxford: Oxford University Press, 2008.

———. *Proslogion.*

Augustine. *Enarratio in Psalmos.*

———. *City of God, VIII–XVI.* Translated by Gerald G. Walsh and Grace Monahan. Washington, DC: Catholic University of America Press, 1952.

———. *Confessions.* Translated by Frank J. Sheed. Edited by Michael P. Foley. Indianapolis, IN: Hackett, 2006.

———. *On Christian Doctrine.* Translated by J.F. Shaw. Mineola, NY: Dover Publications, 2009.

———. *On the Immortality of the Soul.*

———. *St. Augustine's* On the Happy Life: *Translation and Commentary.* Translated by Michael P. Foley. Yale University Press, 2019.

———. *St. Augustine's* Soliloquies: *Translation and Commentary.* Translated by Michael P. Foley. Yale University Press, 2020.

———. *Tractatus in Joannem.*

Basil the Great. *On the Holy Spirit.* Translated by Stephen M. Hildebrand. Yonkers, NY: St. Vladimir's Press, 2011.

Beale, Stephen. "How Protestants Still Get Justification Wrong." *Crisis Magazine,* October 30, 2017. www.crisismagazine.com/2017/protestants-still-get-justification-wrong.

Bellarmine, Robert. *A Commentary on the Book of Psalms.* Boonville, NY: Preserving Christian Publications, 2008.

Benedict XVI. (See also Ratzinger, Joseph.)

———. "Message of the Holy Father Benedict XVI to the Youth of the World on the Occasion of the 22nd World Youth Day, 2007." www.vatican.va/content/benedict-xvi/en/messages/youth/documents/hf_ben-xvi_mes_20070127_youth.html.

———. "On God's Marriage Proposal: Angelus Address at the 2008 World Youth Day Closing Mass." Zenit News. July 19, 2008. http://zenit.org/article-23282?l=english.

———. "St. Paul: Wednesday General Audience." January 7, 2009. www.vatican.va/content/benedict-xvi/en/audiences/2009/documents/hf_ben-xvi_aud_20090107.html.

The Book of Offering According to the Rite of the Antiochene Syriac Maronite Church. Beirut, Lebanon: Patriarcat Maronite, 2012.

Cicero. *Hortensius*.

Corpus Orationum 3.D.pars altera: Orationes 1708–2389. Edited by E. Moeller, J.-M. Clément, and B. Coppieters 't Wallant. Turnholt, Belgium: Brepols, 1993.

Corpus Orationum 4: Orationes 2390–3028. Edited by E. Moeller, J.-M. Clément, and B. Coppieters 't Wallant. Turnholt, Belgium: Brepols, 1993.

The Daily Missal and Liturgical Manual. London: Baronius Press, 2007.

Daniel, Lillian. https://religionnews.com/2013/08/13/answering-the-spiritual-but-religious-an-interview-with-lillian-daniel/.

Dante, *Inferno*. Translated by Henry Wadsworth Longfellow. N.p.: Royal Classics, 2021.

DiPippo, Gregory. "The Ancient Character of the Feast of the Circumcision." *New Liturgical Movement*, January 1, 2019. www.newliturgicalmovement.org/2019/01/the-ancient-character-of-feast-of.html.

———. "Liturgical Notes on the Immaculate Conception." *New Liturgical Movement*, December 8, 2019. www.newliturgicalmovement.org/2019/12/liturgical-notes-on-immaculate.html.

———. "The Origins of All Saints' Day." *New Liturgical Movement*, November 2, 2017. www.newliturgicalmovement.org/2017/11/the-origin-of-all-saints-day.html.

———. "The Station Churches of Septuagesima." *New Liturgical Movement*, February 09, 2020. www.newliturgicalmovement.org/2020/02/the-station-churches-of-septuagesima.html.

Dostoevsky, Fedor. *The Idiot*. Translated by Alan Myers. Oxford: Oxford University Press, 1992.

Ellebracht, Mary Pierre. *Remarks on the Vocabulary of the Ancient Orations in the Missale Romanum*. Nijmegen: Dekker & Van de Vegt, 1963.

Emery, Gilles. *The Trinity*. Translated by Matthew Levering. Washington, DC: Catholic University of America Press, 2011.

Foley, Michael P. "A Reflection on the Feast of Christ the King." *New Liturgical Movement*, October 21, 2020. www.newliturgicalmovement.org/2020/10/a-reflection-on-fate-of-feast-of-christ.html.

———. "Divine Chastisement in the Traditional Roman Missal." *New Liturgical Movement*, October 14, 2020. www.newliturgicalmovement.org/2020/10/divine-chastisement-in-traditional.html.

———. "Divine Do-Overs: The Secret of Recapitulation in the Traditional Calendar." *The Latin Mass* 19.2 (Spring 2010): 46–49.

———. "Drunk Catholic History: Spirits and the Holy Spirit." *OnePeterFive*, August 18, 2015. https://onepeterfive.com/drunk-catholic-history-spirits-and-the-holy-spirit/.

———. "The Reform of the Calendar and the Reduction of Liturgical Recapitulation." In *Liturgy in the Twenty-First Century: Contemporary Issues and Perspectives*, ed. Alcuin Reid, 321–41. London: Bloomsbury T&T Clark, 2016.

————. "Renewing Respect for Christian Despisal." *The Latin Mass* 27.1 (Winter/Spring 2018): 36–40.

Fortescue, Adrian. *The Mass: A Study of the Roman Liturgy*. London: Longmans, Green, and Co., 1912.

Francis de Sales. *Introduction to the Devout Life*. Translator anonymous. Point Roberts, WA: Eremitical Press, 2009.

The Gelasian Sacramentary. Edited by H.A. Wilson. Oxford: Clarendon Press, 1894.

Gihr, Nicholas. *An Explanation of the* Veni Sancte Spiritus. Fitzwilliam, NH: Loreto Publications, 2009.

The Gregorian Sacramentary. Edited by H.A. Wilson. London: Harrison and Sons, 1915.

Gregory of Tours. *Eight Books of Miracles*.

Gregory Nazianzen. *On God and Christ: The Five Theological Orations and Two Letters to Cledonius*. Translated by Frederick Williams and Lionel Wickham. Yonkers, NY: St. Vladimir's Seminary Press, 2002.

Gregory the Great. *Moralia*.

Grossman, Edith. "Narrative Transmutations." PEN American Centre. www.scribd.com/document/230692721/Edith-Grossman.

Guardini, Romano. *The Spirit of the Liturgy*. Translated by Ada Lane. New York: Sheed & Ward, 1935.

Guéranger, Prosper. *The Liturgical Year*. 15 vols. Translated by Dom Laurence Shepherd. Great Falls, MT: Bonaventure Publications, 2000.

Haessly, Mary Gonzaga. *Rhetoric in the Sunday Collects of the Roman Missal*. Cleveland, OH: Ursuline College for Women, 1938.

Harris, Elise. "Benedict XVI: Cardinal Meisner Died a 'Cheerful' Man." *Catholic News Agency*, July 16, 2017. www.catholicnewsagency. com/news/benedict-xvi-cardinal-meisner-died-a-cheerful-man-71628.

Hazell, Matthew. *The Post-Communion Prayers in the Ordinary Form of the Roman Rite: Texts and Sources*. N.p.: Lectionary Study Press, 2020.

Hildegard of Bingen. *Ordo Virtutum*.

Homer, *Odyssey*. Translated by Stanley Lombardo. Indianapolis, IN: Hackett, 2000.

Julian of Norwich. *Revelations of Divine Love*. Translated by Grace Warrack. London: Methuen and Company, 1901.

Jerome. *Epistle* 21.2.

John Damascene. *Second Homily on the Dormition of Mary*.

Knox, Ronald. *The Creed in Slow Motion*. New York: Sheed & Ward, 1949.

Kocik, Thomas. "Review of Gerald O'Collins' *Lost in Translation: The English Language and the Catholic Mass*." In *Antiphon* 22.1 (2018): 107–13.

Kwasniewski, Peter. "The Collects of Advent: Who is Being Addressed, and What Difference Does It Make?" *New Liturgical Movement*,

December 19, 2016. www.newliturgicalmovement.org/2016/12/the-collects-of-advent-who-is-being_19.html.

————. "How Different Are the Pre-1955, 1962, and 1969 Calendars from Christmas into Epiphanytide?" *Rorate Caeli*, January 2, 2021. https://rorate-caeli.blogspot.com/2021/01/how-different-are-pre-1955-1962-and.html.

————. *The Once and Future Roman Rite: Returning to the Traditional Latin Liturgy after Seventy Years of Exile*. Gastonia, NC: TAN Books, 2023.

————. "Patricentric Purism and the Elimination of Liturgical Prayer Addressed to Christ." *New Liturgical Movement*, April 12, 2021. www.newliturgicalmovement.org/2021/04/patricentric-purism-and-elimination-of.html.

————. *Resurgent in the Midst of Crisis: Sacred Liturgy, the Traditional Latin Mass, and Renewal in the Church*. Kettering, OH: Angelico Press, 2014.

————. "Should We 'Despise Earthly Goods and Love Heavenly Ones'? A Liturgical Lesson for Lent." *OnePeterFive*, March 2, 2022, https://onepeterfive.com/despise-earthly-goods/.

————. "Who's Afraid of Predestination?" *New Liturgical Movement*. January 29, 2018. www.newliturgicalmovement.org/2018/01/whos-afraid-of-predestination.html.

Lexicon Recentis Latinitatis. Vatican City: Libraria Editoria Vaticana, 2003.

Lewis and Short Latin Dictionary. Oxford: Clarendon Press, 1879.

Lewis, C.S. *Abolition of Man*. Oxford: Oxford University Press, 1943.

————. *The Great Divorce*. New York: Harper One, 1946.

Magister, Sandro. "Homilies. The Liturgical Year Narrated by Joseph Ratzinger, Pope." http://chiesa.espresso.repubblica.it/articolo/209107bdc4.html?eng=y.

Macken, Walter. "God Made Sunday," in *God Made Sunday and Other Stories*. London: Pan Books, 1962.

Marmion, Columba. *Christ in His Mysteries*. Stamullen, Ireland: Cenacle Press, 2023.

————. *Christ the Life of the Soul*. Tacoma, WA: Angelico Press, 2012.

Missale Romanum, editio typica, 1962.

Missale Romanum, editio typica, 2002.

Mohrmann, Christine. "Confessions as a Literary Work of Art." In *Etudes sur le Latin des Chrétiens*, 2nd edition. Tome I. Edizioni di Storia e Letteratura (1961): 371–81.

My Sunday Missal. Edited by Joseph F. Stedman. New York: Confraternity of the Precious Blood, 1942.

The New Roman Missal. Edited by F.X. Lasance and Francis Augustine Walsh. Palmdale, CA: Christian Book Club of America, 1993.

Newman, John Henry. *Callista*. New York: Cosimo Classics, 1856.

O'Mahony, Kieran J. "Note on the English Roman Missal (2011)." www.tarsus.ie/resources/000-PDFs/Roman-Missal-Letter.pdf. Retrieved June 15, 2020.

Oxford English Dictionary. 3rd edition. Oxford: Oxford University Press, 2007.

Parsch, Pius. *The Church's Year of Grace*. 5 vols. Translated by William G. Heidt. Collegeville, MN: Liturgical Press, 1958.

Pascal, Blaise. *Pensées*. Paris: Georges Crès et Cie, 1919.

Paul VI. *Paenitemini*. www.vatican.va/content/paul-vi/en/apost_constitutions/documents/hf_p-vi_apc_19660217_paenitemini.html.

Pius XII, *Munificentissimus Deus*, 1950.

Plato. *Republic*. Translated by Allan Bloom. New York: Basic Books, 1968.

Pristas, Lauren. *The Collects of the Roman Missals*. London: Bloomsbury T&T Clark, 2013.

———. "The Post-Vatican II Revision of the Lenten Collects." In *Ever Directed towards the Lord*, edited by Uwe Michael Lang, 62–89. London: T&T Clark, 2007.

Prudlo, Donald. "The Anniversary of the Feast of Corpus Christi." *New Liturgical Movement*, August 11, 2020. www.newliturgicalmovement.org/2020/08/the-anniversary-of-feast-of-corpus.html.

Ratzinger, Joseph. *Milestones: Memoirs 1927–1977*. Translated by Erasmo Leiva-Merikakis. San Francisco: Ignatius Press, 1998.

The Roman Missal, 3rd edition. Washington, DC: USCCB Publishing, 2011.

The Saint Andrew Daily Missal. Edited by Gaspar Lefebvre. St. Paul, MN: E.M. Lohmann Co., 1952.

The Saint Andrew Daily Missal. Edited by Gaspar Lefebvre. Bruges, Belgium: Liturgical Apostolate, 1959.

The Saint Joseph Daily Missal. Edited by Hugo H. Hoever. New York: Catholic Book Publishing Co., 1953.

Schuster, Ildefonso. *The Sacramentary*. 5 vols. Translated by Arthur Levelis-Marke. London: Burns, Oates & Washbourne, 1925; repr. Waterloo, ON: Arouca Press, 2020.

Shakespeare, William. *Richard II*.

Serafini, Franco. *A Cardiologist Examines Jesus: The Stunning Science Behind Eucharistic Miracles*. Manchester, NH: Sophia Institute Press, 2021.

Sheed, Frank. *Theology for Beginners*. Ann Arbor, MI: Servant Books, 1981.

Staples, Tim. *Behold Your Mother*. San Diego: Catholic Answers Press, 2014.

Suetonius. *Tiberius*.

Thomas Aquinas. *Summa theologiae*.

Vergil, *The Aeneid*.

Weiser, Francis X. *Handbook of Christian Feasts and Customs: The Year of the Lord in Liturgy and Folklore*. New York: Harcourt, Brace, and Company, 1958.

Wilkinson, Bruce. *The Prayer of Jabez: Breaking Through to the Blessed Life*. New York: Multnomah Books, 2000.

INDEX